Teaching Skills For Dummies®

BESTSELLING
BOOK SERIES

What Makes a Great Teacher?

Some people are born to be great teachers. I'm sure you've come acr‍‍‍‍
instinctively how to teach. But most people have to work very hard to d‍
A great teacher:

- ✔ **Likes the kids and knows how to show it:** Remember why you came ‍‍‍‍ ‍‍‍‍ ‍‍‍‍the first place. Show genuine warmth toward your students; build a bond with them that he‍‍‍‍ ‍‍‍‍them to learn.

- ✔ **Teaches so that the students *want* to learn:** Being a teacher's a creative activity: use your imaginative talents to make your lessons engaging for your students.

- ✔ **Knows that voice and body matter a lot:** Understand that teaching's a *physical* occupation, too. The whole time in your classroom, you're using your voice and your body to communicate with your children.

- ✔ **Creates a positive atmosphere:** Look for the best in your students, rather than focusing on what's going wrong. Develop an atmosphere of mutual respect and understanding, but make sure you stay in overall control of your class.

- ✔ **Understands how to 'police' the classroom:** Classroom and behaviour management are only *ever* about allowing teaching to take place. Get structures, rules and routines in place so that you can do your job without interruption.

- ✔ **Feels passionate about the job:** Teaching's far too important a job for anyone to do it half-heartedly. Use your passion to inspire the next generation. Make them love learning, or a subject, as much as you do. Be a teacher they *never* forget.

Dip into any section in this book to discover more about becoming a really great teacher.

Putting on a Great Performance

I've often drawn an analogy between teaching and acting: once you start to consider this, the parallels are really quite striking. As a teacher, you have:

- ✔ **A stage on which to perform:** Give the students an enthralling, exhilarating, interesting, challenging time in your classroom, and they *want* to come to your lessons.

- ✔ **A show to present:** Your lesson plan's your script – think ahead about where you want the performance to go. But don't forget that sometimes improvisation makes for a thrilling, 'seat of the pants' experience.

- ✔ **An audience watching your every move:** Your students are one of the most demanding audiences you can find. A class can be as hard to please as the most ruthless theatre critic (and senior managers and inspectors can be even harder!), but if they like the show you put on, they should let you know that too.

- ✔ **A character to 'step into':** When you're on that stage, 'being' the teacher, you're not playing yourself. Your teacher character's a version of who you really are, but exaggerated in certain key points (calmer, firmer, fairer, more positive, among many other aspects).

Just like an actor, you have to use your physicality and vocal skills to get the character across. And you have to put on a great show for the full length of the run.

Teaching Skills For Dummies®

Cheat Sheet

Creating a Style of Your Own

You're unique – as a person, but also as a teacher. And as part of what makes you unique, you use a teaching style all of your own. But whatever type of style you use, you need to hone that style to perfection to get the most out of your class. Remember to:

- **Consider your personality.** Your teaching style comes from your personality. Think about which aspects of your character are attractive or appealing, and make the most of them. If you've got a natural flair for comedy, get your students laughing in lessons. If you're the dramatic type, incorporate a sense of theatre into your classroom.

- **Sort out your bad habits.** While you're making the most of your attractive traits, you've got to deal with the unappealing ones as well. Often, doing this is about dampening down your instinctive responses when problems crop up. If you tend to lose your temper easily, work hard at staying calm. If you blush at the slightest mistake, learn how to swallow your embarrassment. Understand how you come across to your students – your style is as much about how they *perceive* you as about how you feel inside.

- **Believe in yourself.** The more confident you appear, the better your students respond. They *want* you to be in control – of the class, and also of yourself. Even if you don't feel confident inside, you've got to exude self-belief if you want to succeed.

- **Build up your communication skills.** Whatever your teaching style, you've got to be a skilled communicator to be a great teacher. Learn how to speak clearly, and with expression – add tone, pace, depth and richness to your voice. Reflect constantly on the messages your body sends to your class – when you appear open, relaxed and welcoming your students feel positive about you.

- **Be positive and firm but fun, with a touch of humanity thrown in for good measure.** Think about the kind of teachers you had as a child, and which ones made you feel that you could succeed. Some were probably stricter than others, but whatever their style, you could tell they genuinely *cared* about whether you did well. That's the perfect recipe for being a really fantastic teacher.

Head to Chapter 2 for more advice on honing your teaching style.

What Makes a Great Lesson?

A great teacher knows how to plan and teach a really great lesson. Doing this is a big task, but the more you practise and experiment, the easier it becomes. Also, working out what to put in your lessons and how to deliver them is one of the most exciting and creative aspects of your role. A great lesson:

- Is varied, appeals to different learning styles and incorporates multisensory activities.

- Is interesting, engaging and memorable; it 'sticks' with the students after the event.

- Gets the students to actually *understand* something new or to develop a new skill.

- Is adapted to students of different abilities so that everyone can access the learning.

Achieving all this isn't easy, but when you get it right, and your students 'click' with that tricky new concept, you get a great feeling. Part II of this book tells you all you need to know (and more!) about creating really superb lessons.

For Dummies: Bestselling Book Series for Beginners

Teaching Skills

FOR

DUMMIES®

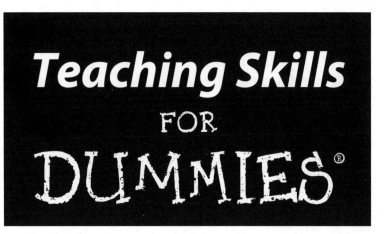

by Sue Cowley

A John Wiley and Sons, Ltd, Publication

Teaching Skills For Dummies®

Published by
John Wiley & Sons, Ltd
The Atrium
Southern Gate
Chichester
West Sussex
PO19 8SQ
England

E-mail (for orders and customer service enquires): cs-books@wiley.co.uk

Visit our Home Page on www.wiley.com

For general information on our other products and services, please contact our Customer Care Department within the U.S. at 800-762-2974, outside the U.S. at 317-572-3993, or fax 317-572-4002.

For technical support, please visit www.wiley.com/techsupport.

Wiley also publishes its books in a variety of electronic formats. Some content that appears in print may not be available in electronic books.

British Library Cataloguing in Publication Data: A catalogue record for this book is available from the British Library

ISBN: 978-0-470-74084-2

Printed and bound in Great Britain by Bell & Bain Ltd, Glasgow

10 9 8 7 6 5 4 3 2 1

WILEY

About the Author

Sue Cowley is a teacher, writer, trainer and presenter. She qualified with a BEd (Hons) from Kingston University. Although she originally trained to teach primary school children, Sue later moved into teaching English and Drama at secondary level. She has taught in schools in London and Bristol, and also at an international school in Portugal. She reached the giddy heights of 'subject co-ordinator' on the career ladder, but made a conscious decision to stick it out in the classroom, rather than moving into management.

Sue is the author of more than a dozen books on teaching, including the best-selling *Getting the Buggers to Behave.* As well as having a big following in the UK, her books have also been translated into various other languages and her work is popular with teachers in China, India, Poland and Slovenia, amongst many others. Sue divides her time between delivering INSET in schools and colleges, writing books and articles, presenting at conferences and on Teachers' TV, and bringing up a young family. She still spends time working with students 'at the chalkface', helping out in local schools.

Sue's belief is that what teachers need above all else is practical, realistic and honest advice about how to survive and succeed in their classrooms. She bases all her work on her own experiences as a teacher and on tips and advice she's been given by others. In her books, Sue guarantees you a 'theory-free' experience. When it comes to teaching, her motto is: 'Whatever works - for the teacher and for the kids'.

Sue loves to spend her spare time reading crime novels or being out in her garden getting muddy. She lives in Somerset, with her partner, her two children and a cat called Herbie.

Dedication

This book is dedicated to Álvie and Edite, with all my love.

Acknowledgements

I'd like to thank Tilak, because this book wouldn't have been possible without him. He makes it possible for me to get on with writing, mostly without interruption. Thanks to you for putting up with me and my disorganised (or rather, 'creative') approach to life!

Special thanks go to my Mum, who passed the 'teaching gene' onto me. They do say that it runs in the family.

I'd also like to give a mention to all those teachers I've worked with and learned from over the years. Thanks for letting me nick your ideas and copy your approaches.

And finally, thanks to all the students who've passed through my lessons - the well behaved ones and the ones who weren't quite so great. I've learned an awful lot from you guys as well.

Publisher's Acknowledgements

We're proud of this book; please send us your comments through our Dummies online registration form located at www.dummies.com/register/.

Some of the people who helped bring this book to market include the following:

Acquisitions, Editorial, and Media Development

Project Editor: Steve Edwards

Development Editor: Tracy Barr

Content Editor: Jo Theedom

Commissioning Editor: Nicole Hermitage

Publishing Assistant: Jennifer Prytherch

Copy Editor: Sally Osborn

Proofreader: Helen Heyes

Technical Editor: Tabatha Rayment

Executive Editor: Samantha Spickernell

Executive Project Editor: Daniel Mersey

Cover Photos: © Rob Walls/Alamy

Cartoons: Ed McLachlan

Composition Services

Project Coordinator: Lynsey Stanford

Layout and Graphics: Christin Swinford

Proofreader: Melissa Cossell

Indexer: Ty Koontz

Brand Reviewer: Carrie Burchfield

Contents at a Glance

Table of Contents

Introduction

*T*eaching is one of the *best* jobs you can possibly do. And if you're a teacher already or thinking about becoming one, then I do hope you agree. Teaching is also one of the most *important* jobs you can possibly do. The future prospects of a whole generation of children lie, at least partly, in your hands. And teaching is also one of the most *difficult* jobs you can do. Okay, it's not brain surgery, but it can be challenging, stressful, frustrating, emotionally draining, physically demanding, high pressure and incredibly hard work.

But for all the tough days and all the challenges, teaching's definitely worthwhile. The joy you get out of helping your students succeed makes worthwhile all the effort you have to put in to get them to work their hardest. The excitement of having a class in the palm of your hand makes worthwhile the struggle you had to reach that moment. And of course, the holidays are great as well.

When I go into schools to work with teachers, I ask them: 'What motivates you to turn up at school every day?' Their initial response is always to laugh: 'I need the salary to pay my mortgage!' But within seconds, they highlight all the bits of the job that really make it worthwhile, all the rewards teaching gives them that money simply can't buy.

Teaching's a vocation, pure and simple. If you're only in it for the money, you're in the wrong job. Okay, the salary isn't too bad these days, but as a graduate you can do something a lot less stressful and earn the same money or more. As a teacher you get the chance to make a difference. And you don't find many jobs that can offer you that.

About This Book

I want reading this book to feel like you're sitting down with a friend for a chat. You've asked her for some words of advice because she's been teaching for a while. She has some commonsense ideas about what does and doesn't work, which she's happy to share with you. Your friend has your best interests at heart. She understands all the joys of being a teacher, but she also know about the demands of the job as well.

This friend of yours doesn't expect you to be perfect, like your head teacher may. She understands that you're a human being and that all your little habits and imperfections are part of what makes you unique. And she knows that in some schools, and with some students, even getting to the point where you can address your class, let alone teach them anything, is sometimes nigh on impossible.

Your friend's keen to give you honest, practical and realistic advice about the things that may actually work in your classroom. She knows that this is what busy teachers really need when they read a book about teaching. She understands that what works in one school or situation may not work in another, but she trusts you to figure out for yourself what works for you. She wants you to try to maintain a positive approach in your classroom, although she fully understands how difficult that can be at times.

This friend of yours also wants you to feel empowered to make changes to your teaching and your classroom practice. She understands that when you're trying to change student attitudes in the most difficult schools, you can feel like a fish swimming against the tide. She knows that sometimes you're very tempted to give up and say 'whatever' as you slap a worksheet on the students' desks.

Your friend wants you to focus on what you *can* change, rather than on what you *can't*. She knows that you can't change your head teacher or senior management (much as you may like to). And you can't change the kids for some other, better-behaved ones (no matter how desirable that may feel at times). But what you *can* change, what you *can* do something about, is your own teaching and your own teaching skills. And that's what she believes this book can show you how to do.

This friend of yours has taught the 'class from hell', but she's also had classes in the palm of her hand. She's taught in many different schools and worked with students of all different ages. She's taught in nursery, primary and secondary schools, with students from ages 3 to 18. She's been a permanent member of staff, but she's done supply teaching as well. She's also watched, worked with and trained many thousands of teachers, both in the UK and overseas. She wants you to know that whatever your teaching situation, she has some understanding of how you feel.

So I hope that as you read this book you feel like I'm that friend of yours. That I'm on your side. I've put the sum total of all my teaching experiences into this book. And I genuinely hope that some of it, and hopefully a lot of it, is valuable to you as you develop your own teaching skills.

My hope is that this book helps you to:

- ✔ Enjoy your teaching and the time you spend with your classes.
- ✔ Develop a teaching style that works for you and your students.

✔ Explore interesting and effective ways to communicate with your classes.

✔ Understand how you can create and deliver high-quality lessons: ones that help your children gain knowledge effectively and also enjoy their learning.

✔ Pick up techniques to help you keep your students focused and engaged and to make your life in the classroom easier and less stressful.

✔ Discover the structures you can use in your classroom that allow you to keep everything and everyone under control.

✔ Explore the many ways to build better behaviour with your classes and create a really positive environment for work.

✔ Handle every situation in the most positive way, no matter how challenging or difficult it feels.

✔ Get to know all the different people you work with and how best to build a sense of partnership and team work with them all.

✔ Deal with all those bits of the job that happen beyond the classroom walls: paperwork and marking, or extra-curricular activities.

✔ Build up a whole battery of teaching skills so that you can deal with every eventuality the job throws at you.

Conventions Used in This Book

A few conventions in this book are designed to help you navigate the text:

✔ *Italics* are used to give emphasis and to highlight new words.

✔ **Bold** is used to show the key concepts in a list.

✔ Monofont is used for website and email addresses.

In order to keep things fair and concise, I've used alternating genders in each chapter.

What You're Not to Read

You'll find some stuff in this book that is interesting, but that you don't *have* to read to make sense of what I'm saying. Sometimes you'll see an icon that asks you to 'Think Of' a situation and how you might respond to it. These sections are great for when you have a chance to sit and reflect on your teaching skills, but you can skip them if you're short on time. Similarly, the sidebars are all asides and, although you might find them thought-provoking to read, they're not critical to understanding the book.

Foolish Assumptions

If you bought this book, I think it's fair of me to assume that you're either a teacher already or someone who is considering going into the profession. I don't cover the ever-changing nature of the curriculum and I don't explore the various routes into the profession; I assume that you'll locate that information for yourself, if you need it. What I *do* focus on is the kind of key skills you'll need to become a really successful teacher. You might disagree with some of what I say, but I hope that you'll be open-minded enough to give even the craziest ideas a try!

How This Book Is Organised

This book has 20 chapters, divided between six main parts.

Inside each chapter are sub-sections about the main topic of the chapter. My aim is to make this book both practical and easily accessible. You should easily be able to find and read the topics that are most relevant to you. You may like to dip in and out of the book or you can read it cover to cover (if you have any time left over after all that marking!).

Part I: Developing Your Teaching Style

The first part of the book shows you how to develop a teaching 'style' that works for both you and your students. You find out how to create an aura of confidence, even when you don't feel like that inside. You examine a variety of different teaching styles to help you figure out which approach works for you.

In this part, you also see how you can use both verbal and non-verbal approaches to communicate with, and connect with, your class. You discover how to make the most of what comes out of your mouth and also how to use your body in the most effective way possible.

Part II: Teaching a Class

In this part, you find out all about how to teach your class so that the students learn loads and everyone gains a positive feeling of success. You see how you can prepare and deliver really good-quality lessons. And you discover the different approaches to your teaching that can help you meet the needs of every student.

In this part, I show you how you can get your students interested in their work and keep them engaged right through a lesson. You also find many ways to push your students to achieve their best and to stay focused on the activities you set.

This part also shows you how to maximise aspects of your teaching outside the immediate lesson – things like assessment, resources and displays. You explore how to incorporate a variety of interesting objects and approaches into your lessons so that you can really get the most out of your children.

Part III: Managing a Class

This part helps you discover loads about the ins and outs of actually managing a class and a classroom. You see how routines and structures can help make your time in the classroom both easier and more effective, and how different classroom layouts affect the way your students work.

In this part, you find out the best strategies to use to handle problem behaviour. You investigate how to get better behaviour from your students; how to maximise your strengths as a classroom manager; and also how to overcome any weaknesses you may have.

You also find out how to develop and maintain a positive feeling in your classroom and how to use rewards and sanctions as effectively as possible. And you explore how to handle the really challenging situations and students and cope with the way these situations make you feel.

Part IV: Dealing with Different Kinds of People

In this part, you find out how to deal with the different kinds of people you need to work with as a teacher. You see how you can develop good, strong and positive relationships with your students, and explore how you may develop the pastoral side of your role.

This section also helps you investigate how you can work effectively with the other staff at your school, and which people you may be best to avoid. You also see how to build up the lines of communication with your students' parents or carers and how to develop the kind of positive relationships with them that help your students to work at their best.

Part V: Succeeding Beyond the Classroom

You find a lot of advice in this section about developing your teaching skills beyond the classroom. Whether you need to sort out that ever-growing pile of paperwork or get involved in extra-curricular activities, everything you need to know is here. You also discover how to take stock of your current situation and plan for your development in the future.

Part VI: The Part of Tens

In this final part, you get some quick, simple and effective tips for dealing with some of the knottier aspects of the profession. You get quick, no-nonsense advice on topics as diverse as engaging with a group and dealing with stress.

This part offers a great 'dip-in' guide for when your time's short but your need's strong. Dive into it and see what you can discover!

Icons Used in This Book

You come across little icons throughout this book. These icons are designed to highlight specific bits of text. These sections give you a particular strategy to use or something important to consider.

Some top techniques, strategies and pointers for you to bear in mind as you develop your teaching skills to the max. Don't forget these techniques: they stand you in great stead in your classroom.

These are practical ideas and suggestions that have worked for me in my classroom. Often they're suggestions another teacher's kindly given to me. Only common sense and realistic advice to be found here!

Watch out! When you see this icon, get primed for some top advice about what to avoid in your classroom and in your teaching.

Take a moment to reflect on things from your own experience or imagine how you may respond to a situation. A chance to think things through outside the pressurised classroom environment.

Where to Go from Here

If you're brand new to teaching, this book contains pretty much every technique I've ever tried, been told or been taught. No matter where you 'land' inside the covers, you can find some practical and honest advice about coping in your classroom. As a new teacher, you may get great benefit from reading this book from start to finish, but you don't do any harm at all if you only have time to dip in and out.

If you have a specific issue in your classroom, then turn to the contents pages to see if you can spot where I deal with it. Often, I cover that issue in more than one chapter. Teaching's a complex business, and sometimes you need to come at your problem from more than one angle to help yourself solve it.

If you're an experienced teacher with plenty of years in the profession, then this book may offer you a reminder of some of the techniques you used to use, but maybe haven't employed for a while. Or it can show you how you *are* doing all the right things, but that sometimes circumstances mean you can't always be perfect.

And if you have a problem that I don't cover in this book, then feel free to contact me via email. I'll see what I can do, although I can't promise an instant solution. To contact me, visit my website, `www.suecowley.co.uk,` and follow the links from there.

Finally, please remember that *no magic wand* exists in teaching. No simple answer solves all your problems. But if you keep plugging away and never stop improving, then with time you become the best teacher you can possibly be.

Part I
Developing Your Teaching Style

'Paperwork? What paperwork?'

In this part . . .

We teachers are a stylish bunch. No, I'm not talking about leather elbow patches on tweed jackets, or dodgy pinafores and sandals with socks. I'm talking about the teaching style you have – a style that's all your very own. I'm going to show you how your style works, and the kind of impact it can have (positive or negative) on your chances of success in your classroom. I share all those little tricks of the trade with you. The ones that make your students *believe* you're in charge, even when you're a quivering wreck inside. You need to project confidence and a belief in your abilities. Get started on building that confident persona!

Chapter 1

Building Your Teaching Skills

*B*eing a teacher is a tricky job – you have so many different areas to get right. You have to develop a style of teaching that works for you and your students. You have to communicate with both classes and individuals, and build up bonds between you and your students. You also have to know how to plan and teach your lessons, so your students get to learn loads, and hopefully have fun at the same time. And on top of all that, you need to build up effective relationships with staff and parents as well. The job's a big one!

But teaching's well worth doing. Being a teacher is one of the best jobs to have. If you get things right, you help your students discover new things each and every day. If you get things right, you *inspire* your students to go on to great things. As the saying goes, nobody forgets a good teacher. This book can help you become the best teacher you can possibly be, and this chapter gives an overview of the challenges that await you.

Developing Your Teaching Style

As a teacher you have your own, individual teaching style – a teaching personality that's as unique to you as your fingerprints. Some teachers take a firm, strict, old-school approach, like the classic sergeant major with his authoritarian manner and loud voice. Other teachers have a fun, relaxed and even comic style, using humour to get the best out of their students.

No one style is right for every teacher, although some styles work better than others. Similarly, no one style is right for every class. Some students respond brilliantly to a teacher who's strict and scary; others become confrontational if the teacher tries to lay down the law. Much depends on the type of students and the sort of class you're teaching.

The more you develop the positive aspects of your teaching style, the better teacher you become. This development's all part of the process of becoming a great teacher. The following sections give an overview of the key characteristics of a successful, confident teaching style, and Chapters 2 and 3 offer a variety of other strategies you can use to develop a style that works for you.

Understanding your teaching style

The key to success is to understand your teaching style: to become aware of which parts of your style work well and how to develop them; and to know which parts of your style aren't so effective and how you can improve them. To develop your teaching style to its peak of perfection, you need to:

- ✔ Reflect on your teaching approaches and how well they're working, preferably *while* you're teaching.

- ✔ Be conscious of how your behaviour in the classroom affects the way your students respond to you.

- ✔ Adapt the methods and strategies you use to suit the way your students respond (again, preferably during the course of the lesson).

- ✔ Vary the approaches you use according to the age and type of students.

- ✔ Adapt the style you use to fit with the mood and 'feel' of the class or of individual students.

- ✔ Watch other teachers in action to see what works and what doesn't.

- ✔ Work out which strategies and style best fit the setting where you teach.

- ✔ Build a style that's confident, definite, aware, positive and flexible.

The better you understand yourself as a teacher, the better your students respond, behave and learn – and the more you can get on with the fun bit, which is, of course, the teaching.

Becoming a confident teacher

I can remember being terrified the first time I set foot in a classroom as a teacher. I had a sick, hollow feeling in my stomach, like you get when you ride a rollercoaster and it drops suddenly down a steep slope. My head was full of self-doubt. Were the students going to like me? Were they going to understand my explanations? Were they even going to listen to me so I could teach them?

Feeling nervous at first is entirely natural. In fact, you should probably be worried if you *don't* feel nervous the first few times you set foot in the classroom, because being over-confident can be a recipe for disaster. If you're too sure of yourself, before you even know the class, you may appear unresponsive to the students sitting in front of you. Take care that self belief doesn't tip over into arrogance or aggression.

Remember that how you feel inside doesn't matter, because you can still project an air of confidence on the outside. Your aim is to develop an air of confidence, self-control and a mastery of everything that happens in your classroom. This comes with time and experience, and with loads and loads of self-reflection. (If you're new to teaching, you can fake this until you begin to believe it.) As a confident teacher:

- ✔ You put on a 'teacher character' – you show that you're in control of the work, the students and, crucially, yourself.
- ✔ You give your students a feeling of security.
- ✔ You take charge of what goes on in your classroom while staying responsive to what the students think as well.
- ✔ You use a firm, fair and fun approach to your role.
- ✔ You adapt the approaches you use to the needs of your students.
- ✔ Your confident, effective approach gives your students the freedom to get on with doing their work.
- ✔ Your confidence shines through in everything you say and do.

Most teachers feel nervous at the start of the school year. When you've been away from the classroom over the summer holidays, you may feel as though you've 'forgotten' how to teach. But teaching's like riding a bike – after you have the hang of it, you never really forget.

Improving how you communicate

Teaching's all about communication. You communicate what you want to your class; they communicate their understanding (or lack of understanding) back to you. Your communication skills can also reinforce or undermine the air of confidence you want to project (discussed in the preceding section). If you look like you mean what you're saying, and believe in yourself, this gives your students a perception that you're confident and in control.

You communicate with your students in lots of different ways – some obvious, some not so apparent. You communicate:

- **By talking to your class:** Well, of course you do! But communication isn't as simple as just opening your mouth and speaking. It's about getting the volume, tone, pace, vocabulary and emotional quality of your voice just right.

- **By listening to your students:** Communication is a two-way street. When you invite a response, by asking a question, use your verbal and non-verbal skills to demonstrate your interest.

- **Through your face and facial expressions:** You can use your eyes and face to connect with a class, or to indicate that you're displeased. A single raised eyebrow can say more than a thousand words.

- **With your hands:** Your hands are one of the most expressive parts of your body. Use them to communicate instructions, commands, praise or enthusiasm. Let your hands do the talking.

- **Through your body postures and positions:** Your students 'read' a lot about you by the way you stand and hold yourself. A relaxed, confident and welcoming posture helps you build relationships with a class.

- **By the way you move around the classroom:** Don't get stuck at the front by the board when the troublemakers are at the back, plotting mischief. Move around the space, a bit like a cat patrolling its territory.

- **Through the way you control the space:** Make clear that this is *your* space, and you are in control of how it looks and how it's used. The students are very welcome inside it, but you're the one in charge.

Strike a balance between verbal and non-verbal communication. Remember that *how* you say something is often more important than *what* you say. Talking too long is a mistake – use other approaches to get your point across.

Develop your communication skills so that what you say is concise and easy to follow. When you give an instruction, keep it short and clear. When you offer an explanation, you can make it longer but keep it succinct. Use plenty of non-verbal cues to keep your students focused on what you're saying.

Remember that your students are continually interpreting your tone of voice and your body language, and responding to the messages you give. Become fully aware of the verbal and non-verbal messages you send your class, particularly the subconscious messages. Reflect on everything you say and do, and the effect that has on your students. Discover how to step outside yourself and see and hear how you appear to your students.

You can find loads of advice about effective verbal and non-verbal communication in Chapter 3.

Managing and Teaching Your Class

Your key job as a teacher is, of course, to *teach*. But the job isn't quite that simple. Not only must you plan, prepare and deliver fantastic, high-quality lessons, you must also manage the behaviour of your students while they're in your classroom. You may prepare the most brilliant lesson in the history of the world, but if you can't get your students to let you deliver it, they never find out how great it is.

You may find a strong link between the way you teach your class and how well you manage the students during their lessons. If you make your lessons interesting and engaging, they're more likely to listen and behave. This isn't a magic formula for solving behaviour issues in a really challenging school. But getting your students to *want* to learn is a good starting point.

Creating fantastic lessons

Creating really great lessons starts with good preparation (most of the time). As you can see in Chapter 4, planning's a tricky business. Your plans may have tons of detail or very little at all. So long as they actually *work* for you, in your classroom, with your students, in your situation, that's what counts.

Don't allow lesson planning to take over your life. Follow the 'Reduce, Reuse, Recycle' mantra in Chapter 4 to limit the amount of time you spend on planning. You can't be an effective teacher if your work takes up every spare minute of every day – give yourself some time out too.

If you're training as a teacher or are new to the job, you'll be expected to give plenty of detail in your plans. As you gain experience, hold onto a few of these more detailed plans, or even just the templates that you used to write them. That way, you can whip them out during inspections or observations.

Fantastic, high-quality lessons have some or all of the following:

- ✔ A clear sense of structure, so your students know where they're going and what they're meant to be doing.
- ✔ A learning objective, so you know what you're aiming to teach.
- ✔ A balance between focused learning and understanding how long your students can concentrate effectively on any one activity.
- ✔ A lot of hands-on, practical activities to keep everyone involved.
- ✔ A good balance of activities – some teacher talk (but not too much), some student-led learning and so on.
- ✔ A sense of forward momentum, created by setting targets to achieve and time limits within which to meet them.
- ✔ High-quality instructions, so the students know what they're meant to do and how they're meant to do it.
- ✔ Multisensory approaches, and activities that take account of how everybody learns best.
- ✔ Interactive tasks, which encourage your students to get fully engaged with their discoveries.
- ✔ Content that reflects the needs and interests of your students, and that they can relate to their lives outside school.
- ✔ Work that's differentiated to the needs of your students, so everyone can feel successful.
- ✔ A sense of fun.

Having said all that, don't put too much pressure on yourself to create multimedia, whiz-bang style lessons. Doing so isn't possible *all* the time. Do your best, but don't be afraid to take your foot off the pedal a bit when you need a rest.

Don't get so hooked up on structure that you forget the reality: some of the best lessons are those that develop organically, in partnership with a class. Sometimes, be brave enough to throw caution to the wind and let your creative side have the upper hand.

Being a brilliant teacher

Some teachers are naturally brilliant: they have 'it'. Charisma, a bond with the children, a natural ability to communicate. Plenty of strategies exist that can help mere mortals to emulate these 'natural' teachers. To become the best teacher you can be, aim to:

✔ Find interesting and imaginative ways to get your students' attention – focus on the creative side of the job as well as the daily routines.

✔ Hold onto the passion and enthusiasm that got you into the classroom in the first place. Aim to be an inspiration to your students.

✔ Maintain your own interest in the job, by keeping things fresh for yourself as well as for your students.

✔ Strive to be the best teacher that ever lived, taking every tip and opportunity to develop that comes your way.

✔ Use your voice and body in an engaging way – communicate your love of knowledge through the way you speak and present yourself to your class.

✔ Be a role model for your students, someone they want to please.

✔ Maintain a sense of humour and perspective at all times.

✔ Be genuine and caring with your students and find ways to engage with them and build relationships.

✔ Build on the natural sense of curiosity everyone has as a young child – make your students *want* to know.

✔ Go against the norm – be a bit subversive, crazy or surprising in your efforts to engage with your class.

✔ Play around with different sensory responses, bringing your lessons to life in a fully rounded way.

The more effort you put into varied approaches, the better your students behave and learn. This isn't an instant solution, but you do have total control – you can be the teacher *you* want to be.

Taking control of your classroom

Your aim is to get the most out of your students while they're with you, whether that's once a week in some secondary subjects or every day in a primary school. You want them working at their peak, so they can discover as much as possible in your lessons together.

You can get the most out of your students by keeping them engaged, using strategies like these:

✔ Ensuring that they stay on task during lessons, setting activities that suit their needs and setting them in a way your students understand.

✔ Building a bank of rules together, so that it becomes 'our' classroom, and you create a feeling of mutual respect and ownership of lessons.

✔ Using targets and time limits to create a sense of focus and increase on-task behaviour.

✔ Incorporating a lot of rewards into your teaching, using positive methods far more than you use sanctions.

✔ Building a sense of pace into your lessons and your teaching, particularly through the way you use your voice.

✔ Helping them to develop their concentration, but understanding how long you can reasonably expect students to focus at one time.

✔ Encouraging them to develop good listening skills and managing the noise levels within the room.

✔ Using assessment effectively, as a method of showing your students where they are now and where they need to go next.

✔ Incorporating a wide variety of interesting and engaging activities within your lessons, so your students *want* to stay on task.

✔ Utilising resources in the best possible way, and thinking about the more unusual types of resources that may inspire your students.

✔ Using displays to develop and extend their discoveries and to make your classroom a more creative place in which to spend time.

With all these strategies in place, your students should get the most out of the time you spend together. They should also look forward to being in your lessons, so they arrive with a good feeling about what's going to happen. Head to Chapters 5 and 6 for more information.

Talking 'bout my generation

Remember that the students you teach are *this* generation, not *yours*. These young people have been brought up in a world that's very different to the one that existed even a couple of decades ago. Even if you're close to your students in age, they're still a world apart from you.

Young people these days know all about their rights. This can be negative in some respects (when they insist that asking them to work is 'against their human rights'). But I'm glad to work with youngsters who stand up for themselves, and who don't allow teachers to demand respect simply because of a supposed position of authority. I want to *earn* their respect, thanks.

Using structures to develop effective learning

As Chapter 7 explains, the way you set up your classroom and the approaches you use to structure your lessons all contribute to high-quality learning. You need to create routines and structures that really work. Establishing these routines is an ongoing process, but after you get the task underway, you free up much more time for the fun part – the teaching.

Get your structures and routines right by:

- ✔ Setting up routines for how students behave within lessons – the way they enter and leave the classroom, how they approach group work, and so on.

- ✔ Adapting the structures you use according to the needs and age of your students, and the kind of environment in which you work.

- ✔ Maintaining and developing your routines over time, so you adapt them until they work optimally for everyone.

- ✔ Taking care to manage lesson time in an effective way, so no one feels rushed, but equally, no one gets bored.

- ✔ Ensuring that you differentiate the activities you use, so that all students can access the work.

- ✔ Being particularly careful about the way you start and finish your lessons or your day, and understanding why this is so important.

- ✔ Using effective approaches and structures for group activities, so the students use this format in the best possible way.

- ✔ Setting up, and adapting, your teaching space so it helps you both manage behaviour and teach more effectively.

- ✔ Exploring the benefits and downsides of various layouts, and being willing to try different approaches to find what works best for you.

- ✔ Managing the students within the space: thinking about where they sit in relation to you, and how this may affect their learning and behaviour.

- ✔ Using the space in an interesting way yourself, as a method of both controlling the class and also making your teaching more effective.

The ideal is for your structures and routines to become 'invisible'. For them to work in such a way that the students don't realise how you're controlling them, even though they're aware that the control's going on.

Handling behaviour in a positive way

Managing behaviour is one of the key concerns for many teachers. After all, if you can't get your students to behave, then you aren't able to teach them properly. Behaviour management is a complex issue, which Chapter 8 explains in detail and you can't find any easy answers. But with time and practice you can get behaviour management right, and make great strides forward, even in the most challenging situations.

To handle behaviour in the most positive way possible, follow these suggestions:

✔ Establish clear expectations at the start of your time with any class: explain the behaviour you want, and what happens if that behaviour doesn't occur.

✔ Use every possible way to get silent attention from your students when you need to address them. Refuse to talk over a class that isn't listening.

✔ Find ways to get your students to maintain their focus, so what you tell them actually sinks in.

✔ Play up to your strengths and take account of your weaknesses. Have an understanding of how your students perceive you.

✔ Build strong and solid relationships with your students, establishing a sense of empathy with the class.

✔ Aim for a confident appearance, even if you don't feel confident inside. Refer to the earlier section, 'Becoming a confident teacher', for an overview, and Chapter 2 for pointers on projecting confidence.

✔ Keep calm as much of the time as humanly possible. Think about the triggers that cause you to lose your temper, and find ways to avoid them.

✔ Be consistent, and aim to treat each and every student in a fair and equitable way.

✔ Maintain a bit of distance between yourself and your students – don't try to be their friend, because they honestly don't *want* you as a mate!

✔ Stick to your guns – once you've set your standards, don't get drawn into endless debates about what is and isn't fair.

✔ Steer well clear of aggressive approaches: avoid getting angry when a student is difficult, since this only exacerbates the problem.

✔ Be clear about the school policies for dealing with behaviour, making sure that your sanctions and rewards follow the whole-school approach.

✔ Match the strategies you use to your own situation – understand that what works well with one set of students may not be helpful for another.

This last point is vital for getting behaviour management right. You can find lots of suggestions and strategies in this book, so choose the ones that work in your own unique classroom situation.

While most of the behaviour issues you face are low level, you also need to understand what to do when a more serious incident develops. Examine your approaches ahead of time; when a challenging situation arises, you need to be sure what action to take.

To handle challenging behaviour effectively, check out these ideas:

- ✔ Develop a clear understanding of why some students may become confrontational with you.

- ✔ Be honest about how you sometimes contribute to the tensions that arise in your classroom.

- ✔ Develop a teaching style that circumvents the need for students to become confrontational – be positive, assertive, calm and fair.

- ✔ Understand the kind of approaches that work best in defusing a confrontation, and be aware of your legal position.

- ✔ Look for support when you need it and consider joining a union as a source of back-up and advice.

- ✔ Take care to handle the aftermath of misbehaviour for yourself, as well as for the student. These incidents affect you too; take this into account after the event.

- ✔ Know the kind of approaches you can take with the most difficult classes, and discover ways to win them back.

- ✔ Understand how to deal with really difficult individuals, adapting the strategies you use to the specific situation or student.

- ✔ Have plenty of ideas about how to manage your own stress levels and to stop yourself from getting too caught up in your work.

Remember that these high-level incidents are rare in most schools. If you work in a really challenging situation, insist on the support and back-up you need when the worst does happen. Go to Chapter 10 for more on dealing with challenging situations.

Creating a positive classroom climate

In addition to using strategies to manage behaviour and control your class, the ideal is for you to create a climate where good behaviour and hard work are a matter of course. Make your classroom feel like a great place to be – look for the positive, rather than focusing on the negative. To create a positive feeling in your classroom, you need to:

- ✔ Be friendly, welcoming and positive with your students – make them feel that you're happy to work with them, and that you want the best for them.

- ✔ Use rewards and positive ways of motivating your students; avoid negative approaches to classroom and behaviour management.

- ✔ Maintain and build on your positive climate throughout the school year, taking particular account of times when standards might slip.

- ✔ Keep a handle on your moods and emotions, and refuse to allow yourself to respond in a negative way when students mess you around.

- ✔ Discover how rewards work. Understand that some students are naturally self-motivated, whereas others need external motivators.

- ✔ Use sanctions in a positive way. You do need to punish, but you should aim to do so in a way that may actually change the student's behaviour.

- ✔ Give your students choices about how they behave – help them understand that their actions have consequences.

With both you and your students in a positive frame of mind, your time spent in the classroom is much happier, and much more effective. Go to Chapter 9 for more in-depth information.

Getting to Know the Main Characters

You come across a whole host of characters in your role as a teacher. Obviously, the students themselves are the main players. But you also need to develop a sense of team work with the other staff at your school. Plus you have to build up partnerships with parents and carers to help you develop your students to their fullest.

Building relationships with your students

When you relate well with your students and they feel that you have their best interests at heart, you're bound to get better results in your classroom. Building up these bonds takes time and commitment, but the results that you get are well worth the effort you expend. To build strong, positive relationships with your students, you must:

- ✔ View them as *people* and not just as pupils.

- ✔ Get to know their names quickly and use them frequently.

- ✔ Adapt the way you handle different students according to students' needs.

✔ Help your students develop into fully rounded people. Teach them life skills, such as being cooperative and respectful, as well as developing their academic side.

✔ Develop the pastoral side of your role. If you work as a form tutor or primary class teacher, focus on helping your students develop as people, as well as on getting them to learn.

The more students you teach, the harder you may find developing a bond with each one. If you're a secondary teacher working with hundreds of different students, you have a hard task ahead of you. You can still make headway, though, by following the advice and guidance in Chapter 11.

The vast majority of young people *want* to build up good relationships with their teachers. Don't let them get too close, though. You need to maintain a certain distance so you can do your job effectively.

Playing your part in the staff team

Although your role as a teacher can seem quite isolated, in fact you play a key part in the bigger team at your school. This team includes both teaching and non-teaching staff. From the caretaker to the lunchtime supervisors, everyone has a vital part to play. To become an effective team member, you should:

✔ Understand and respect the different roles that various staff play in the daily life of the school.

✔ Remember that all these roles support the whole-school ethos – and that no one job is more deserving of respect than another.

✔ Look for support when you need it, and make sure that you give support to others as well.

✔ Find ways to work effectively with support staff in your classroom. Understand that these people can make a huge difference to your students' chances of success.

✔ Get to know the 'right' people and avoid getting caught up with the 'wrong' ones.

Every school or setting has its own particular challenges when working as a staff team. Whether your school has only a few members of staff or over a hundred, you benefit yourself and your students by working effectively together. Go to Chapter 12 for details on how to be part of an educational team.

Handling parents

As a teacher, you come into contact with all sorts of parents and carers – from those who want nothing more than to support you in working with their children, to those who make your life as difficult as they can. In truth, the vast majority fall somewhere in between. Yes, they do want something from you (a good education for their children), but they're happy to give something in return.

To work effectively with parents and carers, you need to:

✔ Build up the lines of communication – let parents know what goes on in your classroom and show them ways to support their children at home.

✔ Use the same kind of strategies with parents that you use on a tricky child: be polite, fair and reasonable, but stick to your standards.

✔ Follow up on every offer of help – whether that's volunteers to help with readers or a parental 'expert' to come in and talk with your class.

✔ Make sure that you report good news to parents as well as contacting them when things are going wrong.

The parents' evening is an opportunity to talk with parents and carers and a great time to set targets for future improvement. You may feel a bit nervous at your first few parents' evenings. Follow the advice in Chapter 13 to help you.

Building Your Skills Beyond the Classroom

Your role as a teacher doesn't stop at the classroom door. You must also handle all that paperwork and cope with your marking load. And on the positive side, you should think about developing yourself and your career for the future. Building your teaching skills beyond the classroom can have a powerfully positive influence on the work you do with your students. Part V tackles these issues in detail.

Dealing with paperwork

You need to be ruthlessly efficient if you're not going to let paperwork take over your life. Stick to the approaches I give in Chapter 14 and you should be able to keep things in check. Check out these additional tips:

✔ Be ruthless about binning the papers you don't need.

✔ Deal instantly with those bits of paper that need a response.

✔ Pass paperwork on so it becomes someone else's problem.

✔ Avoid creating a huge 'to do' mountain for yourself.

✔ Use your time as effectively as possible.

✔ Create a clear and simple 'to do' list when you have a lot going on.

A great piece of advice about time management is to try to handle each piece of paper *only once*. Although, to be honest, if you can manage that, you're a better, more efficient person than me!

The school report is one very important type of paperwork. It's one of the main ways in which you communicate with parents and carers. Reports allow you to show where your students are doing well and to set clear targets for improvement. But reports can be incredibly time consuming to write, especially if you teach a large number of different classes. Factor this into your timings when you know reports are coming up.

Balancing your marking

You may find a tension between the need to get books 'looking' marked and the actual value of the marking you do in educational terms. If you want to, you can spend every waking hour marking books in great detail and still not feel you've done everything. To keep your marking load reasonable, and to get the best value out of the marking you do, you should:

✔ Use a variety of approaches for marking – detailed marking, a quick tick and flick, marking for specific areas of improvement and so on.

✔ Avoid setting too many activities that involve a lot of marking at any one time.

✔ Balance the type of tasks you set throughout the week, so you spread your marking load.

✔ Get your students involved in assessing each other's work; this isn't only helpful for you, but educationally valuable for them.

✔ Make sure that your students *read* what you've written, so they actually benefit from the marking you do.

Some subjects generate a lot more marking than others. Be aware of this when you're teaching a writing-based subject or topic. If you teach a subject where the students do a lot of written work, consider how you can find the time to get everything marked. Chapter 14 has all the information you need.

Working with your students beyond the classroom

One of the most enjoyable ways to develop your teaching skills is to get involved with your students beyond the classroom. This may mean taking part in some extra-curricular activities. Doing so is a really great way to boost your skills and also to develop positive relationships with young people. Of course, another great way to develop yourself as a teacher is to take your class out on a trip, or to hitch a ride on a trip that someone else has organised. For many young people, a school trip is one of the most memorable experiences they have at school. Go to Chapter 15 for ideas and advice on how to teach and interact with your students beyond the classroom.

Reflecting on and developing your skills

All the time as a teacher, you want to reflect on your skills and find ways to develop them further. This may mean taking an additional qualification that adds to your classroom practice. It can involve preparing for, and learning from, observations and inspections.

Perhaps the most useful approach is to develop the ability to reflect on your own classroom practice in an informal manner, learning from the mistakes you make in your lessons and also celebrating your successes. For more thoughts about building your skills in this area, go to Chapter 16.

Chapter 2

Understanding Teaching Styles – and Developing One That Works for You

The trick to successful teaching is to approach it with confidence and aplomb, to develop a teaching style that oozes self-belief and self-assurance. This isn't easy – if you're new to teaching, you may feel unsure of yourself and of what you expect from your students. The problem is, your uncertainty's communicated to your students, and they respond by messing you around.

When you achieve a confident teaching style, you look like you're *meant* to be there, delivering the low-down on the subject. You look like you're *happy* to be there, passing on your love of learning. In fact, you look like you're downright *excited* to be there – because when you get things right, few jobs are as rewarding as being a teacher.

Putting on Your Teaching Character with Confidence

When you stand in front of a class, you shrug off your normal self and take on a teacher 'character'. You're not the same person as when you're busy at home or out relaxing with friends. Putting on your teacher character is all part of developing your own, personal teaching style.

Your students want you to be a character who's:

- ✔ **In control of the work:** They need to feel secure about what happens in your lessons. That way, they can get on with learning.

- ✔ **In control of yourself:** Students don't want to be subjected to a teacher with ever-changing moods, or one who loses the plot and screams.

- ✔ **In control of your teaching space:** Show your students that this space is yours, and that you're in control of what happens within it. That way, your students feel happy and confident about being in your classroom.

- ✔ **In control of them:** They want a teacher who can keep everyone in line. Again, this helps them feel safe and secure.

Teaching is a play with many characters: the educator, the parental figure, the social worker, the welfare officer, the administrator, the nose wiper. And you don't just have to learn how to play *one* role, you have to play them all.

Picking the right character

When you put on your teacher character, you not only have to look confident, you also have to pick the right role to suit your situation. The teacher character you portray varies according to:

- ✔ **The age of the students:** If you work with students of different ages, you must adapt your character to suit. You may use a strict and firm character with young students, and a more informal, relaxed character with older ones.

- ✔ **The needs of the students:** A class full of students with learning difficulties is a very different kettle of fish to one containing high flyers. Weaker students need you to boost their self-esteem; bright ones may need pushing to achieve their best.

- ✔ **The type of class:** A lively, naughty class requires a firm hand; a timid, quiet class needs a gentler approach that draws them out.

> ✔ **The time of day/week:** On a Monday morning your character may have a 'let's wake up and get going' personality; on a Friday afternoon you may need a 'let's focus and get this done before the weekend' one.

> ✔ **The setting where you work:** A rural grammar school needs one kind of character; an inner-city comprehensive needs another. In a selective setting, you may need to play the 'old-school' teacher, whereas in a mixed, urban school, you may have to use a more relaxed approach.

As you gain experience you adapt your character instinctively to the situation, until you hardly need to think about it at all. That is, until you move to a new school, and then you have to create your character all over again!

Appearing confident – even when you're not

If you appear confident, your students feel safe and happy in your presence. Your confidence shines through in the way you move, speak, interact, deliver the subject and relate to the class. That's not to say that just because you have an aura of confidence you never experience problems. Some days students just don't seem to 'get it', no matter how well you explain a task. On other days a class may take against you or student behaviour may spiral out of control. But if you exude confidence and really believe in yourself, you keep a positive frame of mind. And you're in a good position to deal with any problems that crop up.

Even when you just pretend to have confidence, you actually build a real sense of confidence at the same time. In turn, you boost your approaches to teaching and improve your control of your classroom.

The art of bluff

You can't do much to *force* your students to work hard and behave properly. The option of physically chastising them no longer applies; you're not meant to terrify them either. But still, you have to make them believe you're in charge. This is where the 'art of bluff' comes in. If you really, truly *believe* you're in control, that belief comes through in the way you present yourself. Sometimes, bending the truth a little helps to keep your students in line.

Some indications that a bluff may be useful include the following:

> ✔ **Your level of experience:** Students often ask young teachers: 'Are you a new teacher, Miss/Sir?' What they mean is 'Can we get away with misbehaving for you?' Even if you're a new teacher, you can truthfully answer: 'I'm new to this school, but I'm wise beyond my years in spotting nonsense.'

✔ **What you're teaching:** Say 'We're going to do some really exciting stuff today' in a convincing tone and you may fool your students. No matter whether you're teaching algebra or conjugating verbs, if you make the subject sound cool you start the lesson with a positive feeling.

✔ **How great the rewards are:** The quality of the rewards you give to your students isn't relevant – how you make them sound is. 'I've got three fantastic stickers/reward slips/postcards home to give out today' makes them sound worth earning.

A fine line exists between a bluff and an outright fib. You must decide how far you're willing to go. Some teachers get away with the most outrageous lies – the students don't actually *believe* what their teacher says, but they happily join in with the joke.

Spiders and snakes – they're more scared of you than you are of them

Standing in front of a class you don't yet know is a nerve-racking experience. Lots of them are facing only one of you. If they refuse to work or start to mess around, you have to get them back under control all by yourself. This situation is a bit like when you were in the interview for your current teaching job. Yes, you felt terrified inside, but somehow you managed to convince your potential employers that you were the right person for the job. Think about:

✔ The kind of frame of mind you had in the interview.

✔ How you overcame your internal fears, or whether you even used those nerves to help you get the job.

✔ How you made yourself appear in control and confident, even though you didn't feel like that inside.

✔ Whether you used any psychological tricks or strategies to help you get through the experience intact.

Remember that saying about spiders and snakes: 'They're more scared of you than you are of them'? Imagine yourself coming across an unfamiliar dog in the park. The dog is off its leash, and you can't see an owner anywhere. You flap around and panic. The dog senses your nervousness and strikes out. Now imagine yourself staying calm: you capture the dog by its collar and hold onto it until its owner arrives, with no sense of alarm. It's the same with students – they feed off your emotional state. Look fearful and they bite; keep cool and they're reassured.

Staying calm and cool means you respond rationally and deal with difficult situations in a considered way. You can find many tips about keeping your cool in Chapter 8.

Too good to be true?

I once met a geography teacher who told me a story about how he rewarded his class. It was a definite case of 'the art of bluff' and how students are happy to go along with the joke where the teacher means well.

The teacher explained to me that his girlfriend loved celebrity magazines. When she finished reading them, she passed them onto him, and he kept them in a pile in his stock cupboard.

When he noticed someone working well in his class, this teacher slipped into his stock cupboard and found a photo of a celebrity that the student admired – David Beckham, for instance, for the football-mad boys. He tore out the photo and 'autographed' it with a message from the celebrity to the student.

'Do they really believe that you have David Beckham in your stock cupboard?' I asked him, incredulous. 'Of course not,' he said, 'but they love the idea. It's a kind of in-joke between me and the kids.'

Exploring Different Teaching Styles

A key component of your teaching character is your teaching style. Teaching styles aren't 'one size fits all': as many different teaching styles exist as teachers. Your style comes out of your normal personality, but the two aren't the same thing. You may choose a relaxed style, with a comic twist; you can decide on a firm and strict style. No harm lies in experimenting with different styles until you find the one that best suits your students and your situation. 'Whatever works' is a great motto to stick by. Remember that no 'right' or 'wrong' applies to teaching styles. Figure out what works best for you and your students and then do it.

Your style isn't your personality, but it does evolve from what you're like as a person. You can try to adopt a different persona in the classroom, but the 'real you' shines through, no matter how much you try to hide it. You'd also have to keep up the act, even when you didn't feel like it. Your style tells your students a lot about you and your approach to life in general, and to teaching in particular. Better to be a version of yourself, with some 'new and improved added extras', than to try to create a whole new persona that just doesn't fit or suit you.

After a while, your teaching style becomes second nature. It varies over the course of a term but at the heart of it is your own, unique teacher character.

Many new teachers start out with a style that's too relaxed and friendly out of the mistaken belief that, if the students like you, they behave for you. For a while this approach often works, but then the students start to push at the boundaries, and as their 'mate' you don't feel in a position to tell them off. You're not their mate; they don't have to *like* you to work hard for you. Keep a distance between yourself and your students. Then, when you do have to discipline them, they're going to respond much better. (For lots more ideas on finding the right balance, see 'Maintaining a distance' in Chapter 8.)

'Old-school' style – strict and scary

This style's from the past, authoritarian and teacher-led – the students must do as they're told without question. Such a style was born in the time when children were meant to be seen and not heard. It sits rather awkwardly with modern attitudes about young people.

Not everything about an 'old-school' style is negative, however; some of the approaches work well within a modern style of teaching. For instance, a firm and no-nonsense approach can pay dividends, as can high standards and clear routines. You'll want to avoid shouting, though, and you might like to crack the occasional smile.

Look at the list of attributes below to see which ones may work for you, and which you should avoid.

Some attributes of the 'old-school' teaching style include:

- ✓ A firm, no-nonsense approach – the teacher's definitely in charge.
- ✓ High standards – lining up the class before the lesson, insisting students stand when another teacher enters the room.
- ✓ A focus on punishment to sort misbehaviour, rather than on rewards to encourage good behaviour.
- ✓ Smiles are rare – no hint of a friendly attitude toward students.
- ✓ A tendency to shout at a student or a class.
- ✓ A 'chalk-and-talk' method of teaching, where the teacher stands at the front to deliver the lesson.
- ✓ Tasks done individually, rather than in groups.
- ✓ More time spent on writing activities than on speaking ones.
- ✓ A reliance on 'expert' texts, such as textbooks and reference books.

You can incorporate some of these attributes – for instance the high standards – into your classroom to good effect. This style is more often used in high-achieving, high-discipline settings, such as independent or grammar schools.

The 'good old days'

You may have heard people referring to the 'good old days', a time when children did as they were told, when they respected authority figures and when schools were an oasis of calm and hard work. Some people believe that corporal punishment created this magical state. Others blame television, computer games or even E numbers in foods for the downward slide in standards.

I argue that the 'good old days' are a myth – as you get older, you paint the past in rosier and rosier hues. And we easily forget that, only a few decades back, some students were in a state of pretty much constant fear of their teachers (me included).

Yes, you do find problems with levels of respect for teachers in some schools. Changes in society itself, and within the way schools are organised, have made a teacher's job harder in a lot of ways.

But I still much prefer the current state of affairs, where students stand up for themselves and their rights. This makes teaching more challenging, but that challenge makes you a better teacher.

 Look around your school or setting and think about the styles different teachers use. Many may employ a modern teaching style, but some may have an old-school style. (And some may revert to this style when under pressure.) Do any teachers use an old-school style successfully? Who are they, and why does the style work for them? Often, the old-school teachers are older members of staff with a reputation, or those in positions of authority.

'Modern' style – firm, fair and fun

With a 'modern' style, you take charge of the classroom in a positive way. You offer a firm, fair but hopefully fun approach to teaching. You accept that students have rights (they remind you frequently of this to make sure you don't forget). You encourage them to take control of their learning and to develop independence.

This is the 'ideal' teaching style. You know when to crack down, but you're reasonable in your demands. You let the class have fun, but you make sure they don't push at the limits. A modern teaching style focuses on learning. It's about getting the right conditions in place to let your students get on with their education, and it revolves around some key concepts. You must:

- **Be assertive.** Control the classroom – be confident, certain and definite about what you want. Use a firm approach and stay calm at all times.

- **Stay positive.** Use rewards to motivate students, looking for the best in everyone. Focus on what goes right rather than on what goes wrong.

✔ **Be consistent.** Treat all students equally, applying the same standards to everyone. If you say 'no chewing gum', follow through on that every time.

✔ **Foster independence.** Encourage your students to take control of their learning. Set tasks that require independent study and group work. Give them your trust, and they should repay it with hard work and focus.

✔ **Keep up to date.** Take an interest in recent cultural developments and find ways to incorporate them into your teaching. You don't have to *like* the latest music/novel/film/trend/fad, just use it to your advantage.

✔ **Know when to be flexible.** Understand why consistency is important, but see the need for flexibility as well. View your students as people, not robots, and appreciate that sometimes they need delicate handling. Know when to bend the rules rather than break your relationship with a class.

✔ **Be creative.** Be inventive and imaginative in delivering your lessons. Spice them up with interesting resources, multisensory activities, visual presentations.

✔ **Have a sense of humour.** Laugh with (but not at) your students. Don't object if they laugh at you when you do something stupid. Don't be too precious about yourself. Humour helps everyone relax, it lightens the atmosphere and helps your students learn more effectively.

✔ **Show respect.** Never ask for respect without giving it. Show respect to your students and they should give it back to you. Be polite at all times. If your students don't give you respect, refuse to sink to their level.

Balance is essential, but it's very hard to achieve. You must strike a balance between consistency and flexibility: when to crack down on misbehaviour, when to use a lighter touch. You must balance work and fun: understand when to push a class and when you're flogging the proverbial dead horse.

You know if you're doing it right because you and your students are enjoying the experience. When everything just clicks into place and the lesson goes smoothly and to your expectations, you've got the balance right. You need this balance personally, as well as professionally. Do the best you can as a teacher, but don't tire yourself out in pursuit of an impossible goal.

A head teacher I know told me that his motto is *'Be reasonable, but don't reason with them'*. This is a great maxim for achieving a modern teaching style. Set reasonable standards and expectations, both for yourself and your students. Make sure that what you ask is fair, and that you ask for it in a firm way. Then refuse to get pulled into justifying yourself to your class.

Unusual teaching styles

Most teachers use a straightforward style – the firm, fair and fun style this chapter describes. Some teachers take things further, using a style that develops from an eccentric personality. In teaching 'crazy is good' – if your students aren't sure what's going to happen next, they stay on their toes. You may come across these kinds of teachers:

✔ **The drama queen:** She does everything with a flourish and a sense of boundless enthusiasm. She refers to the students as 'dahlings' or 'luvvies.'

✔ **The classroom clown:** She loves to play practical jokes and tell rude stories. The students feel relaxed and enjoy her lessons, but if they push too far she cracks down hard.

✔ **The art school drop-out:** She wears wild and outrageous clothes, smeared with paint. She believes in free expression and the creative potential of each individual.

✔ **The sergeant major:** She models her style on an army sergeant. The students understand that she shouts so they do their best.

Examining Your Own Teaching Style

To develop a top-notch teaching style, you must examine the style you use and the effect it has on your class. You learn this process of self-reflection and self-examination as you gain in teaching experience.

Put yourself in your students' place – see yourself as they see you. Remember what sitting in class listening to a teacher drone on was like for you. Imagine yourself as a student in your own lesson: what do you need to change? Hold up a mirror to your style to see how it looks from the other side.

You can examine your teaching style while you're 'in action' (if you're lucky by filming yourself, as Chapter 3 suggests) and learn how to adapt your approaches during the course of a lesson.

What works for me?

Your style must work for your students but it must also work for you – you're the one who has to use it! Your style must be something that you can 'switch on', day after day, week after week. You may well find you have lots of enthusiasm at the start of the school year, but as the term drags on your energy levels dip.

To find a style that works for you, make sure it:

- ✔ **Is easy to maintain:** Choose a style you can keep up over the course of a school year. Consistency is important because it lets your students know where they stand.

- ✔ **Isn't too teacher-intensive:** Avoid a style that's emotionally or physically draining. A lot of shouting is hard to sustain, counter-productive and can damage your voice. Too much 'chalk and talk' is tough on you. Most of the time, make your students do most of the work.

- ✔ **Is interesting:** Develop an approach that keeps your interest. Make sure your students find your style captivating as well.

- ✔ **Helps you stay calm and relaxed:** Demonstrate impressive levels of self-control to your students. Find a style that helps you stay calm.

- ✔ **Doesn't get you into pointless confrontations:** Find a style that lets you maintain high standards, but doesn't get you into a lot of arguments with students. Work out whether pushing a point achieves anything.

What works in my setting?

Your style must suit the setting where you teach. You may need to use a very different style if you work in a small pre-school, a large comprehensive, a suburban independent school, an inner-city academy, tutoring students out of school, with adult learners or in a young offenders' institute.

Your style needs to reflect your priorities. Imagine that you teach students who are highly motivated, have pushy parents and your management team has a clear structure for sanctions in place. In this instance, your focus is probably on getting through lots of work, because you're unlikely to be worried too much by behaviour issues.

Now imagine that you teach students who are poorly motivated, have parents who don't care and the sanctions systems at your school just don't work at all. In that situation, behaviour management is going to be a priority. Your focus will be on showing your students why learning and school are important, and on re-engaging them with the idea that learning can be fun. You're definitely not going to get them under control with an 'old-school' strict approach.

Work out the best style for your setting by asking yourself these questions:

- ✔ **What do my students expect?** Be realistic about how your students *expect* you to teach them. Are they comfy with quite a strict and firm approach, or is a slightly relaxed style more likely to get good results?

✔ **What do my students need?** You use a different style for a 5-year-old child and a 30-year-old mature student. Work out what your students need from you and give it to them, at least in part.

✔ **What do other teachers do?** Look around your setting to see how other teachers work. How do they adapt their styles to suit the students? See which styles work well – and then nick bits of them.

✔ **What do parents/carers/managers expect?** They pay your wages, so give them the style they expect. You can get away with a little bit of subversion (it's great fun), but don't push things too far.

I've taught students of all ages, from 3-year-olds to 50-year-olds. Although my basic teaching *methods* are similar, my *style* varies hugely.

What works with my students?

After teaching for a few years, you've become confident that you know what works. Your teaching style is sorted and you get a great response from your students. Unfortunately, nobody mentions this to the students at your next school. You walk into your first lesson and it's a riot. You use the style that worked so well before; your students completely ignore you.

This situation isn't fictional – this happened to me, and it may happen to you when you change schools. What works with one bunch of students can fail miserably with the next. Students vary hugely from school to school, and from area to area. The students you teach are unique; adapt your style to them.

To develop the right style for your students:

✔ **Never patronise them.** Don't speak down to them or assume that you know what they're thinking or feeling. Watch that you use age-appropriate methods and vocabulary – you won't speak to 15-year-olds in the same way you address 5-year-olds. Learners of any age are sensitive to being patronised, so don't do it.

✔ **Understand their issues.** Your students have issues, such as family break-ups, conflicts within a community, poverty, addiction and so on, that are nothing to do with school, with you or with your teaching. Understand their situations and take them into account to develop your style.

✔ **Ask them for information and feedback.** Your students are the experts on themselves, so ask them to tell you about what they're like. This information is invaluable in building a strong and positive relationship and developing a style that works with this particular group.

✔ **Big them up.** However deprived your students are, believe they can achieve great things. See every child as a 'golden child'. Be the person who believes in them – the one who makes a difference. Remember that being a teacher is never just about teaching but is about being a role model and hopefully an inspiration, too.

✔ **Respond instinctively to them.** Get a 'feel' for your students and respond instinctively to their needs. Listen carefully to what they tell you, and the subtext of what they say as well. 'Read' their moods and their body language for signs of conflict or low self worth. This is a hard skill to learn – it involves being relaxed and responsive. You know when you've got it.

In teaching, you learn all the time. When you move to a new school or setting, you get a chance to try adding a few new aspects to your style.

Reflecting on your challenges

View any problems as a chance to reflect and improve. By learning to reflect you build a style that best suits your students. After a bad lesson or day, ask yourself:

✔ Did I do or say something that triggered the problem?

✔ How did I react when things began to go wrong?

✔ Did I adapt to the situation, or keep going in the same way?

✔ Did other factors contribute (the weather, a problem in a previous lesson, a disrupted timetable)?

✔ Could my lesson planning have been a factor in adding to the problem?

✔ What can I learn from this experience so that I do things differently next time around?

Remember, reflection isn't about negative self-criticism, it's about positive soul searching to make yourself the best teacher you can be. As well as reflecting by yourself, ask other members of staff for their thoughts and impressions about what happened.

Don't always blame yourself when things go wrong. Sometimes a problem is nothing to do with you and your style – the student was just having a bad day. Other times something you do (or don't do) contributes to the problem. See mistakes as an opportunity to develop, but don't be over-critical of yourself.

Developing Your Teaching Style

After you have the bones of your teaching style in place, find ways to develop it further. Start to experiment with interesting forms of communication – adapt the way you use your body, perhaps experimenting with how far you can use hand signals to 'talk' to your class. Try out some unusual lessons to see how your students react – for example, get them to take on the character of astronauts, setting up your room as a spaceship, for a study of the solar system.

View your style as a 'work in progress' – something that's never quite finished, but which grows and develops over time until it's as close to perfect as possible.

Playing around with verbal and non-verbal communication

Your verbal and non-verbal skills are a key part of your teaching style. You use them to control and communicate with your students and also to engage and interest a class. Play around with the way you speak and the way you use your body. Experiment to see the kind of effects it can have on your class. You can find a lot of detail about verbal and non-verbal communication in Chapter 3. Think about the following to get you started:

✔ **How can I play around with volume?** If you normally use a loud voice and have a tendency to shout, experiment with using a very quiet volume instead, to see whether it improves your students' focus. If you like a strict, old-school style, see whether it works equally well using a quiet, deadly tone.

✔ **How can I experiment with tone?** If you're reading a story to the class, try making it sound *really* spooky, or *incredibly* exciting. How far can you go before your students give you a weird look as though to say 'you're crazy, miss'?

✔ **What can you do with your face?** Take a look in a mirror and try out some different looks. What does it 'say' when you raise a single eyebrow? This is a classic look for the 'old-school' style of teaching, but it can work equally well with a more modern style.

✔ **How can you use your body?** Try out different postures when you're waiting for your class to fall silent. Experiment with hands on hips, arms folded, or arms by your sides to see which one projects the style you prefer to use.

> ✔ **How can you be more inventive with the space?** Experiment with teaching from different spots in the room – the sides and back, as well as the front. If you're using a modern style, but experiencing behaviour issues, try changing the layout of the desks to the old school rows.

You may be more strongly aware of how you speak, but your body language often 'says' more to your students than your voice ever can. Watch out for the negative messages that your body language can send. Make sure you don't:

✔ Stand in one spot, back against the wall.

✔ Drop your shoulders inwards and curl in on yourself.

✔ Bite your lip or a nail.

✔ Refuse to make direct eye contact with students.

✔ Stay as far away from the troublemakers as you can.

All these mistakes suggest a lack of confidence and an unwillingness to get engaged with the students.

Varying your lessons

The way you structure and deliver your lessons says a great deal about your style. The content you include tells the students what kind of teacher you are or want to be. Your lessons are based on the curriculum you teach, but you can typically adapt the content to suit your own needs and style. You can find loads of information about structuring and delivering really great lessons in Chapters 4, 5 and 6.

If you opt to use an old-school style, you assume that your students will behave well and work hard whatever kind of lesson they receive. In an old-school style lesson, the teacher often insists on long periods of focus, and tends to lecture students without inviting any feedback. Where this style is in use, you often find a 'chalk and talk' approach where the teacher writes notes up on the board and the students copy these down. The old-school style promotes a teacher, rather than child, centred approach.

In recent years, the impact of learning styles in schools has been widely discussed. As a result, even those teachers who do have success with an old-school approach have been encouraged to make some changes to their lesson planning and delivery. If this is your preferred style, consider whether you might incorporate some of the more modern elements discussed below.

To ensure that your style feels fresh, modern and interesting, you need to:

✔ **Suit the lessons to the students.** Keep your standards high, but don't demand the impossible from your students. If you ask them to write in silence for an hour every lesson, expect rebellion. Balance focused work with some time off for good behaviour.

✔ **Incorporate their interests where possible.** Find out what your students are 'into' and use it in some way in your lessons. Keep an eye on the latest playground crazes. When you spot an interesting one, incorporate it into your teaching.

✔ **Use plenty of exciting and engaging resources.** Take time to find resources that spark your students' curiosity. This gives a clear message: 'I am willing to put effort into creating interesting lessons for you.'

✔ **Let some lessons develop organically.** Occasionally, let a lesson develop of its own accord. Pounce on an idea a student offers; or bring in a resource and see where the class wants to go with it. Be flexible and responsive and you 'connect' with your students.

✔ **Aim to appeal to everyone.** Your students are good at different things. Some of them love writing, others enjoy drawing or practical, hands-on activities. Appeal to everyone by incorporating a variety of tasks into your lessons: something thoughtful, something active, something creative. The more different tasks you include, the more likely you are to strike a chord with all your students.

You can't appeal to every student with every lesson. Some work is boring or hard, no matter how well you deliver it. Some students aren't interested in the topic you're covering. Make sure that the majority of your lessons excite or at least interest your students by following these ideas and those I offer in Chapters 4 and 5. If you do this, most students will pay you the compliment of behaving well and working hard in those lessons that aren't so exciting.

Chapter 3

Making the Most of Your Communication Skills

*T*eachers are communicators: communication is at the heart of what you do every time you stand in front of a class. You speak to the students. They (hopefully) listen to you. But communication isn't just about opening your mouth and talking. It's also about:

✔ How your voice sounds.

✔ The particular words you decide to use.

✔ The messages your body sends.

✔ How your face looks.

✔ The way you control the space.

Of course, communication is a two-way process. You communicate *with* your students, rather than *at* them, and by being open to what they tell you, you build a positive and effective relationship together.

In this chapter you find out how to communicate really effectively with your students. And the better your communication skills, the better the behaviour and learning you get in your classroom.

Examining What You Say and Do

Human beings have an instinctive urge to connect with each other. As a teacher, you must form a connection with each of your students, whatever their age, attitude or abilities. Forming this connection is about bringing all of your communication skills into play.

Quality communication matters because:

- ✔ **It helps you 'click' with individuals and classes.** The continual process of communication helps them feel that you know and respect them.

- ✔ **It's vital for effective classroom and behaviour management.** You must communicate what you want to your students – that way, they know how they are meant to behave.

- ✔ **It sends a very clear message about you as a teacher.** It says, 'I care about building bonds with you'.

- ✔ **It allows quality teaching and learning to happen.** You communicate what you want the students to learn, in a way they understand.

- ✔ **It makes your classroom a fun and interesting place to be.** You come across as a vibrant, interesting person to spend time with.

Improving your communication skills is a process of learning and experimenting, rather than an instant 'fix'. With time and experience, you find yourself becoming a more and more effective communicator.

To become a really great teacher you have to be self-aware. The whole time you teach, be conscious of how your voice sounds and how your body looks. Imagine you're an actor, up there at the front of a class, putting on a performance. Get your role right and your audience is captivated; get it wrong and they start to drift away.

Put yourself in your students' shoes. Ask yourself: 'How do I look and sound from *their* perspective?' If you figure that out, you have some chance of understanding why they are (a) fidgeting, (b) dozing off or (c) about to riot.

Communication's all about perception

Many times, I've stood in front of a class and felt absolutely terrified: as a new teacher, as a supply teacher, on my first day at a new school. But I've always tried to appear confident on the outside, to hide my inner fears.

If you look scared or tense, your students quickly pick up on it: a nervous tremor in your voice, a lack of direct eye contact, these send clear signals about your inner state of mind. And if the students suss that you're worried, they seize the opportunity to pressurise you even more.

Often, students aren't fully aware of why they react to you in a particular way. Their reactions may be almost entirely subconscious, especially if you work with young children. But whether or not your students are conscious of their perceptions, they still act on what those perceptions tell them.

How you feel inside doesn't matter – no one can know that unless your body or voice gives them clues. What matters is how your students *perceive* you. Most of the time, if you look and sound confident, then that's how you come across.

Understanding the subconscious messages you send

Even as you work at becoming more self-aware, many of the messages you send to a class remain stubbornly subconscious. We all have those little habits and tics – chewing a nail, biting a lip. Ask yourself:

- ✔ **What do I do with my face when I'm feeling tense?** Think particularly about your eyes and your mouth – this is often where tension shows.

- ✔ **What do I do with my hands and fingers when I'm under pressure?** If you're a nail biter, you may subconsciously take this habit into your classroom.

- ✔ **Do I take up a particular body position when I'm feeling threatened?** You may have a tendency to close in on yourself, or to turn your back on a class.

- ✔ **Do I remember to move around the room when I'm nervous?** You could find yourself frozen close to your board, rather than getting in close to those troublemakers at the back.

- ✔ **How does my voice sound when I'm feeling tense?** Your voice is particularly responsive to stress – does it crack, tighten or rise under pressure?

- ✔ **What do my clothing choices say about me?** Consider the kind of message your clothes are sending to the class. Do you look too formal or informal? Match your outfit to the messages you want to send.

> ✔ **Do I have any vocal 'tics' or phrases that come out in stressful situations?** You probably have some repetitive phrases that you're not conscious of using. Mine are 'okay, right', 'so' and 'well'.

The ideal is to be in a continual state of self-evaluation and self-awareness – to be conscious of what your body and voice are doing at all times. The more experienced you get as a teacher, the more this becomes second nature.

Making Magic with Your Mouth

As a teacher, you can do some magical things with your mouth and your voice. What you say, and the way you say it, has a hugely powerful effect on a class's behaviour and work. If you pitch the tone, volume, pace and emotional quality of your voice exactly right, you find that your students suddenly become much more positive and responsive towards you.

Teachers speak in the classroom for many different reasons. You use talk to inform, to explain, to inspire, to reason, to insist, to question, to discuss. Speaking is a central part of being a teacher, so getting it right pays dividends. To 'make magic' with your voice, you need to:

> ✔ **Be clear:** Say what you need to say in as few words as possible, without any ambiguity.

> ✔ **Sound interesting**: Speak in an engaging, imaginative and enthusiastic way.

> ✔ **Sound relaxed**: Don't allow internal tension to come through in the sound of your voice.

> ✔ **Sound confident and in control:** Put across the impression that you're in command of the class and the space.

> ✔ **Play with pace:** Use the speed at which you speak to give a sense of energy and forward motion, or alternatively to calm things down.

> ✔ **Keep a lid on excessive emotion**: Don't let negative emotions show through when you speak.

Our voices play a key part in the way other people perceive us. To see for yourself how true this is, conjure up the sound of someone's voice in your head – really hear that person speaking. You may want to choose someone famous, like a politician or an actor, or someone familiar from your daily life. How does the sound of that person's voice contribute to your overall impression of them? Do you *like* the vocal sound, or does it irritate or depress you? Chances are, the way you respond to the voice feeds into how you feel about that person.

Benefiting from volume

The volume levels you use depend on what you're doing. When you're addressing a whole class, you must talk loudly enough to be heard. When you're talking with an individual or a small group, you adjust the volume levels downwards. Finding the right volume levels for each situation is a key teaching skill to master.

Talking loudly can become a habit. You're trying to enthuse a class and you get carried away. Or a class is winding you up and your voice begins to get louder and louder. Become conscious of the sound of your voice. Make regular checks on your volume levels. About 90 per cent of the time, you're probably talking too loudly.

The quieter you are as a teacher, the more your students have to listen in order to hear you. Watching students perk up their ears to hear you is a bit like watching a turtle poke its head out of its shell: that slight forward motion with the ear towards the teacher is a good sign that you're getting the volume right.

Speaking more quietly also affects the sound quality of your voice in a positive way. A quiet volume tends to lead to a more relaxed, conversational-sounding teaching voice. In turn, this relaxes and calms your students.

Think of your voice as like a piece of music on a stereo. Sometimes you want to turn the volume right up to make sure everyone can hear and that the music has an impact. At other times, you need a quieter sound to help create an aura of relaxation. Just as with a stereo, learn to turn the volume of your voice up and down to suit your needs. Watch to see how your students are responding – do they look interested, or have they 'tuned out'? Adapt the volume you use to make sure that you keep your class fully engaged.

No one likes to be shouted at. Shouting's just not polite. And more than that, it shows that you've lost control of your emotions. Shouting at your students when they're misbehaving is like waving a red rag in front of a bull: doing so encourages them to behave even worse. Sometimes you have to raise your voice, to show that you're not happy about a situation. But when you do raise your voice, make sure you do so from a position of emotional self-control, and not when you're completely furious. That way, the voice you use comes from your diaphragm, and not from your throat. You *sound* like you're in control, because you are.

Remember that if you start out loud, you then have nowhere to go. But if you normally sound relaxed and reasonably quiet, even the slightest rise in your volume level has an impact. Save your loudest voice for any really serious or dangerous situations.

Getting to the truth about tone

Tone is all about how you inflect your voice – change its timbre – to express emotion, passion or interest. It gives an insight into your inner state, whether that's your actual state or something you're pretending to feel. Tone can tell your class that you're happy, scared, excited, nervous, irritated, interested, curious and so on.

Just as an actor or public speaker uses tone to enhance the connection with the audience, so do the most effective teachers. Of course, you've got to pitch it at the right level for your student audience. With young children, plenty of tone is great. With older students, avoid excesses of tone – the students may perceive it as being patronising.

Tone is important in your teaching for lots of reasons:

- ✔ **It makes your voice sound interesting**. Consider the difference between someone talking in a complete monotone, and someone telling a spooky story in a really scary-sounding voice. I know which one I prefer to listen to, and so do your students.

- ✔ **It helps you gain and keep a class's attention.** Your students often respond more to the *sound* of what you say than to the actual words you use. This is particularly so for younger students, and for those learning a second language.

- ✔ **It gives clues and cues to help students learn.** They judge what you want by listening to the tonal quality of your voice. If you sound enthused, this sends them cues that something interesting is going to happen.

- ✔ **It makes your face and body come to life.** Try telling an exciting story, using lots of tone – you may find that you can't help bringing expression into your face, and you probably move around too. Adding tone forces you to teach in a more interesting way.

- ✔ **It helps you manage student behaviour**. You can use tone to tell a class that you're not impressed with their behaviour. Again, they probably pick up more clues from the sound of your voice than from what you say.

Varying tone for maximum effect

Some types of tone work really well in different classroom situations. When you're teaching, try sounding:

- ✔ Excited: *'We've got some really fun things to do today.'*

- ✔ Interested: *'I'm really going to enjoy exploring this topic.'*

- ✔ Curious: *'How can we find out an answer to this?'*

- ✔ Amazed: *'Wow, I didn't know that!'*

When you're dealing with problematic behaviour, try sounding:

✔ Surprised: *'I can't believe you're behaving like this.'*

✔ Disappointed: *'You're really letting yourself down with that behaviour.'*

✔ Puzzled: *'Why on earth would you want to do that?'*

These tones suggest that your normal impression is that the students are brilliant. And the only appropriate response to misbehaviour is to be amazed.

Keeping negative emotions under control

Your voice can be a bit sneaky, a bit of a gossip – it loves to give away all your inner secrets. And this is especially so when we come to emotion. Emotion is probably the hardest thing of all to keep secret. Nerves make your voice crack, stress makes your voice hard and tense, but humour makes it sound relaxed and pleasant to hear. Remember, every time you let your voice betray negative emotions such as fear or anger, doing so:

✔ Shows your students they have some measure of control over you.

✔ Encourages them to repeat the behaviour that got the emotional response in the first place.

✔ Can scare or even terrify your more nervous students.

✔ Increases your stress levels.

One great way to stop emotion from leaking into your voice is to learn how to stay calm when you face difficult classroom situations. This sounds easy, but it's surprisingly hard to do. You can find out lots more about keeping yourself calm in Chapter 8.

Playing with pace

Pace is a powerful tool in verbal communication. Use a fast pace to liven up an unenthusiastic class, or a slow pace to calm down a bunch of excited students. Play around with different speeds while you're teaching, to see the effect they have on your class.

If you've got lots to get through in a fast-paced lesson, then the speed of your voice gives your students the cue to work quickly. Similarly, if you want a calm and focused approach to the work, you can cue the students into this fact with the speed of your voice.

Think about the length of individual words. Single-syllable words are great for when you want to grab a class's attention – that rapid-fire, 'machine gun' effect is difficult to ignore. Longer words are useful when you want to slow down a situation, for instance with an over-excited class.

Think of words as though they're chewing gum. You can stretch them out like elastic, you can spit them out quickly and you can vary the pace within each one. So you may say 'c . . . a . . . l . . . m . . . d . . . o . . . w . . . n' to settle a lively class, or 'Right! Eyes on me now!' to a group who are losing focus.

Picking the right words

Good verbal communication is not just about *how* you speak, it's also about the words you choose. The vocabulary you use with your class has a direct impact on the quality of learning and behaviour in your lessons. You need to use language that is:

- ✔ **Clear and unambiguous.** Say what you mean, and mean what you say. Use as few words as possible to get your meaning across – that way you keep the students' interest and attention.

- ✔ **At the right level for the student or class.** Don't use vocabulary that's far too complex for your class, but don't over-simplify your language for more able or older students.

- ✔ **Structured and focused.** Speak in a linear and well-ordered way, rather than hopping about from one idea to another.

- ✔ **Formal enough to fit the occasion.** Take care to limit your use of slang and colloquialisms, which give an informal feel to what you say and make it appear less important or meaningful. Students who don't have English as a first language could find these words hard to understand.

- ✔ **Interesting and engaging.** Use words that gain and keep your students' attention – 'fun', 'exciting' and 'adventurous' are all good.

The most crucial time to get language right is when you give instructions: if the students don't know what you want them to do, they can't do it, and they may well veer off the task.

Giving high-quality instructions is surprisingly hard. Have you noticed how, when you explain a task, moments after beginning the activity a bunch of hands go up with students asking 'What are we meant to do?' Avoid this by getting your instructions right in the first place.

To give clear, effective instructions, follow these steps:

1. **Give a 'cue' as to when the students should start, for instance: 'When I tell you to start . . .'**

2. **Make a statement about the task: what should be done, and how it should be done (in pairs, with discussion, etc.).**

3. **Set a target for how much they must achieve: five ideas, three sentences, ten pages, for example.**

4. **Set a time limit so the students know how long they have to do the task.**

5. **Agree a signal to show when you want the class back, for instance putting your hand in the air.**

6. **Check for understanding, by asking a student to explain the activity back to you.**

7. **Ask whether students have any questions.**

8. **Say 'go!'**

This is a lot to remember, and you need practice to get it right. But before long you whiz through each of these steps instinctively. For a more detailed explanation of this technique, see Chapter 4.

Teachers often develop the habit of using rhetorical questions. You know the kind of thing I mean. A student says 'You're an old cow!' and you reply 'What did you say?' To which the accurate answer is 'I said you're an old cow!'. Don't phrase what you say as a question, unless you actually want an answer. Get into the habit of making statements rather than asking questions. So instead of asking 'Why aren't you working?' say 'I want you to get on with your work right now'.

Keeping to the point

Teachers spend a lot of the time talking. Often, teachers spend *too much* of the time talking. Be honest: are you just a little bit in love with the sound of your own voice? Certainly, you probably became a teacher because you love to explain, to inform, to engage. This enthusiasm can easily tip over into too much talk. I willingly admit that talking too much is one of my own worst teaching sins.

As you talk to a class or an individual student, learn to read the signs that say 'we're switching off'. Many students do a very good impression of listening, when in reality your words are not actually reaching their brains. And when you see those signs (fidgeting, looking away, tipping on chairs), switch to a more active style of teaching as soon as you can.

A good rule of thumb for maximum concentration span is the students' age plus two. So with a class of 5-year-olds, you have about seven minutes before they start to lose interest. With a class of 16-year-olds, you get a bit longer. But remember, you don't *have* to use all of those 18 minutes!

Taking care of your voice

Your voice is absolutely central to your job as a teacher – if you can't speak, you can't teach. Your voice is the equivalent of a musician's instrument, an essential tool for doing your job. But unlike a musician, you only have one voice, and you can't send it away to be repaired. You absolutely *must* take care of your voice, especially if you plan to be teaching for many years. You can't afford to thrash it or trash it like a guitarist in a rock concert.

To take the best care of your voice:

✔ **Develop a good vocal technique**: Speak from your diaphragm and not from your throat.

✔ **Don't talk more than necessary**: Get your students to do the talking rather than lecturing them for long periods.

✔ **Avoid shouting as far as is humanly possible**: Yelling's very bad for your voice, as it can strain and damage it.

✔ **Don't force a whisper either**: This is equally bad for your voice.

✔ **Use pre-agreed silence signals to gain the attention of a class, rather than shouting over noise**: Try hands up for silence, clapping a rhythm, standing with arms folded looking mean.

✔ **Drink plenty of fluids while teaching and in your breaks**: This keeps your vocal chords well lubricated.

✔ **Stick to water if you can**: Avoid milky drinks because they encourage your body to produce mucus.

✔ **Take care of your physical health.** Be aware that smoking, and drinking alcohol and too much tea or coffee can also damage your voice.

✔ **Rest your voice whenever you can**: Spend some quiet time outside the classroom. Relax and sit in silent contemplation at least once a day.

Letting Your Body Do the Talking

Good communication is not just about using your voice effectively; you can also 'say' a great deal with your body. Controlling the signals you send with your body is hard – often they're almost entirely subconscious. Become more self-aware, and learn to understand the role that your body plays in high-quality communication. For a more detailed study of this fascinating subject, you may like to read Elizabeth Kuhnke's *Body Language For Dummies* (Wiley).

The eyes have it

As the saying goes, 'the eyes are the window to the soul'. You probably don't have any desire to peer into the souls of every student you teach, and you certainly don't want them delving into yours. But making direct eye contact is a great way to bond with a class and to manage student behaviour.

Watching yourself in action

The first time you see yourself teaching can come as a bit of a shock. I was never brave enough to video myself at work in the classroom. But when I was asked to present some programmes for Teachers' TV, I finally got to watch myself 'in action'.

If you do get the chance to see yourself teaching, you may find this an alarming, but worthwhile, experience. Some schools now have special observation classrooms, with small cameras in place, so that teachers can see themselves at work. On film, those parts of your personality that you imagined to be subtle and charming come across as irritating and off-putting. Vocal 'tics' are all too obvious when you see and hear yourself talk at a class.

Things are not all bad though. You may also spot some things that you do subconsciously, things that help you connect with your students. Overall, seeing yourself on film is well worth doing if you get the chance.

When you look someone directly in the eyes, you make an instant kind of connection. That person feels that you are paying attention to them, that you have noticed them as an individual. Using eye contact is a great way to create a strong relationship.

You use your eyes to communicate different messages and meanings in different situations:

- ✔ **Direct eye contact with lots of individuals.** Use lots of this at the start of lessons, to 'click' with students and to ensure you have their attention.

- ✔ **'Deadly stare' at one individual.** Use a quick, pointed glance to say 'I've spotted what you're doing and I don't like it'.

- ✔ **Swift glance around the room.** This gives an overview of how a class is getting on and whether all the students are focusing on their work.

- ✔ **Removing all eye contact from a class.** This says 'I'm waiting for you to give me your attention' or 'I'm not happy at all'.

Experiment with using eye contact in different ways. Doing so can feel quite hard work at first, but you soon build eye contact into the bank of different communication strategies that you use with a class.

When you're talking one on one with a student, don't feel that you must always make direct eye contact. This is especially so when you're giving a sanction. Some students perceive direct eye contact as aggressive. Others feel uncomfortable about looking you directly in the eyes, perhaps because of cultural differences. Instead, crouch down alongside students, with your body facing in the same direction as theirs. You can still talk and be heard, but you remove some of the pressure from the situation.

Eyes to the right

Many teachers teach to their dominant side, although most are not aware that they're doing this. What this means is, if you're right handed you tend to focus your eyes and your body on the right-hand side of the room. The students on your far left get the least of your attention. If you're left handed then the opposite applies.

Be conscious about whether you're teaching more to one side of the room than the other, and make a concerted effort to overcome this dominant side tendency. Remind yourself, several times during a lesson, to check that you're looking at everyone in the class.

Facing the facts

Your students spend a large part of every day looking at your face. While there's not much you can do to change your facial appearance (barring cosmetic surgery), you can certainly play around with your facial expressions.

Most of the time, aim to keep a relaxed, happy but firm expression on your face. This lets your students feel that you respect and care about them, but also that you're in control of the class. If any behaviour problems crop up, change your expression to one of surprise, disappointment or irritation, as appropriate. Again, make your rational side decide how your face should look, rather than allowing your emotions to show through in your expressions.

Spending some time looking in the mirror is worthwhile, to get a better sense of how your face appears to your students. Practise subtle expressions such as a frown, or a single raised eyebrow. This very minor facial change says a whole host of things, including 'excuse me!', 'really?' and 'oh yes?'.

Helping hands

I love to teach with my hands – I really can't help it. When I'm working with a class my hands start to move around, almost of their own accord. Your hands are such an expressive part of your body: they can click, twist, grab, clap, gesticulate and so on. Make the most of hand movements and gestures – let your hands do the talking!

You can say a whole host of things to a class using very simple hand signals. These signals are pretty much universally understood (although do watch for cultural variations if you teach in a far-flung part of the world and you're not completely au fait with local traditions). Hand signals are especially useful for classroom management, because they can indicate your wishes to a whole class of students at once. In fact, you should almost be able to manage your class with hand signals alone.

You can use your hands to say:

- ✔ 'Well done' – using a thumbs-up gesture, clapping or giving a 'high five' to an individual.

- ✔ 'Please listen' – putting your hand behind your ear to indicate you want the students to pay attention.

- ✔ 'Silence please' – placing your index finger on lips and waiting until the students notice.

- ✔ 'Stand up' – moving both hands, palms upwards, in a lifting motion to show that the students should stand up from their chairs.

- ✔ 'Stop!' – moving both hands, palms down, in a cutting/crossing motion, or alternatively putting one hand up, with your palm facing the class.

The more frequently you use your hands to give commands, instructions and praise, the more quickly your students respond.

Perfecting posture and body position

The overall appearance of your body sends subconscious messages to your class. You may stand, hands on hips, looking mean while you wait for a class to settle. You can fold your arms and glance at your watch to tell a class 'I'm waiting'. Becoming more conscious about what your body 'says' is a great way to boost your teaching skills.

You've probably developed a particular spot in your classroom where you stand when you want to address the class. You may have done this instinctively or made a conscious choice about it. This 'silence spot' or 'attention spot' is a useful indicator that you want the students' attention. If you haven't got a 'silence spot' already, then develop one with your class. Go to stand in the same spot every time you want the students to stop and listen. Over time, you find they respond more and more quickly.

To make the most of posture and positioning:

- ✔ **Aim to maintain an upright, open body stance**: This suggests an air of confidence and relaxation.

- ✔ **Keep your head high and erect:** This helps you maintain a good overall posture.

✔ **Make sure you keep your neck and shoulders relaxed:** Don't allow any tension from your body to move into your upper back.

✔ **Avoid turning your back on a class, especially an unruly one:** Stand sideways to write on the board, to avoid the classic classroom problem of a paper missile attack from your students.

✔ **Crouch beside an individual to talk privately:** Keep your conversations one to one, especially if they're about behaviour. That way, you avoid raising the stakes for the student.

✔ **Aim to 'touch all four walls':** Move to all the different parts of the classroom during the course of a lesson. Doing so ensures that you visit and connect with every individual in the room.

The whole time they're with you, students are making conscious and subconscious decisions about how to work and behave, based on their reading of your body language.

Taking Control of the Space

Wherever and whoever you teach, you must send a clear signal to your class that they're in your space, and that you're in control of it. While the students are very welcome inside the space, your role is to ensure they behave and work properly while they're there. You can do this by using body language and movement within the space. You also communicate with your class by the way that you set up and manage your room. You can find lots more ideas about structuring your teaching space in Chapter 7.

You may not have the luxury of a permanent space of your own. Perhaps you have to move around from room to room, going to the class, rather than the class coming to you. This nomadic existence can be both wearing and a cause of discipline issues. If you have to teach in a temporary space of some kind, making a clear non-verbal statement about who's in control is even more important. Use some or all of the techniques described below to help you do this.

You can take control of a space in many different ways. You may:

✔ **Move around the space at will.** Imagine you're a cat, prowling your territory. Don't get stuck at the front beside your whiteboard, when all the troublemakers gravitate to the back. Ideally, make sure that your students never quite know when you may be coming up behind them.

✔ **Teach from the back as well as from the front.** This adds variety, and shows that you can reach and teach from all parts of the room. Ask the students to keep facing front and to listen to your voice, rather than turning to see you.

✔ **Get close to any troublemakers.** You can solve many behaviour issues by moving towards a student and placing a hand on his desk. This indicates: 'I've noticed and I will do something about the behaviour if it continues.'

✔ **Seat the troublemakers where you want them.** You might want to move some of your more difficult students to the front, where they have no chance of hiding their behaviour. A seat near the front is also useful for any students who need extra support with their work.

✔ **Control the way that the students enter and leave the space.** Stand at the door when the class members arrive, inviting them into the room and dealing with any uniform issues as appropriate. I've always made a point of asking students to stand behind their chairs at the end of a lesson. This helps ensure that the space is tidy, and gives a good sense of closure to the session.

✔ **Create and use a seating plan.** Seating plans are a great way to establish that you're in charge of the room, because you're saying where the students sit. You can offer 'free choice of seating' as a reward for a set period of good work and behaviour.

✔ **Rearrange the furniture to suit your needs.** You don't have to stick with the way that a room's normally arranged. Consider what works best for you and your students. Also think about the kind of messages you'd like to communicate through your room layout. A great tip is to sit in every seat in the room to check on each student's viewpoint. You may even rearrange the furniture during a lesson (but if it's not your room, make sure you put it back to rights afterwards).

✔ **Decide what goes on the walls.** Put up some posters and displays to mark the room as your space. This is also a great way of rewarding and motivating your students.

✔ **Have clear rules about what goes where.** Be in charge of saying where resources, books, pens, bags, etc. are placed. Again, this indicates that you're in control of the space.

With all these strategies in place, you communicate to your students that the classroom is your space, and they respond with better work and behaviour. You also feel more in control, which provides a boost to your confidence levels.

Part II
Teaching a Class

In this part . . .

If you're going to get the very best out of your students, you need to plan for, and deliver, really high-quality lessons. And doing that involves more than you may imagine. I show you how to get your students engaged and how to keep them focused right through your lessons. Teaching's a *creative* activity as well as an intellectual and physical one. In this part I outline how you can use your imagination to get the very best results. And have some fun at the same time!

Chapter 4

Preparing and Teaching High-Quality Lessons

*W*hen you plan and deliver a really high-quality lesson you feel great. Your students understand a new concept or learn some new skills. They take charge of their learning and really enjoy the activities you set for them. When a lesson goes wrong, or when your students just don't seem to 'get' the concept you're trying to put across, you don't feel so great.

Creating a good lesson is a bit hit and miss and isn't just about the amount of effort you put into preparation and delivery. Sometimes a well-planned lesson turns into a disaster when you teach it. Other times, a lesson that you barely planned at all turns into one of your finest moments in the classroom. Or a lesson that works well for you with one class may fail miserably with another. All of this is part of the unpredictable but exciting nature of the job! A great deal of the time, what happens isn't your fault. The gods of teaching are fickle and have an odd sense of humour!

In this chapter, you can find a lot of tips for getting things right when planning and teaching great lessons. The more experience you get, the more you get a 'feel' for what works and what doesn't.

Remembering Your Own Teachers

As the saying goes, 'no one forgets a good teacher'. (And to qualify this, you remember the bad teachers even better.) You want to be a 'good teacher', a teacher your students remember long after they've left your class. You want to have a long-lasting influence on the students you teach – to make a difference to their lives.

Think back to when you were at school and summon up a memory of a teacher you remember as being a positive influence, or even an inspiration. Take a few minutes to consider the following:

- ✔ What was she like?

- ✔ What made her memorable?

- ✔ How did she use her voice and her body in the classroom?

- ✔ What kind of lessons did she deliver?

- ✔ How did she respond to you and your work?

- ✔ Did she say or do something specific that sticks in your mind?

- ✔ What kind of teaching style did she have?

Now think of a teacher that you didn't like or didn't get on with. Again, take a few minutes to consider:

- ✔ What you felt was 'wrong' with this teacher.

- ✔ Why you remember her as someone who you didn't 'click' with.

- ✔ Whether she did anything 'wrong' with her voice or her body in your lessons, or whether you simply found her style boring and uninspiring.

- ✔ What kind of lessons she delivered.

- ✔ Whether the problem was more about the subject she taught than the teacher herself.

- ✔ Whether she ever said or did something that upset you and your classmates.

- ✔ How other students at your school felt about and responded to this teacher.

- ✔ What kind of teaching style she had.

Finally, write down three words or phrases that describe the teacher who gave you the positive memories, and do the same for the teacher you remember in a negative way. Can you use anything in what you've written to inform your own teaching practice?

When I ask this question during the in-school training sessions that I run, some common factors crop up in the teachers that people describe. The memorable, inspirational teachers are those:

- Who believed in you – ones who saw your potential.
- Who made you feel you could do a subject really well – that you had a particular aptitude for it.
- Who trusted you and gave you a bit of free rein – those who allowed you to do unusual or interesting activities.
- Who had a passion for a particular subject that came across in the way that they taught it.
- Who were inspirational in some way, either about a particular subject or on a more general and personal level.
- Who made you feel that they saw you as an individual.

How wonderful to be a teacher that your students remember: you live on long in the memories of the students you're teaching right now. Even when they're no longer under your direct care, you still remain as a vital factor in their lives.

Preparing and teaching really high-quality lessons is something that the 'teacher you remember' probably did really well. You might not have realised it at the time, though, because the better the lesson is, often the less 'prepared' and the more 'responsive' it feels.

Planning for Success

Planning is a funny business. You must work out, ahead of time, exactly what you're going to teach in a lesson. You must figure out how to deliver a new concept or some new information. You also need to consider how the students are going to respond to the activities you set.

When you're planning a menu for a successful lesson, think about these three key ingredients:

- **Flexibility:** Your plan needs to be adaptable in the event of unforeseen circumstances – the TV blowing up, the students arriving ten minutes late, the activity proving to be completely beyond them. You also have to be flexible about the needs of different students (see 'Dealing with Differentiation' further on in this chapter).

✔ **Simplicity:** You must be able to refer to your plan with ease. No point having ten pages of detailed notes, you simply don't have a chance to read them in the hurly-burly of the average classroom.

✔ **Suitability:** Your plan needs to 'fit' the students you teach – not too hard or too easy for them, containing activities that keep them engaged, and making sense and feeling 'real' to them.

The problem with lesson planning is that so many variables come into play. You plan a lesson that requires excellent concentration, but the students arrive in a skittish, wired-up mood. You decide to take the class on a treasure hunt outdoors, but five minutes before the lesson, the rain begins. Be prepared for every eventuality, and have plenty of ideas for back-up activities that work in any situation.

The components of an effective plan

Only one thing makes a 'good' plan: it actually *works* for you and your students, during the lesson where it's used, and it helps them to learn something (whether or not this was quite what you intended). You may feel comfy with a lot of detail; you may need only a few scribbled notes. Of course, senior managers and government inspectors may see things differently, but the reality of planning is about getting good-quality learning to take place.

An effective plan can contain some or all of the following, depending on the level of detail you want or need:

✔ A title.

✔ A list of aims or objectives.

✔ Details of the skills the students should learn (sometimes referred to as *WALT* which stands for 'We Are Learning To').

✔ Information about the 'success criteria', for example, what the students need to demonstrate to show they have achieved your objective (sometimes known as *WILF* which stands for 'What I'm Looking For').

✔ Information about any students in the class who have special needs.

✔ A list of any differentiated tasks.

✔ Details of resources, equipment and classroom layout.

✔ A list of activities.

✔ Timings for each activity.

✔ Intended outcomes for each activity, or for the lesson as a whole.

✔ Specific starter, middle and plenary sections to the lesson (in other words, a beginning, middle and end).

> ✔ Information about evaluation and assessment.
>
> ✔ Extension and homework activities.

The amount of information you include depends on your level of confidence in teaching the lesson – the more confident you are, the less detail you need. It also depends on how well you know the students and their needs, and on whether someone else is observing or inspecting the class.

When you train as a teacher, you put a ton of detail in your plans. Your college tutors demand this and you must comply to pass your course. Detailed plans do have their good points. They help you to think ahead of time about how a lesson may run, and to reflect on how it went after the event. But with time and experience, you need less and less detail in your plans to get through a lesson intact. You 'think on your feet' and adapt an exercise that isn't working to suit how the students respond. You have a mental store of quick activities that you can use to fill in a spare ten minutes or to give you some thinking time while you work out what to do next. A good idea is to make a folder for yourself in which you keep some fun and simple back-up lessons, photocopied sheets and activities.

The three Rs of lesson planning: Reduce, reuse, recycle

In the spirit of environmentally friendly living, embrace the three principles of reducing, reusing and recycling your lessons. These three approaches help you minimise the amount of work you have to put in, they make your plans more productive and they increase the shelf life of the lessons you create.

Follow the three Rs:

✔ **Reduce:** Reduce the amount of detail in your plans to the bare bones. Then you can refer to the plan more easily. You can also be more adaptable, learning how to think on your feet during a lesson. You can always plump out the detail when managers or inspectors are likely to visit. Find ways to reduce the amount of planning you do as well, by begging and borrowing lessons and lesson ideas from other teachers, and from the Internet. You can also reduce your planning load by using the second and third Rs below.

✔ **Reuse:** Often, you teach the same topics, themes or books to a series of classes, or to the same age group, for a number of years. In these instances, reusing your plans (or someone else's) from previous years makes sense. Don't do it so often that you get bored and stale with what you're teaching, but don't make unnecessary work for yourself by planning everything afresh.

✔ **Recycle:** When a lesson gets a bit stale, why not 'recycle' it? This may mean cutting out the dull stuff and adding some new activities. It can involve incorporating a new resource, or using the same exercises for a different text. You can recycle ideas as well as entire lessons – if an interesting scenario works well with one class (a crime scene, for instance), then consider how you can adapt it to work with another age group. Try getting together with other staff to see whether you could share and recycle each other's plans as well.

Whenever you get the chance, write some brief notes on your plans just after you've taught them. You can put a tick by activities that go well and a cross by those that don't. You can also scribble a few pointers for next time round. That way, when you revisit the plan in the future, you should remember how it went at the time and what needed changing. Ask your students for some feedback on which bits of a lesson worked well, and which bits need changing.

No plan, no problem?

Nowadays, the 'powers that be' want everything in education to be measured, targeted and delivered in a specific way. As well as doing your teaching, you must *prove* what you do by documenting it. Not so many years ago, a teacher sometimes went into a classroom with just a vague idea in her head about how the lesson may proceed (or even with no idea at all). She possibly began a session by asking the children: 'What do you think we should learn about today?' Shocking, isn't it?

Well no, it's not shocking at all. Because this approach means:

✔ You respond to what your students want and need, at the exact moment you're teaching them.

✔ You have a responsive attitude in your lesson – you react to what's actually happening, rather than trying to predict what may take place.

✔ You're more likely to be creative in the approaches you use, because thinking on your feet can spark off some really interesting ideas.

✔ You can incorporate the students' ideas, needs and abilities into the work you devise.

✔ You can be flexible with timings – if an activity is working really well, or taking longer than anticipated, you can carry on with it rather than stopping halfway through.

✔ You can go off at a tangent if an interesting idea crops up.

Of course, I don't recommend that you take this approach all the time, but once in a while, try it and see what happens. You may be pleasantly surprised at the results. You can also try using this approach in conjunction with a pre-planned lesson – if an activity you planned isn't working, respond by throwing it away, rather than slogging on regardless.

Having said that, be aware that some classes or lessons need more structure than others. You should use a very highly structured approach with:

- ✔ Students who tend to misbehave – the clear structure says 'I know what I'm doing and where we're going, so don't try to mess me around.'

- ✔ Young students – the clear structure says 'I will take care of you and lead you through the lesson, so don't worry about anything except learning.'

- ✔ Subjects that need the students to take a logical series of steps in order to learn a skill or understand a concept (some maths or science topics, for instance).

- ✔ Lessons where you need to get through a lot of stuff.

The section 'Structuring a Quality Lesson' explains how to create a structured lesson plan.

Structuring a Quality Lesson

You create the lesson structure during your planning stage (although lessons rarely run exactly to plan). Getting the structure right can mean the difference between a highly successful lesson and one that descends into chaos. To structure a quality lesson, you must:

- ✔ Decide exactly what you need to teach – a concept, an idea, a skill, a technique.

- ✔ Work out how best to get this across to your students.

- ✔ Plan a series of activities that flow well, leading one into the other in a logical way.

- ✔ Consider how long each activity should take to do.

- ✔ Establish whether your students are able to sustain focus and motivation long enough to complete it.

- ✔ Think about the best way to start and end the lesson – aim to begin with a gripping, engaging activity, and finish with one that rounds things off.

After you're sure of the lesson structure, think about how you're going to communicate it to your students when they arrive at your lesson.

Mapping your journey

A lesson is like a journey. When you set out on a journey with a specific destination in mind, you look at a map before you go (or you programme your sat nav to get you there!). If you're wise, you think ahead about the best route, how long the journey is likely to take, any detours you may need to make or the best spot for a break.

The same applies to a lesson. Your 'specific destination' is to achieve the objective of your lesson. Your 'map' is your lesson plan. The 'best route' is the kind of activities that help you get to your destination. And those detours and planned breaks are all about knowing when a class may lose focus, or need to switch to a different kind of activity. Mapping your lesson journey ahead of time also helps your students.

They understand where they're going and how they're going to get there.

Your 'map' can come in all different shapes and sizes: the traditional lesson plan, flow charts, mind maps, tree diagrams – whatever works best for you.

Sometimes, of course, you go for a walk or a ride without a specific destination in mind – you go simply for the pleasure of the journey. These are the type of 'organic' lessons described in this chapter, the ones without a detailed plan. And sometimes, these are the most interesting journeys of all.

Sharing the lesson's structure with your students

As well as your lesson *having* a structure, your lesson plan must also have a *sense* of structure. This means giving your students the feeling that your lesson offers a clear, well-thought-through and logical way of teaching that particular topic. In your own mind, this may well be true. But if your students don't feel the same, or don't understand what the lesson structure is meant to be, problems and confusion may arise.

Just because you know what the lesson structure is doesn't mean your students do as well. Make the structure clear for the students at the start, so that they know where they're going and how they're going to get there. Give them an overview of the journey you're going to take together, by talking it through before you set off.

Add a sense of structure to your lesson by:

- ✔ Having a list of the lesson activities on the board or on a worksheet, which you go through with the class at the start of the lesson.
- ✔ Giving the students details about what the lesson objective is and how it can be achieved.
- ✔ Talking about the success criteria for the lesson.

✔ Making sure the students know the skills or understanding they need to demonstrate to show that they've achieved these criteria.

✔ Explaining the activities that the class is going to do, how long they may take and what they should learn in each one.

Use the term *WALT* ('We Are Learning To') to tell the class what they're learning to do in the lesson, and use the term *WILF* ('What I'm Looking For') to explain the kind of skills, attitudes or attributes you want to see from them.

After you've given the class a sense of structure, your students understand where the lesson is going and what they're going to do in your time together.

Even though you need to give your students this sense of structure, don't spend ages doing it! Aim to devote around five minutes to making the structure clear, but once you've done that, dive straight into your lesson. Otherwise you run the risk of your students becoming bored or restless and beginning to mess around.

Formats for success

Some lesson formats work better than others, because they take into account the way in which students learn. The format you use depends on the age of the students you teach and also on their ability levels. You may use a lesson with a few longer activities, requiring extended periods of concentration, for older, more able students. You can use a lesson with lots of short activities for young students, or for those with poor focus.

To be successful, your lesson format needs to:

✔ Take account of your students' concentration spans (which are about their age plus two, with an absolute maximum of about 20 minutes for optimum learning).

✔ Include plenty of hands-on, practical activities whenever possible, to keep students focused and engaged.

✔ Balance teacher talk with student discussions or activities.

✔ Offer a balance of short, fast-paced activities and some longer, more in-depth ones.

✔ Have clear targets and time limits for activities.

✔ Give a sense of forward momentum, of moving toward an end goal.

After you've finished writing your lesson plan, take an overview of the pace of the lesson and the kind of focus it requires from your students. Aim to see the lesson from the viewpoint of your students: which activities may they pounce on with pleasure; where may their attention flag and how can you avoid this?

How to set activities successfully

The way in which you set an activity for your class affects how the students do that task. The ideal is for you to give clear instructions, for the students to get straight down to work when you've finished explaining the task, to remain on it for the whole time and to come back to you quickly when the activity is finished. This is tricky to do, though. The following steps should help you get it right:

1. Start by saying 'When I say go...' This 'cue' creates a moment when everyone begins the activity. It means your keen students don't start before they know exactly what to do and that your less-motivated students receive a push to get going.

2. Set a time limit for the activity, giving a visual back-up, either writing the time on the board or using your fingers (e.g. three fingers for three minutes). Ask a student to confirm what the time limit is, to check for understanding.

3. Give details of the amount that students must do in this time: three lines, ten ideas, two pages and so on.

4. Explain the activity in a clear and concise way. Again, check for understanding by getting a student to repeat the task back to you and then clarifying any uncertainties.

5. Make it clear how the task is to be done: in groups, pairs, individually, with or without talking, talking quietly, making notes, with ideas to feedback, etc.

6. Agree a 'stop signal' with the class, to show when you want the students' attention or that the time for the task is over. This signal may be something like three sharp claps, raising a hand in the air, or something more inventive, such as flicking off the overhead lights in your room.

7. Check to see whether students need you to answer any questions about the task.

8. Say 'go!'

This all sounds terribly complicated, but after you and your students get the hang of it, it's very quick. Here's an example of a teacher setting a short written task: 'When I say go, you have three minutes to come up with five ideas for improving our playground. Elena, how many ideas? Yes, five, that's right, well done. You can talk about this in your groups, and I want everyone to make a note of their ideas. When the time is up, I'll clap three times and by the third clap I want you to stop, be silent and ready to listen. Any questions? No? Then off you go.'

When to let your lessons develop organically

Although structure is useful, in some situations you can let a lesson develop organically. Just like a plant, your organic lesson grows from a seed. This 'seed' may be the germ of a good idea, an interesting resource or scenario or a puzzling question that you and your students want to answer.

Sometimes a highly structured lesson starts going wrong. Perhaps you chose the wrong activities when you planned it. Maybe the concept you're trying to teach is too complex for the students at the moment. When this happens, don't be afraid to let the lesson become more organic. Set a quick task for the class while you mull things over. Then throw in a fresh activity that you think up on the spot and see what happens. Allow the lesson to move laterally, away from its original content or purpose.

Remember, even if the lesson doesn't go exactly as you originally intended, that doesn't mean it can't be successful in teaching the students something new. Always think about what *has* been achieved. If a student learned one new thing, you've been successful, even if it wasn't the thing you originally intended.

Delivering a Brilliant Lesson

You feel wonderful when a lesson goes perfectly and the students 'get' exactly what you want them to learn. While having a good, clear plan is vital, the way in which you deliver the lesson is equally, if not more, important. This comes down to you and your teaching skills, and the kind of activities you plan to use. A really brilliant lesson includes some or all of the following elements:

- A great mix of short, forward-moving activities, or a single really special one.

- Multisensory approaches, which appeal to all your students' senses.

- Activities that appeal to a range of learning styles – some visual, some auditory, some 'hands-on' and practical.

- Multimedia approaches, using ICT (information communications technology like computers), video, music and so on.

- Imaginative and creative approaches to learning.

- Something unusual, different or surprising.

- Skilful voice usage – a lot of high-quality tone and pace, with just the right levels of volume.

- Interesting use of your body, with plenty of hand gestures, facial expressions and a lot of movement around the room.

- A feeling of enthusiasm for the subject you're teaching.

- A sense of energy, excitement and pace.

    ✔ Or, conversely, a feeling of calm, concentration and focus.

    ✔ The feeling that you're interested in, and believe in, the potential of all your students.

You'll also find that a really great lesson gets you some really great feedback from your students. When a student says to you, unbidden, 'I really enjoyed that lesson, Miss', you can consider the day a special one.

You can find much more information about using creative, imaginative and multisensory approaches in Chapter 5.

Getting their attention

The beginning of the lesson is the key time for getting things on track. Find effective ways to get your students' attention at the start of the session (use the verbal and non-verbal strategies I talk about in Chapter 3). Make sure you sweep the students along in the pace of all the exciting things that are going on. That way, you have a good chance of keeping them engaged for the entire lesson.

You can grab your students' attention at the start of a lesson in many ways. You may:

    ✔ Start with an activity that gives the class a shock, a surprise or one that makes them laugh. Literally, opening with a 'bang!'

    ✔ Begin on a really positive note, by saying 'I have three great rewards to give out today' and then outlining what these are.

    ✔ Create a sense of mystery and involvement by showing the class an object that inspires curiosity or giving the students a puzzle to solve.

    ✔ Make the lesson sound really gripping, by saying 'We're going to do some really exciting stuff today!'

If your students find it hard to settle at the beginning of a lesson, aim to work out why this happens, so you can solve the problem. They may be coming from a very active, hectic lesson and need some time to quieten down. Perhaps they come straight to you from break and take a while to get back into the right frame of mind for work.

When you lose a class at the start of the lesson, getting them back is incredibly difficult. All kinds of things can go wrong, for instance a class turning up late or the students simply refusing to settle and pay attention. If a class is notoriously difficult to settle or the students are always delayed, open with a starter activity while the students are trickling in. Employing this tactic is far better than getting yourself and your students stressed by attempting to get silent attention at the start.

Passion and inspiration

You came into teaching because you love working with kids, and because you're passionate about learning, or about the subjects you teach. (And if you didn't, then you've probably chosen the wrong career!) If you can find ways to put your passion across to your students, you get much better work and behaviour from them. You also hopefully inspire them to great things in the future. At the very least you show them that learning's important and can also be fun.

To show your passion for learning and to be an inspiration to your students, take the following advice:

- ✔ Be enthusiastic and energetic as much of the time as you can. (But being like this all the time is the way to wear yourself out.)

- ✔ Use your voice and body to put across your love of the subject – plenty of movement, hand gestures, vocal tone.

- ✔ Use creative, imaginative and inspirational approaches during lessons.

- ✔ Be willing to experiment with your teaching: sometimes it goes wrong, but other times it's a huge success. Your students appreciate you making the effort to spice up their lessons and take some risks on their behalf.

- ✔ Be a great role model for your students – someone they can look up to and aspire to be like.

- ✔ Remember to laugh when things go wrong; show your human side as well as your inspirational teacher character.

- ✔ Be genuine with your students – they sense if you don't mean what you say.

- ✔ Care about the success of each and every student you teach.

Teach with passion and you become the kind of teacher who inspires your students to work hard and do well. You also enjoy your lessons and your teaching much more.

Getting the content right

The requirements of the curriculum you teach or the syllabus you deliver dictate your lesson content. But you can deliver the same content in a lot of different ways. Often, the most straightforward approach (via textbooks, or through teacher-led lessons) isn't the most effective in terms of how much and how well the students learn. This is particularly so if you have a tricky class and your students present you with behaviour issues. But however hard or easy the class, matching the content to what best suits your students is always important.

As you plan and deliver the lesson, make sure that you include:

- ✔ **The right level of content for your students** – not too hard, so they feel at sea and unable to learn, but also not too easy because this makes them feel bored and unchallenged.

- ✔ **The right type of content** – aim for something that interests and engages your students, as well as matching the curriculum requirements, at least part of the time.

- ✔ **The right kind of activities** – ones that allow your students to maintain focus, to stay on task and to learn what you intend.

- ✔ **Activities of the right length** – long enough to help students develop sustained concentration, but not so long that they lose focus.

One of the trickiest things is to work out how to engage your students and keep them engaged throughout a lesson. You can find suggestions about how to do this in Chapter 5.

Making concepts concrete

Your skill as a teacher lies in taking an abstract concept (division, metaphor, coordinates, the past tense) and turning it into a concrete activity that your students can do in order to 'get' that concept. The kinds of approach you use depend on the age of your students, and also on their ability levels. Here are some examples across a range of subject areas:

- ✔ **Division (maths):** Making and serving pizzas. Divide up the ingredients into quarters or eighths (onions, pepperoni and so on), then cook the pizzas and divide them equally between the students.

- ✔ **Population spread (geography):** Make jam sandwiches using white bread and butter. The students try to spread butter from the middle of the bread outwards. This shows how populations tend to 'clump' in the middle, then gradually lessen as they spread outwards.

- ✔ **Eyewitness accounts (history):** Ask a fellow member of staff to run into your classroom, pretend to slap you around the face, then run back out. The students must write an eyewitness account of what they saw, including details of what the person did, what they were wearing and so on. Compare the results to see what different students noticed and what they missed. This shows how unreliable eyewitness accounts can be.

- ✔ **Use of forensic evidence (science).** Set up a crime scene in your room, then ask the students to act as police detectives, finding forensic evidence, testing for fingerprints and so on.

The more imaginative, inventive and creative you are in teaching the concepts within a subject, the better your students respond and the more long lasting their learning is.

Personalising the learning to the learners

Personalising learning is about making it relevant to *these* students, with *their* lives and at *this* particular moment in time. Your students want and need to see how the lesson applies to them – why a particular topic, subject or skill is important to learn; what doing an activity or lesson enables a student to do in the future, and so on.

The ideal is for you to individualise the learning to each student. In reality, this is pretty much impossible unless you work with individuals, or with a very small group. But when your students feel that what they're learning is relevant to them and that it fits exactly with their needs, they become much more engaged with the work that you set them.

To personalise the learning you do to the learners you teach, ask yourself (and your students) the following questions:

- What are your students really 'into' – what interests do they have both inside and outside of education?
- How can you incorporate these interests into your lessons?
- What skills do your students already have?
- Which skills do your students still need to learn?
- What concepts do your students already understand?
- Which concepts have your students not yet grasped, but need to know in order to progress?
- How can your students evaluate their progress?
- How can your students use this evaluation to see where they need to go next?

Encourage your students to participate in setting their own learning goals, assessing how they're getting on and in working out how they can best reach the next target.

Making lessons topical

Sometimes school can feel a bit isolated from real life. But your students are aware of what's going on in their world, whether local issues or international stories. And they spend more hours outside school than they do inside it – home life is 'real life' to them. A lesson based on something that's happening in life outside of school feels more relevant and significant to your students.

To make the learning in your classroom more topical, you can:

- ✔ Use a current news story to inspire a lesson or deliver a topic, for instance a political scandal or relief efforts after a disaster.
- ✔ Choose an issue that's in the local media and get your students to give their views on it. For example, whether a new supermarket on the outskirts of town may affect the local high street shops.
- ✔ Incorporate a famous person into your lesson, for instance as a 'client' for whom your students must work.

By giving your lessons a connection to the wider world, you show students that learning is not just an abstract thing – that it has meaning in their everyday lives – and help them to relate to and better remember the concepts you teach.

Dealing with differentiation

Differentiation basically means adapting tasks and the way they're done to suit your individual students. In the average-sized class of around 25 to 30 students, setting a different task for each one isn't feasible. However, if you work with small groups, you may well have the time and opportunity to differentiate for individuals. Even in a large class, you can adapt the activities you set for both the weakest and the most able students.

Don't make too much of a fuss when you're giving out differentiated work to a class. Your less able students don't want their weaknesses highlighted, and your more able students might complain if they have to do a harder activity. Get everyone on task before you go and explain a differentiated worksheet to those students with learning difficulties.

You may come across and use various different types of differentiation. The main types include:

- ✔ **Differentiation by outcome:** Your students do the same work, but each one produces a different end product. (This approach is a bit of a cop-out, because it doesn't actually require the teacher to differentiate at all!)
- ✔ **Differentiation by task:** You set different tasks for students with different needs or with differing levels of ability. You may group your students into ability sets and then set a different task for each one.
- ✔ **Differentiation by resources:** You give your students different resources to use, depending on their ability levels. You may give your more able students a more complicated resource to use (the resource can be a textbook as well as an object).

✔ **Differentiation by support:** You use teaching assistants or support staff to support targeted individuals or groups. Often, teachers focus their support staff on working with lower-ability students. On occasions, make sure that you give your high-ability students support as well, to stretch their learning that bit further.

The amount of differentiation you manage to include depends on the needs of your students, and how much time you're willing or able to devote to adapting lesson activities for different abilities.

One very easy way of differentiating, particularly for the top end of the ability range, is to give your students extension activities to complete. Your students can choose from a range of activities that you offer them, or you can set specific activities for particular students. Offer extension tasks for homework to the most able, or set projects that your gifted students can take on to another level. Take care to use other approaches in addition to this to ensure that you differentiate fully for your most able students.

Keeping lessons interactive

Modern students are used to a lot of interactivity. This interactivity infuses their lives, particularly through new technologies, such as computer games, the Internet and digital television. Your students like to use interactive activities because these help them stay focused and get the most out of your lessons.

Interactivity can take many different forms. Your students may be interacting:

✔ With each other, for instance during a discussion activity.

✔ With you, during a Q&A session.

✔ As individuals, for instance by dictating the direction of their learning, or the way in which a story develops.

✔ With the resources you bring into the lesson.

✔ With the visual stimuli you show them.

✔ With a text or any type of written materials.

✔ With ICT resources, such as games and quizzes.

✔ With displays, for instance adding information to a 'working wall' (a display that progresses during a series of lessons).

✔ With hands-on, practical activities.

Must, should, could

The 'must, should, could' approach is very useful for planning, differentiating and assessment. It allows you (and your students) to differentiate how much an individual student needs to do. The idea is that you divide the lesson activities into three parts:

✔ Those that everyone **must** do.

✔ Those that everyone **should** be able to do, or should at least have a try at doing.

✔ And those that the more able (or faster working) students **could** attempt once they've finished everything else.

Dividing the work up in this way allows you to set a series of tasks, and then to encourage your students to push themselves to complete as much as they can. You may be surprised at how keen some of your less able students are to complete the 'should' and 'could' activities as well. Peer-group approval can be a very powerful incentive.

The more interactive your lessons are, the more your students get involved and engaged with their work. And the better they behave and learn for you. Take care, though, not to over-stimulate your students and get them over-excited. Aim for a balance of some calmer and other more exciting activities and lessons.

Don't forget the fun!

Don't forget that learning works best when it's fun. And that means fun for the *teacher* as well as for the students. If you enjoy delivering a lesson, it comes across in the way you teach it. If you're bored or unsure about teaching a lesson, this shows up just as clearly.

When your students are having fun, they're more relaxed. And a relaxed person learns much better. Laughter helps increase the blood flow to the brain, and consequently is great for encouraging learning and retention. You can feel a bit scared when the whole class is laughing, because you worry whether you're able to get them back. But wait a few minutes for the dust to settle and your students should come back to you of their own accord.

To put the fun in your lessons, check out these tips:

✔ Work out what makes your students laugh, and use it frequently. For some students the trigger is silly jokes and toilet humour, for others it's little stories and anecdotes from real life, for others the fun is in the lesson activities themselves.

✔ If you make a silly mistake, laugh at yourself and let your students laugh at you too. (But be careful about laughing at them – some young people are much more sensitive than adults.)

✔ If you have a 'class clown', let her entertain the students from time to time, rather than always cracking down on her silliness.

✔ Offer activities that give light relief such as quizzes, games and ones using formats nicked from the TV.

✔ Smile at students, frequently and with genuine warmth! Don't believe that saying about 'don't smile until Christmas', it just isn't true.

If your lessons feel more like fun and play than like work, you're on to a winner. And the best compliment of all is when a student says to you, 'We didn't do any work today, did we?' Because you know that they *did*.

Chapter 5

Getting (and Keeping) a Class Engaged

....

In This Chapter

▶ Understanding how to engage and connect with your students

▶ Building a sense of curiosity into your lessons

▶ Appealing to different kinds of learner

▶ Taking multisensory approaches to your teaching

....

*T*he key to really high-quality teaching and learning lies in getting your students engaged, and keeping them that way. Imagine having the class in the palm of your hand, hanging off your every word, fully engaged in every activity you set. This reaction is certainly not possible with every class or in every teaching situation, but it's an ideal for which you can and should aim. And when this engagement does happen, oh what a feeling!

You know when your class is engaged, because you sense that the students are interested in, curious about and fascinated by what you're teaching and what they're learning. And when they feel like this, they can't help but be fully involved in the lesson. Plus, once you have your students engaged, they don't think about misbehaving or going off task. They're far too busy getting on with their learning.

The Keys to Engaging Your Students

Sometimes engaging with your students is relatively easy – they're keen to work and enjoy being at school. Other times creating that sense of engagement is far harder. The students may be disaffected with learning or with school, or you may have to overcome serious behaviour issues.

Creating connections

You engage with your students by building up a strong relationship: not only with you as their teacher, but also with the learning that's happening in the lesson.

Your students can tell if you care about them and what makes them tick. They can feel if you have a passion for discovery and for the subjects you teach. And above all else, they can tell if you're someone who *likes* them and *wants* them to succeed. Sometimes you may have negative feelings about a class, a student or a lesson but as a professional you need to hide your emotions and work on building relationships.

For your students to engage with you and your lessons, they need to form a connection – to get the feeling that everything 'clicks'. In life you meet a whole host of different people: some you may instantly like and want to get to know better; others leave little impression on you, or you may even actively dislike them. In the classroom, you must try to replicate that feeling of wanting to be connected, of wanting to work together.

 You can use many different approaches to create an engaged connection between you, your students and your lessons. Many of these approaches are simply good general practices for you as a teacher. Make sure that you:

- ✔ Use eye contact with individuals when they make a suggestion or answer a question, for positive as well as negative behaviours.

- ✔ Make plenty of use of students' names; again, remember to do this for positive as well as negative reasons.

- ✔ Move toward a student when he makes a contribution to the lesson – foster the sense that he's included and connected.

- ✔ Allow your students a sense that they're contributing to what goes on in the lesson: that the lesson isn't all about what you say they should do, it's about what they *want* to do as well.

- ✔ Take an interest in them, their lives and their interests outside of school.

- ✔ Build a feeling of teamwork and partnership, for instance by using inclusive language such as 'we' and 'us'.

- ✔ Create lessons that your students *want* to participate in and that you enjoy teaching. Find out more about this in 'Creating engaging lessons for modern students', later in this chapter.

As you get to know your students better over the course of the year, you soon understand which approaches help them to connect and which ones are less useful in forming these links.

Creating engaging lessons for modern students

As an individual teacher, you probably have little say about what goes the school or the setting as a whole. You're not able to change the overa ethos, or alter overnight the motivations of the students you teach. However, you can certainly make a difference through what and how you decide to teach them. Creating engaging lessons isn't always an instant solution to handling a difficult class, but it's certainly a useful and practical method for getting your students to listen and to learn.

It may only be a few years since you yourself were at school, or it may be an awful lot longer. But however young or old you are, you still don't teach *your* generation. Modern students are very different from those just a decade or so ago. Many changes have occurred in the world in the last few years, particularly with the advent of new and interactive technologies.

As a teacher, you must adapt how and what you teach to suit the students who are actually sitting in front of you at that very moment. No point harping on about how things used to be, about a 'golden age' when students were willing to learn by rote, when they behaved impeccably, when they respected teachers as authorities. (As far as I'm concerned, that time never really existed.) The time you teach is *now*; the students you teach are of and from that *now*.

George Bernard Shaw said, 'It is all that the young can do for the old, to shock them and keep them up to date.' When the young people you teach are driving you round the bend, or when they simply don't learn in the way you had assumed, this is a very useful quote to bear in mind.

Modern-day learners are used to, and respond well to, approaches that are:

- ✔ Interactive
- ✔ Based on new technologies
- ✔ Relevant to their day-to-day lives or to contemporary concepts
- ✔ Big, colourful, visually interesting
- ✔ Hands-on and practical
- ✔ Creative and imaginative
- ✔ Multimedia – a mix of music, video, Internet and so on

Of course, you still need to use many of the more traditional approaches, and your students still need to know how to write essays, make notes and so on. But remember that life in the 21st century is changing all the time – as someone who works with young people, you have to change with it.

As a teacher, you're encouraged to map out your lessons ahead of time, rather than to allow the students to direct where they want to go with their discovery. While this is great for 'getting through the curriculum', it's not so great for fostering a burning sense of curiosity. Even though you structure many of your lessons for your students ahead of time, don't forget to allow them to have a say in what goes on, for at least some of your time together. You can do this by:

- **Making the lesson content relevant and topical:** Relate the lesson to something that's a current fashion or 'craze', or show how what they're learning relates to life in the wider world.

- **Letting your students direct some of their learning:** You can do this in many ways. Consider these examples:

  - Presenting an interesting object or resource to the students and seeing where they want to go with it. For example, introduce a topic by asking: 'What do you want to find out about this?'

  - Using open-ended, organic lessons – ones where the students direct the content more than the teacher does.

  - Being willing to go with at least some of the lateral suggestions – those questions that move you sideways from the pre-planned course of your lesson but which are interesting to explore – and ideas that your students bring up.

- **Personalising the lesson to the students and their learning styles:** Head to 'Looking at Learning Styles', later in this chapter, for a full discussion on learning styles.

- **Using your voice and body in an engaging way:** Move around the space, making lots of eye contact, to really connect with all the students in the class.

- **Adding props, resources and imaginative scenarios to the lesson:** Aim to create some real-life scenarios that the students recognise or enjoy – for example, a fashion show in a languages lesson or a Roman settlement in a history lesson.

Of course, you still need to control the learning, because otherwise the students may never cover certain areas of the curriculum. You also have to teach them the skills, such as focus and concentration (take a look at Chapter 6 for more advice on how to do this), that they need to be successful learners. These skills help them fully connect with and engage with their work. Actively teach them these skills, and insist that they use them within your lessons.

You can inspire a sense of curiosity and engagement in many different ways. The way you do this depends on the age of your students, and on the subject or subjects you teach. To my mind, one of the keys for you as a teacher is to retain a bit of childlike curiosity and excitement yourself. Be a 'big kid' and try to see life from your students' perspective.

Creating a sense of curiosity

Young children have a powerful sense of curiosity, of 'wanting to know'. They discover their world through interacting with it. They have an innate urge to ask and answer the question: 'What happens if I do this?' When a young child comes across something new or unknown, he tries it out, handles it, experiments with it to see what happens. And as any parent with young children knows, this sense of curiosity is so strong that you must 'toddler proof' your home against all potential hazards.

Sadly, the modern education system has a habit of knocking this sense of curiosity out of students. When young children first start school, they get some emphasis on learning through play and exploration. But before long, the pressure to acquire skills and achieve targets means they move away from this natural, inquisitive state. Be aware of this, and be conscious of how these pressures may affect your students' engagement with their work.

A key part of your role as a teacher is to help your students feel a sense of curiosity, so they once again *want to know*. You can create, or rather *recreate*, this feeling through what and how you teach. Harness your students' natural sense of curiosity in your classroom to help them engage with their work.

Think about the kind of things that make *you* feel curious or interested. Some people get this feeling by solving a puzzle or a crossword, others by delving deep into a topic or concept that they don't yet fully understand. How can you use these approaches in your classroom? And what kind of skills can your students use in activities based on a sense of curiosity? Read on to find some suggestions.

The power of puzzles in getting students engaged

Puzzles appeal to the innate sense of curiosity in the human mind. You can capitalise on your students' urge to work out the answers to tricky questions by using puzzles as a form of activity in your lessons. In the classroom, puzzles can take many different shapes and sizes. For instance, you may get your students to do:

> ✔ **Traditional puzzles,** such as crosswords, word searches, quizzes and tests, Sudoku puzzles, 'gameshow'-style quizzes and treasure hunts. You can incorporate these puzzles into a lesson as a quick starter or recap activity, or perhaps as a longer activity within the lesson itself.

✔ **An entire puzzle-based scenario you set up in your classroom.** This puts a really engaging twist on the more commonly used puzzles. You can do any of the following:

- Set up a crime scene and ask the students to figure out 'whodunnit'. Add a lot of clues and get your class theorising about what happened.

- Show the class a handbag that someone's 'left behind' in the staffroom – can they puzzle out whose it is by looking at what's inside?

- With younger children, 'kidnap' a class toy, leave some clues behind and get the students to work out where the toy's gone.

Ask your students to work as 'detectives' to solve the puzzles, and throw in a few red herrings for good measure.

You find that your students really engage with and enjoy these activities. And at the same time, they use a whole host of higher-order thinking skills, such as theorising, analysing, deduction, lateral thinking and imagination.

You can link puzzles and problem solving to many subject areas. As the students delve into the handbag, they begin to build a character for a story they're writing in English. As they examine your crime scene, they pick out evidence and use forensic techniques to identify 'whodunnit'.

Some subjects, such as science, are full of naturally occurring puzzles that someone in the past has figured out for themselves. 'Why does the apple fall from the tree to the ground?' is one very famous example. Aim to recreate the moment at which the question first struck someone as being something that needs an answer. Encourage your students to come up with their own thought paths about these age-old questions.

Surprising ways to get students engaged

Often, fostering engagement with a lesson is about working against the students' perception of what school *should* be like. When you present your students with something different, unusual or surprising, it encourages them to 'think out of the box' and to question their normal view of what school and learning are all about. It incorporates an element of theatricality into your classroom – a sense of drama that's great for engaging your audience of students.

Three tactics that work particularly well in a lesson are hiding, surprising and shocking. Below are some thoughts about how you can utilise these tactics in your own classroom.

Hiding

When something is 'hidden' from sight, you naturally become more curious about it, wondering what may be there. Revealing the 'something' creates a sense of interest, shock or engagement. You may hide the following items:

✔ Words, quotes or questions in an envelope, with a note on the front saying 'DO NOT OPEN' to heighten your students' sense of curiosity. Their urge to open that envelope really helps you to focus them on the activity.

✔ A precious object, such as a golden key, somewhere in your classroom or school grounds. The students must work out how to find it by following a series of cryptic clues. Again, you recreate the urge to find something that is such a key part of many childhood stories and memories.

✔ A person! I saw this done once in a drama session, and it had a wonderfully powerful effect. A couple of teachers wheeled a large box into the room and then proceeded with their presentation. About halfway through the session, the lid of the box sprung open and out climbed the head teacher. Without even acknowledging that the class was watching, he walked slowly across the room and out of the door. This presentation really made the class think about how they might use the unexpected in their drama, and also about subverting audience expectations. Needless to say, the event was the talk of the college for weeks afterwards.

I often use the idea of hiding as part of my classroom management technique. For instance, I may duck under my desk to calm myself down if a class is starting to wind me up. Or I may 'disappear' outside the room for a moment to shock a class into silence. The question 'Where's she gone?' is often enough to get the class paying attention again.

Surprising

To achieve a surprise, you need to do something completely unexpected in the context of a school. You may:

✔ Completely black out your classroom and ask the students to imagine that it's a haunted house or an alien spaceship. During the lesson they move around the space using only torches and creating a story of their own. The darkness creates a strong sense of atmosphere within the lesson and forces the students to really focus on building their story.

✔ Get your students to create their own surprises by designing and making some Jack-in-the-boxes. They can test these out on students lower down the school to see whether their surprises work effectively.

✔ Teach part of your lesson wearing a blindfold to explore the concept of trust, and how we give and receive it. Explain to the students that you're going to be relying on your sense of hearing and that you're trusting them to behave themselves even though you can't see them. This takes nerve (and you need to do it with a class who won't simply respond by rioting, or by getting up and leaving the room), but it can be very powerful.

Don't overdo your surprises – if you use them too often they begin to lose their impact.

I've found as a teacher that if you appear to be a little crazy, slightly on the edge, the students tend to enjoy it and respond really well. Partly, they love a teacher who's not afraid to make a fool of himself. And partly, I suspect, they don't want to tip you over into completely losing the plot. Of course, this only works if it's part of your natural style, but I've met a surprising amount of teachers who do confess to a liking for the 'edge of insanity' approach!

Shocking

Shocking your students takes things one step further. It's definitely not something to do regularly, because this takes the element of surprise away (see the preceding section). In addition to shocking your students through an aspect of your lesson, you can also shock them through something that you, the teacher, do.

You need to be a certain type of character to get away with shocking your students. You must have a good relationship with them, and your shock shouldn't be something so extreme that it scares, worries or completely unnerves them. Be conscious of how old your students are and whether shocking them is appropriate in the context of your setting.

Here are a few suggestions for 'shocks' that you can get away with in most classrooms/schools. All of the following are taken from real lessons, my own and those of other teachers:

- ✔ **The can of dog food:** The teacher starts the lesson by eating from a can of dog food, and then asks the students whether they want a taste. The lesson is for Design Technology, about looking at packaging – should you believe what you read on the label, and how can you go about making packaging tamper-proof? (Don't worry, the teacher hadn't completely lost the plot! The can of dog food was 'rigged' – it had been emptied out, washed and then refilled with a mixture of Mars bars and jelly to look like dog food.) This one certainly got the class's attention, and has gone on to be one of my favourite anecdotes when I'm training teachers.

- ✔ **Teacher on the run:** The teacher enters the room and jumps up onto the front desks. He then runs down the row of desks in the centre of the room, with the students throwing themselves out of the way to avoid him. There's no particular 'learning objective' to this – doing this simply gets everyone's attention. (A teacher I had as a child did this; he eventually became the head teacher of the school.)

✔ **Write your obituary:** When I was fairly new to teaching, I was trying to think of a way to do the classic 'write about yourself' task in an English lesson, but in a more interesting way. I came up with the idea of getting the students to write their own obituaries, about all the exciting things they'd done during their lives. You need to check before you use this approach, just in case any of your students has recently lost a loved one. But it's certainly a more interesting way to approach what's usually a fairly mundane task. This activity helps the students to question the idea of what's interesting about themselves and to consider what great things *they* might leave behind them.

The great thing about giving your class a shock is that the event tends to reverberate around the school. After the lesson, the students talk to their friends about what happened. These other students view you as a teacher with an 'interesting' reputation. And if your students are never quite sure what to expect when they come to your lessons, they're far more likely to turn up in an engaged frame of mind.

Looking at Learning Styles

The idea that different people have different learning styles is a fairly recent innovation. It came about through the work of American professor Howard Gardner, who proposed that people have 'multiple intelligences'. Gardner identified seven types of intelligence:

✔ **Verbal-linguistic:** This type of learner enjoys working with words, both written and spoken, and likes to learn by reading, note taking, listening to lectures and so on.

✔ **Logical-mathematical:** These learners are good with numbers and logic and enjoy reasoning, calculations and abstract ideas.

✔ **Bodily-kinaesthetic:** These students love to use their bodies, and enjoy subjects such as PE and dance. They learn and remember best by moving and doing, rather than by reading or writing.

✔ **Spatial-visual:** These learners have strong spatial awareness and enjoy visualising and manipulating images in their minds.

✔ **Musical:** These learners are skilled at performing, composing and appreciating musical patterns.

✔ **Interpersonal:** These students are great at interacting and empathising with others, learning best by working with others and using discussions and debates.

✔ **Intrapersonal:** These learners excel at introspection and self reflection, preferring to learn on their own and often having a developed ability for philosophical thinking.

No one falls into only a single category; your students may excel in several of these areas.

Although Gardner didn't directly relate his theory to the classroom, many educators have adopted his ideas as a way of helping their students engage with their lessons and with their learning. Looking around the average group of students, you can easily see that they learn best in different ways. Some love to get 'hands-on' with the work, others are good at discussing ideas in groups, while some prefer a highly visual approach.

Some schools use a simplified version of Gardner's work to help teachers plan and deliver lessons that appeal to different learning styles. Many schools use the term *VAK* (which stands for 'visual, auditory, kinaesthetic') to encourage a more rounded approach to teaching and learning. By appealing to these three different approaches that learners might prefer, you help the students engage with the lesson. You also ensure that they learn as effectively as possible and retain that learning after the lesson.

Teaching for different learning styles in the classroom

Taking Gardner's work to its logical conclusion, teachers need to identify each student's preferred learning style and then adapt the work to suit each individual. But if you have a class of around 30 students, you're not going to be able to differentiate each activity to suit the learning style of each individual.

The theory of 'learning styles' encourages you to include a range of tasks in your lessons. When you're planning your lessons, aim to incorporate plenty of variety. The vast majority of lesson activities appeal to two or more types of learning style. For instance, you may look at some percussion instruments while talking about the sounds they make, and then get 'hands on' to try them out. You can find out much more about using a variety of activities in Chapter 6.

When planning, the VAK acronym works as a useful reminder to include a variety of tasks. For instance, in a primary maths lesson about division, you might use:

✔ **Visual:** The class looks at various images on the electronic whiteboard (circles and squares, for example), students come to the front to divide these into halves, quarters and so on.

✔ **Auditory:** The students call out the answers to various mental maths problems involving division.

> ✔ **Kinaesthetic:** The students work in groups, receiving paper shapes which they must cut up into halves, quarters and so on.

You can take this activity one step further by adding a multisensory element such as food; for instance, dividing ingredients for a pizza (see 'Creating multisensory lessons' further on in this chapter).

Getting hands-on for learning

The classic old-fashioned lesson from a few decades back appeals to students who prefer to learn using language or logic. The teacher lectures the class and the students make notes (verbal-linguistic) or shows how to solve some problems and the students work on some examples (logical-mathematical). Occasionally the teacher adds a little bit of visual stimulus for good measure – reading a textbook that has some pictures in it, for example.

With the old-school approach students rarely have a chance to move around or get involved in practical, hands-on activities. But find ways to use kinaesthetic approaches in your lessons and you not only appeal to the greatest number of learning styles, you also tend to incorporate more multisensory approaches.

As the saying goes, we remember only a small fraction of what we read, a little more of what we hear, but we remember most from direct, purposeful experience or from teaching something to others (see Edgar Dale's *Cone of Experience* for the origins of this saying). Students love to learn by *doing* something, by getting hands-on to learn about how they can use a material, how a concept works, how an experiment can help to demonstrate a theory or prove a result. Learning that's practical and hands-on is also generally more memorable for a class.

Consider the advantages for your classroom management too:

> ✔ Those students with the most challenging behaviour are often those who respond best to practical, hands-on activities.
>
> ✔ When students are actively involved with touching, using or holding something, they're less likely to be talking or being disruptive.
>
> ✔ Students (particularly the youngest) find focusing on chatting harder when they're doing something with their hands.

You may be tempted to avoid letting difficult students get 'hands-on', because of concerns over how they may behave when doing practical activities with many resources. However, if you can bring yourself to trust your students and to take the risk, much of the time these approaches are successful. Even when getting hands-on doesn't work, you still learn a lot about useful behaviour-management techniques.

My approach has always been to take a few risks in the kind of learning I ask my students to do. Doing so helps your students to engage with, and be interested in, the activities you set. You also stretch yourself as a teacher – your creative skills and your classroom management ones as well.

Developing activities for different learning styles

The types of activity you use depend on the kind of subject or topic you teach. But whatever activity you want your students to do, you can usually approach it in a number of different ways. As you plan, look at how many different approaches you can apply to a task or an activity, to make it appeal to the maximum number of learners and the broadest range of learning styles.

Following is an example of how you may create tasks that appeal to learners with a variety of learning styles, taking the topic of sorting in a primary maths class:

1. **Divide the class into groups (interpersonal style).**

2. **Give each group a box of Smarties and ask them to sort the Smarties into a pile for each different colour (spatial-visual and bodily-kinaesthetic styles).**

3. **After separating the Smarties, instruct them to count and record the number in each pile (logical-mathematical style).**

4. **Ask the students to talk together about how to display this information in a visual way (verbal-linguistic and spatial-visual styles).**

   This display can take the form of a pie or bar chart or even a spreadsheet.

5. **After creating the visual display, they present their findings to the class (interpersonal and verbal-linguistic styles).**

6. **Each student writes a short, individual account of how they approached the task, reflecting on what they did well (intrapersonal style).**

7. **Finally, they all get to eat the Smarties!**

During this task, the students use all or most of the different learning styles. They also have to practise a bit of self-discipline so they don't eat the Smarties until the end.

Creating Multisensory Lessons

You can help your students engage with their work and make your lessons more memorable by using multisensory approaches. Of course, your students use their senses all the time (looking at and listening to you, holding a pen and so on). But the idea is to find multisensory activities that are inspiring, exciting and interesting. This helps your students engage with and retain the work they do.

When you sit down to plan a lesson, consider the options for incorporating a range of sensory responses. If possible, aim to include each of the five senses in some way. With some lateral thinking this is possible right across the curriculum subjects. In many ways, the senses link very closely to the multiple intelligences discussed in the preceding 'Looking at Learning Styles' section.

Why the senses are key

The senses are key to effective learning for so many different reasons. People interact with their world mainly through their sensory responses to it. Even when you're not aware of using your senses, they're still there, helping you understand your world, keeping you out of danger, allowing you to appreciate beauty and so on. When your students use their senses in your lessons:

✔ They're encouraged to engage with the work.

✔ They remember the learning they do.

✔ Students with different learning styles find the lessons appealing.

✔ Your lessons are more interesting.

✔ You encourage a variety of responses and students use a wider range of thinking skills.

Young people often lead very busy lives, with a lot of sensory information bombarding them (television, computers, music and so on). But much of this sensory information is 'second-hand' and one-dimensional, devoid of that emotional link they get when they experience things at first hand.

 Aim to recreate the 'real world' as fully as you can in your classroom, to help your students fully engage with what they're learning. You experience a big difference between looking at a picture of the sea, and standing with your feet in the water, smelling and tasting the salt in the air and feeling the wind on your skin. Take your class out on trips and visits whenever possible. And at the very least aim to bring resources and objects into your classroom, so that students can experience aspects of the world around them at first hand.

Using the five senses

You can find a whole host of ways to incorporate the senses of sight, hearing, touch, taste and smell into your lessons. When you're planning a lesson, consider how you can add in opportunities to use some or all of the senses. For instance, to inspire a poem or piece of creative writing, your students may:

- ✔ Take a walk in the school grounds, to look at the natural world around them.
- ✔ Listen to extracts of classical music inspired by nature.
- ✔ Feel a range of natural materials: leaves, twigs, stones.
- ✔ Taste and smell some of the fruits (blackberries, elderflowers) that are native to the UK.

In a history lesson looking at time lines, your students may place different sensory items on a line according to their historical period. They can:

- ✔ Look at pictures of historical buildings, to identify architectural features from different time periods.
- ✔ Listen to musical extracts from the past and match these to the images of buildings.
- ✔ Feel a variety of textured building materials (bricks, straw, clay, wood, metal, plastic) and establish when these were used, or make some models with them.
- ✔ Identify the smells that were common at different periods (wood smoke, raw sewage) and when these smells were superseded by new technologies (electricity, mains drainage).
- ✔ Read about, cook and taste foods from different time periods: gruel, foraged wild nuts and berries and so on.

You can have one table each for the different senses, with the students circulating the room to 'visit' each one. With such a wide multisensory input, students engage with the learning and use various learning styles in many different ways.

Of course, using all the senses isn't possible all the time, or in every subject. And doing so means some extra work for you. But even if you only do it once in a while, you may be amazed at how much better your students respond, and how much better you feel about your lesson.

Sniffing out the forgotten sense

Did you know that smell is the sense most closely associated with long-term memory? The slightest whiff of a scent from the past is enough to take you back to memories long since buried (especially where those memories have negative connotations). But if you think about smell, it's also the sense least utilised in the typical classroom. How often do you ask your students to use their sense of smell while they're learning?

Think back to when you were at school and try to conjure up the smell of your school canteen. My own primary school canteen smelt of cheese-and-onion pie, a smell that made me feel nauseous. Even all these years later, I can still pull that smell out of my memory. And when I come across the same smell in my day-to-day life, it brings the memories from my youth flooding back – and it still makes me feel sick. What smell do you remember from your own school dinner days? And what kind of memories, feelings and associations does that smell evoke?

You can use the sense of smell in your teaching in a whole host of different ways. How you do this depends on the age of the students you teach, and also on the subject or subjects you deliver. You can ask students to:

- Smell a range of herbs to inspire some creative writing.

- Sniff some spices as a way of starting off the study of India in geography.

- Take a scent tour of the school, collecting examples of the smells (both pleasant and unpleasant) they find around the buildings and grounds.

By using their sense of smell, your students engage with the work they're doing and retain it in their memories. They get that first-hand experience that's so vital for connecting with the world.

Playing with the senses

You can create some lovely effects by playing around with the different senses. This adds interest to lessons, and also encourages your students to think about how they rely on their senses working together to perceive their world fully.

One way of 'playing with the senses' is to remove a sense from your students. This encourages them to use their other senses in a new and fuller way, and also to think about how life must feel for people who have a sensory impairment. You can ask your students to:

- ✔ Draw a picture while wearing a blindfold.
- ✔ Write using the 'wrong' hand, or with one hand behind their backs.
- ✔ Direct a blindfolded partner around an open space.

I visited one school which had a unit for visually impaired students. All the teachers were asked to spend some time in another teacher's lesson wearing a blindfold, so that they could experience a lesson from the student's perspective.

Another interesting approach is to cross the senses with each other. So your students may:

- ✔ Describe a scent in visual terms; for example, what does the smell of baking bread look like?
- ✔ Explain what a taste feels like; for example, what may the sour, bitter taste of lemons be like to touch?
- ✔ Create a soundscape or piece of music based on looking at a picture, for instance of the ocean.

These activities allude to a rare condition known as *synesthesia*, where an individual's sensory perceptions are mixed, so that he might 'hear' colours or 'smell' numbers.

Chapter 6

Getting the Most Out of Your Students

In This Chapter

▶ Keeping students focused on a task

▶ Exploring the best methods of assessing your students

▶ Utilising interesting resources in your lessons

▶ Getting the best out of displays

As a teacher, you want to get the very best out of each and every one of your students. However, you only have a limited amount of time to spend with them: a few hours each day in the primary classroom, perhaps as little as an hour a week in some secondary subject areas. The secret is to get students to gain as much knowledge as you possibly can in the time you have together. In this chapter, you find out how to do just that.

Chapter 5 explores how to engage and interest your students through different ways of preparing and delivering lessons. In this chapter, you discover how to keep your students focused on the lesson activities and how to ensure that they gain as much as they possibly can during class time. A key part of this is helping your students develop the more generalised skills that aid their learning, such as focus, concentration and listening effectively.

Keeping a Class On Task

The more time students spend on their tasks, the more knowledge they acquire when they're in your lessons. Yet one of the biggest frustrations in the classroom is that when you explain a task, you set the students off to work, and a few minutes later you see that several (or many) of them are drifting off task. Fortunately, you have many different teaching strategies at your disposal to keep a class focused, as the following sections show.

Introducing the activity

One of the keys to keeping a class on task is to introduce the activity properly in the first place. You must introduce it so that all the students understand exactly what they're meant to do, and then they get on and do that to the best of their abilities, in the time you've allowed. This sounds fairly straightforward, but actually it's one of the trickiest aspects of classroom practice. After you understand how to introduce activities in the most effective way, you save yourself a lot of stress, and also encourage your students to work to their utmost.

Each time you set a task, you need your students to understand a variety of things, as outlined in the first column in Table 6-1. To see how this works, imagine you set a quick group discussion activity. You're looking at the topic of forces, and you want to start by getting the students to think of different ways of moving from one place to another. In the second column of Table 6-1 are examples of how you can introduce the discussion task.

Table 6-1	Information to Give When Introducing an Activity
Information to Convey	*Example*
What they have to do	'I want you to think of as many different ways of moving from one place to another as you can.'
How much they have to do	'Try to come up with at least ten ideas . . .'
How they should approach the task	'. . . working in groups with one person writing down everyone's suggestions.'
How long they have to complete the task	'I'm going to give you three minutes to try and find at least ten ideas.'
What a successful finished piece should include (you may give a couple of examples to help, or encourage your class to think of a couple of examples to get everyone going)	'Aim to find as many different forms of transport as you can, for instance walking is one way that people move, but they can also travel in a car and in other forms of transport.'
What they should do if they finish ahead of time	'If you get ten ideas before the three minutes are up, then see if you can get another ten!'
How you intend to get the whole class back to you at the end of the time	'When you hear me clap three times like this, that means the time is up, and I want you to stop talking and wait for me to continue.'

You have a lot of information to get across! To make sure that your students hear and understand all the information they need, follow this advice when giving instructions:

- ✔ **Keep your explanation concise and to the point.** If your explanation goes on for too long, your students may stop listening half way through. And if they don't listen to your explanation first time round, you're going to get that irritating chorus of 'I don't know what to do' as soon as the activity begins.

- ✔ **Be willing to recap the instructions before your students get going, depending on how well they normally listen and understand your explanations.** Do this by asking one of your students to summarise what you've said, and then clarifying any areas of misunderstanding. Choosing the student who's least likely to have been listening can work well – this encourages her to listen better in future!

- ✔ **Find a way to stop students from jumping into the activity before you've delivered the instructions.** Some students are itching to get going; so keen to start that they can't wait for you to finish explaining the task. Often, these students are the highly motivated ones in your class: the keen ones, rather than the difficult ones. But a few minutes into the activity, these students have to ask you for a recap on what they're meant to be doing, because they didn't listen properly first time around. Although your students being desperate to get going on their work is great, you don't want to have to spend half your time reiterating the task.

  You can avoid this problem by using the 'When I say go . . . ' technique. This involves 'training up' your children so that they don't start until you say so. Here's how the technique works. Before you begin to outline any task, say: 'When I say go I want you to . . . ' If any students begin the work before you have finished your explanation, simply ask: 'Did I say go yet?' When you've finished explaining the task, say: 'Three, two, one, go!'

  Ask that your students put their pens down on the table before you begin your explanation. By doing this you ensure that they don't have anything to fiddle or write with until you've said 'go'.

- ✔ **Be very clear about the _how_ of the activity: Explain exactly _how_ the students should work while they're involved in the task.** If you don't say otherwise, they probably assume that they're allowed to talk while they're working. Be specific too as to whether they should work in pairs, groups or on their own. And be precise about how much, and what kind, of talking (if any) should go on. You can find some more suggestions about how to set activities successfully in Chapter 4.

Using targets and time limits

You can create a sense of purpose, and encourage your students to stay on task, by setting targets and time limits for each activity they do. Generally speaking, people work at their quickest and most efficient when a deadline's approaching. And the more important you feel meeting that deadline is, the more likely you are to finish the task on, or even ahead of, time.

Imagine you set a task for your class, but you aren't specific about how long they have to do it, or how much you want them to do. You tell them that you want them to come up with 'some ideas' on a topic, and then you set them off to work. Think about how they may respond to this vague approach. Are they likely to approach the task with a sense of purpose? Or may they work for a bit, then drift into non-work-related chatter?

Play around with the kind of targets and time limits you set, until you find out what best suits your class. You also need to adapt the time limits according to what the task actually involves. To ensure that your time limits work as you want them to, remember to do the following:

- ✔ **Choose a limit that's reasonable to the task.** For simple discussion or idea-gathering tasks, time limits can be fairly short: two, three or five minutes. Save longer time limits for lengthier activities requiring more concentrated focus, perhaps ten or fifteen minutes at a go.

  Avoid going much beyond 20 minutes for any single task. This is about the maximum length of time that people (even adults) can maintain their optimum concentration levels.

- ✔ **Give your students reminders of how long they've got left, particularly toward the end of the specified time limit.** I tend to do a reminder at one minute, then at ten seconds, ending with a countdown from five to zero.

- ✔ **Chop longer activities up into shorter chunks, with time for feedback or a break in between.** For instance, when writing an essay your students may first write a plan, then feedback on what they've done, before moving on to write the introduction, and so on. You can also pause the class every five or ten minutes or so when they're doing a longer task. Call everyone back together to see how they're getting on, to review progress and to see whether they have any questions.

- ✔ **Have times during the year when you practise long periods of focused concentration (up to an hour), especially for older students.** Set up most of these long activities as individual work, done in silence, in test conditions. This helps older students prepare for the reality of sitting exams.

You may feel unsure about setting a lot of short activities, perhaps because you're worried about getting the class back to you after each one. But even with the most difficult classes, the more they practise coming back to you, the quicker and easier getting their attention becomes.

You don't have to adhere exactly to your pre-set time limits. After all, your students are unlikely actually to be timing you; they're hopefully too busy focusing on the task. If toward the end of your time limit you sense that the students haven't had long enough to do the task properly, stretch the time out a little. Conversely, if you realise that most of them have finished and you're only part way through the time, you can cut it down a little to suit.

Incorporating rewards

By using a series of short, targeted tasks as explained in the preceding section, you have the chance to incorporate a lot of rewards into your teaching, some for each task that gets completed. These rewards need not be anything complicated, they can be as simple as a smile, or saying 'well done' to the students. Many of your students gain a sense of achievement simply by meeting the targets you set.

When you're gathering ideas, one of the best 'rewards' of all is to get a student to read out her answers. Having the entire peer group listening to, and gaining from, someone else's ideas is a very effective way of sharing information and motivating your students.

You can find ideas for getting rewards right, and the kind of rewards you may like to use in your classroom, in Chapter 9.

Creating a sense of pace

The way you introduce a task affects the way your students approach it. Aim to create a sense of pace and forward momentum so that the students move quickly on to the task, and stay focused while they're doing the activity. You can do this using many of the verbal and non-verbal communication strategies outlined in the following list:

- ✔ Introduce the task using an excited-sounding tone in your voice.
- ✔ Describe the activity in a way that makes it sound interesting and motivational.
- ✔ Add plenty of pace to your voice – use a mixture of different paces, within sentences and also within words.
- ✔ Set clear time limits and targets to give that sense of forward momentum.
- ✔ Use your body, hands and face in an expressive way, to give a feeling of energy and impetus.

You find that, most of the time, your students respond to the sense of pace you create by getting straight down to work and by focusing hard on the task. (For more information on effective communication, head to Chapter 3.)

From time to time, set up a task by framing it as a 'competition'. This spin helps encourage your students to get going quickly on the activity, and to complete it to the best of their ability. I find these competitive tasks most useful for encouraging motivation during group work, for instance when you're asking everyone to brainstorm ideas in a group. At the end of the task, give everyone a sense of success by saying something like: 'Hands up if your group got five or more ideas . . . well done . . . now if you got ten or more ideas . . . ' and so on. That way all the groups feel they've done well, and you can identify which group has 'won' by getting the most suggestions or answers.

Putting pace into your lessons is quite teacher intensive – you need lots of energy and enthusiasm. You can't do it all the time, so save pace for when it has the most effect. Perhaps at the start of a lesson, to get your students going, or with a particularly tricky class who are hard to motivate.

While you want to encourage a sense of pace and impetus, don't overdo things and go too far in the opposite direction. You don't want your students to feel harried while they're working, or to get so flustered they can't get going on or complete the activity. Aim for a feeling of positive motivation, but don't instil a sense of panic. Balance times of high energy and pushing forward with the work, and times when the students settle down to a calm, quiet task.

Fostering Focused Learning

Overestimating your students' ability to focus is easy. I'm sure all teachers have done this (I certainly have). You need to give quite a lengthy introduction to the lesson, but half way through the students begin to lose focus and start to mess around. Or you set the class a task that you reckon takes half an hour of good concentrated work, but after 15 minutes you notice that they're already going off task.

The older your students are, the more important their ability to concentrate for long periods is. To be successful in their exams, they must be able to focus for an hour or two at a time. This doesn't happen overnight – developing the necessary self-discipline to do this requires time and training. If you teach a class of students who are taking formal, external examinations, make sure that you build these skills with them as a part of their course.

You need to be realistic about how long your students can focus for at any one time. If you push them beyond their maximum concentration span, they're likely to go off task and begin to misbehave. Far better to limit the time they spend on any one activity than to have to deal with behaviour issues during the task.

Different types of task involve different kinds, and amounts, of concentration:

✔ **Listening to the teacher talk:** This task requires a high level of focus from your students, because they must make sense of what you say and try to retain it. Remember, even if your students are listening silently, that doesn't mean that what you're saying is actually going in.

✔ **Whole-class Q&A sessions:** These times aren't quite as intensive as periods spent listening to you speaking. The interactive nature of Q&A sessions gives a buzz and a more relaxed feeling to the activity. Do find ways to encourage all your students to join in, rather than letting a few of them do all the work while the others opt out.

✔ **Individual written work:** This task needs good concentration, particularly for younger students whose writing skills are still developing. Aim for silence in your classroom to help your students to concentrate.

✔ **Discussing a question in groups:** This task is less 'focus intensive', because students can opt in and out of the activity as others talk. Although they must listen to each other, the concentration they require isn't quite as high as when you're explaining a subject or activity to the whole class.

You should aim to mix and match the types of task to suit your students best: a bit of listening, a bit of discussion, some individual work and so on.

A good rule of thumb for concentration spans is a child's age plus two. So a child in a Reception class is able to concentrate on one activity for about six or seven minutes. By the first year of secondary school, your students are able to focus on any one task for about twelve or thirteen minutes at a time.

Developing focus and concentration

A common complaint in the modern classroom is that students 'just can't concentrate'. Many demands exist on young people's attention: toys, television, radio, computer games, the Internet, mobile phones and many more. Students are used to multitasking, paying attention to many different activities at the same time.

In the classroom, you want your students to pay full attention to the particular concept, idea, information or skill they're studying. The ideal is for them to achieve fully focused, concentrated attention on the activity, whether that's listening to you teach or doing a task during the lesson. This full and complete engagement is an important part of effective learning.

Concentration-building strategies

Just as you teach your students new skills within a subject area, so you can also teach them how to focus and concentrate. Indeed, concentration is a vital skill for gaining knowledge and one they must master to succeed in their exams. Build up your students' concentration by:

- ✔ Gradually increasing the length of time over which you ask them to concentrate on a single activity.

- ✔ Incorporating some silent working time into lessons, so that everyone has a chance to focus without interruption.

- ✔ Eliminating unnecessary distractions, such as students wandering the room, tapping pens or calling out questions.

- ✔ Praising them for their concentration skills, as well as for good work and behaviour.

- ✔ Having an expectation that everyone can focus fully on an activity – that your students must respect one another's right to learn.

- ✔ Using exercises specifically designed to build concentration skills (see below for some suggestions).

As part of your work on developing concentration skills, incorporate some short focus exercises into your lessons or your daily routines. You can use these exercises as:

- ✔ A quick starter activity before the main lesson begins

- ✔ A way of breaking up longer periods of concentrated work

- ✔ A short break between different subject lessons in primary school

- ✔ A calm-down and focus time at the end of a lesson

Exercises to enhance concentration

Although focus exercises are typically found in drama lessons, you can use them as a brief starter, 'break-out' or plenary activity in any lesson. You can try the following:

- ✔ **Backwards counting:** Close your eyes and count backwards from 10 to zero (or from 50 to zero) in your head. When you finish, open your eyes and wait silently for everyone to finish.

- ✔ **Backwards spelling:** Close your eyes and spell your full name, backwards, in your head. What did you have to do to be able to spell it?

- ✔ **Mirrors:** Face your partner and nominate one person to lead. Imagine you're looking into a mirror. Follow your partner's moves *exactly*. Someone watching you shouldn't be able to tell who's leading and who's following.

✔ **Paired stare:** Working in pairs, stare into your partner's eyes without blinking or laughing. Keep the stare going as long as possible. Afterwards, talk about what caused you to lose concentration. Is this easier with someone you know or with a stranger?

✔ **Register order:** Rather than taking the register yourself, ask the students to call out their names *in register order.* You force them to concentrate really hard by doing this – they must listen to slot their name in at the right moment.

✔ **Statues:** On the command to 'freeze', everyone must freeze completely still like a statue. They mustn't move at all (they can breathe, obviously). Start with a minute or two, then gradually develop the length of time over which your students do this activity. This is an excellent exercise for finishing off a lesson in a calm and focused way.

The more often you do these exercises, the better your students become at them. I've found that students love to have a bit of time in class to settle themselves and focus, ready to work.

Developing good listening skills

All students must master the skill of effective listening: not just listening in silence, but also taking in and understanding what you're saying to them. Thankfully, this is something you can help them with as part of your teaching routine. The more you work with your students on listening, the better they get at it.

Some students are very adept at giving the *appearance* that they're listening, but the meaning of the words just doesn't seem to sink in. What you're after is active listening, listening in which every student extracts the relevant meaning from what you're saying. Make sure that you use vocabulary that's at the right level for your students – not too complex, but not so simple that you sound patronising.

To encourage and develop good listening skills, you can try asking your students to:

✔ Listen for a key word and raise a hand when they hear it.

✔ Draw an image while they're listening, for instance doodling some random pictures (a surprisingly good tactic for enhancing focus).

✔ Listen out for three key words that you identify before you begin to talk. The students could raise a hand when they hear the word.

✔ Identify three key points in what you say and give feedback on these after you finish talking.

✔ Practise listening activities, for example closing their eyes and listening to noises inside the room, then just outside and then far beyond. They can then talk together about what they heard.

The better your students can listen, the more they get out of the times when you need to talk to them in the classroom. When their listening's really focused and they take in what you say, your life's much easier. You have less need to repeat yourself or to explain a task several times to different individuals around the class.

Managing noise levels

A key part of your classroom management role is to regulate and manage the noise levels of your class. Of course, a buzz of noise when all the students are on task is very different to the racket of a class out of control. But even if your students are working happily and with good motivation, you still need to control the noise levels, particularly if you're working with young children. Some teachers prefer a very quiet classroom; others like a buzz of noise for all or most of the time. The noise level you use depends on the age group, subject and type of students you teach, but also on your school ethos and your personal preference. What you don't want is uncontrolled and ever-increasing noise, especially if it's unrelated to the work.

Managing noise levels is vital for a number of very good reasons. Perhaps most importantly, high noise levels are very stressful, for both you and your students. This is especially so if your class is noisy for all or most of the day. Your students find it much easier to focus, concentrate and learn if you regulate the noise levels in your classroom, and ensure that they don't get too high.

In addition, as noise levels rise, the situation gets worse and worse because everyone has to speak more loudly to be heard. If you let the noise level spiral out of control, pulling the volume back down again is hard, and you may end up using your voice to quieten your class. If you frequently call out over a noisy class, this can be very damaging for your voice. In addition, a really rowdy class affects the work going on not only in your classroom, but in other classrooms close to yours as well. Having the noisiest class in the school can be rather embarrassing!

Most students find controlling the noise in the classroom by themselves quite hard. You need to take an overview of the noise levels and help your students discover how to regulate themselves. Follow the advice outlined in the following sections.

Use a noise-o-meter

Using a 'noise-o-meter' of some kind is a very effective way of helping your class to understand how noisy they're being. You can draw a chart on your board, with a line rising up to a 'crisis point' if the noise gets too much. You can also ask an individual student to act as a 'noise monitor' and gauge the noise levels in the room. And if the noise does get too much, have some kind of strategy in place, for instance stopping the class and insisting that they work in silence for a few minutes.

Explain what voice goes with what situation

Talk with your class about the different kinds of 'voices' they should use in different situations. Discuss what these voices mean, and get your students to practise them until they understand exactly what they mean. You can divide your voices into:

- ✔ Silent zone, for when individual work's going on.

- ✔ Paired voice, for when the students are working in twos.

- ✔ Small group voice, for when group discussions are taking place.

- ✔ Large group voice, for instance when speaking in a debate where a lot of other people need to hear what you're saying.

- ✔ Playground voice, which you should only hear when the students are outdoors at break time!

When silence is golden

Most of the time, I insist that my students work in complete silence when they're doing individual work, especially if the task involves writing. I do this for a number of reasons:

- ✔ If they have no need to discuss the activity, then a silent classroom's the best environment in which to work.

- ✔ Most students find focusing easier with no distractions, such as noise, in the room.

- ✔ If you set this standard early on, your students don't think to question it.

- ✔ Saying 'no talking' rather than 'talk quietly' is much easier, because you don't have to define what 'quietly' means. Plus, if you do let students 'talk quietly', they're unlikely to stay all that quiet for very long.

- ✔ Getting used to the discipline of working in complete silence is very helpful for your students, so that when they do exams they're accustomed to working in this way.

- ✔ On some (admittedly rare) occasions, you can get on with doing some work of your own while the students are working silently.

When your students are working silently, you might ask them if they'd like some quiet, calm music in the background. On special occasions, or when the class is working especially well, you may allow them to bring in some music of their own to play. (A word of warning, though – check the lyrical content first for inappropriate language.)

In Chapter 3, you can find out all about how to use your voice to control behaviour and encourage good work practices. When you're thinking about the sound levels in the room, think about how your own voice contributes to the quantity of noise.

A quiet classroom is the best environment for teaching and learning – too much noise can be hugely stressful for you and for your students. If you want your students to control their noise levels, you have to know how to control your own. Model the kind of speaking you want your students to use: don't drone on endlessly unless absolutely necessary; only speak as loudly as you need to be heard; add plenty of interest to your voice with tone and pace; and avoid shouting as far as humanly possible.

Using a Variety of Tasks

The most interesting and engaging lessons are those that offer students a variety of different tasks – these are the lessons that help your students get the most out of your time together. They also ensure that you appeal to the different ways in which your students learn (see Chapter 5 for more thoughts on learning styles). Using a variety of tasks also encourages your students to retain their focus right through the lesson.

The traditional lesson format is still very prevalent in many schools. This format involves a teacher introduction to a topic, followed by some kind of student activity, typically individual writing using worksheets or textbooks. But this approach is at odds with the way many modern students like to learn and the way research shows they learn best. You shouldn't feel the need to pander to what your students *want* to do in lessons. However, you should certainly question how well the approaches you use encourage your students to stay focused and to learn.

Being stuck doing one thing for a long time starts to get boring, even if you're an adult. This applies doubly so for children. As you've seen previously in this chapter, the maximum concentration span for effective learning doesn't extend much beyond 20 minutes. Young people are used to flitting from one activity to another outside of school – they may send a quick text, look up something on the Internet and listen to music, all pretty much simultaneously.

Although part of your role as a teacher is to encourage extended focus, you also need to take into account the limits of your students' concentration spans. By using a variety of tasks you can spice things up, and help your students stay focused on and get the most out of their learning. By studying the same idea, concept or skill using a variety of different formats or approaches, your students are far more likely to retain their learning in the longer term.

Hallmarks of a nicely varied lesson

When you sit down to plan a lesson, take an overview of your plan to check whether you're including a good variety of tasks. A well-balanced and varied lesson may include the following:

- ✔ A brief teacher introduction, using visual aids such as pictures, video clips or props.
- ✔ A time for students to discuss and gather ideas, to talk in groups or to explore resources.
- ✔ Some interactive question-and-answer time, to gather the ideas together.
- ✔ Some movement between groups, to share the students' ideas around.
- ✔ Some 'hands-on' activities that get everyone involved, preferably involving multisensory approaches.
- ✔ A plenary activity in which students present what they've discovered to the class.

Of course, the exact nature of what you do depends on the age of the children and on the subject you're teaching. But in most instances, and in most subjects, achieving a good mix of activities is fairly straightforward.

Achieving variety across different subjects

Traditionally, certain tasks are associated with certain subjects: writing in an English or Literacy lesson, experiments in a Science lesson, drawing in an Art lesson. Often, though, you can usefully take a task that fits in one subject and utilise it in another. For instance, if you're teaching young children to recognise letter shapes, you can get them to:

- ✔ Practise making the letter shapes in the air with a finger
- ✔ Sing the letter sounds and use percussive instruments to make a different noise for each one

> ✔ Create letter shapes with their bodies
>
> ✔ Create sculptures of different letters, using Plasticine or clay
>
> ✔ Draw the letter shapes in chalk on the playground floor
>
> ✔ Cook biscuits in the different letter shapes

As you can see, these activities cross a range of subject areas: Music, Drama, Art, Cookery and so on. These cross-curricular links mean that students are getting to know the shapes, while simultaneously developing a skill from another subject (such as how to cook a biscuit).

Certain subjects sit well together naturally. History has many links to Literature; Biology, Physical Education and PSHE topics are often inter-related. But you can often create the most interesting combinations by putting together two activities, subjects or topics that seem diametrically opposed. This creates interest for your students, allows for tasks that have plenty of variety and also encourages you to think creatively when you're planning lesson activities.

So you can:

> ✔ Draw a graph (Maths) to show the levels of dramatic tension in a short story (English).
>
> ✔ Measure the distance (Maths) that students of different heights can skip, hop and jump (PE).
>
> ✔ Go on a nature trail (Science) and create a collage (Art) using the materials you collect.
>
> ✔ Design and make some clothes (Design Technology) from different time periods (History).

The most engaging lessons often call on your students to mix and use skills and ideas from several subjects at once. This approach can also lead to some very interesting lateral thinking and creativity, from both you and your students.

Making the Most of Resources

The basic definition of a 'resource' is anything you bring into the classroom to boost and improve your students' learning. Your resources can be as diverse, interesting and exciting as you care to make them. The more unusual the resource, often the better the response from the students. Resources certainly help you get the most, and the best, out of your students during lesson time.

Keep an eye out in your everyday life outside of school for anything that looks interesting and may play a part in your teaching. For instance, the other day I received a gift in a giant cardboard tube. As a teacher, I was just as interested in the giant tube as in what was inside it! And the tube's already made a successful appearance in my teaching.

Different kinds of resource

The kinds of resource you use can be as varied and interesting as you like. The only real limits are the cost and availability of the resources, and of course the safety of your students while they're using them. Don't be afraid to experiment with some more unusual resources. The worst that can happen is that your class gets over-excited, in which case you get to exercise your classroom management skills to the max!

Your resources can include the following:

- Everyday, or unusual, objects (for example, a huge cardboard tube for work on building a telescope, or some paperclips to set off a 'twenty uses for' thinking skills activity).

- Props to add to a dramatic scenario (for example, playing cards, coins and a matchbook to add to a 'crime scene' gambling scenario).

- Materials relating to the subject (for example, metal and wood for some Science work on studying different materials).

- Clothes, for you or the students to wear (for example, a Roman helmet to start off a History lesson on the Romans, or white coats for some work as 'government scientists').

- Accessories (for example, hats, bags, shoes, jewellery for building a character study for a story, or to recreate a fashion show).

- Natural materials (for example, a skeleton leaf and some crystals for some close observation drawings in Art).

- Living things (for example, some herb plants to smell to spark off sensory writing in English, or some mini beasts for a Science topic).

- People (for example, parent volunteers to help children with their reading, or experts such as journalists for a newspaper project).

- Music and radio (for example, as an inspiration for creative writing, or simply some background music as a reward).

- Images (for example, photos of different holiday destinations to spark off writing postcards, or images of different historical characters for a History topic).

✔ Video (for example, film from a previous year's school production, for the students to write their own theatre reviews).

✔ ICT (for example, the Internet as a research source for any topic you care to mention).

The more creative you get with your resources, the better your students respond, the more focused they should be on their work and the more they get out of the lesson.

Gathering resources, bringing them into school and working out where to store them can take a fair bit of time and organisation. Over the years as a teacher, you collect a range of resources that you know work really well with your classes. To my mind, gathering and looking after these materials are well worth the time and effort in terms of the knowledge that the students get out of them, and also because of the general improvement in behaviour and focus that they elicit.

Getting hands-on with resources

Whenever possible, letting students get hands-on with resources is a great idea, rather than you standing at the front with a resource to show it to the class. This helps your students get the most out of the resources that you've brought into your lesson. Before you do this, though, think carefully about the management issues involved. Ask yourself the following questions:

✔ How and when are you going to allow the students to handle the resources? You may have them on the desks for a starter to get your children inspired, or you may prefer to keep a tighter rein, getting volunteers up to the front to handle them.

✔ Do you have enough resources so that the students have one each? If not, how are you going to manage the sharing of the resources? If your resources are limited, you may have a single table for them, which the students visit in groups. You may decide to pass resources from group to group, giving a time limit for looking at them.

✔ Are any safety considerations involved in using these resources in your classroom? You may need to do a risk assessment before the lesson. If you have the services of a technician (for instance, in Science) she could help you ensure safe use of the resources.

✔ How can you ensure that the resources don't get damaged? Insist on sensible behaviour, otherwise the resources are taken away immediately. Leave enough time at the end of the lesson for clearing up, and check the resources as they're handed back in.

> ✔ How are you going to collect the resources at the end of the lesson? You may ask students to place the resources in the centre of desks. You could go around the room collecting them. With older students, you may ask for volunteers to gather them.

Don't let these management issues put you off the idea of using lots of resources. The more practice you get in handling resources in a lesson, the easier and quicker doing so becomes.

Unusual ideas for resources

I love to use resources in an unusual way – probably because I trained as a drama teacher! But whatever the subject you teach, you can use unusual resources, or use common or garden ones in an unusual way.

Here are a few suggestions to get you thinking:

> ✔ Put several resources together to create an entire scenario, for instance a crime scene, a French marketplace, a building site.
>
> ✔ Wear some clothes and play a 'character', building a story within which your students learn.
>
> ✔ Create an atmosphere in your classroom using lights, blackouts, music, sound effects and so on.
>
> ✔ Get some visiting artists into your school: writers, musicians, sculptors.

Of course, you don't have to do this all the time, or in all of your lessons. But every once in a while, do let your 'big kid' out and get creative with the resources you use.

Flour babies

Often, the skills don't lie so much in the resources you use, but what you do with them. One example of this is my 'flour babies' activity, which I've used several times. Although these days you can get 'real' babies to do this topic, to my mind using a bag of flour adds humour and creativity to the approach.

The idea is that you give a bag of flour to each of your students – this is their 'baby', and they must treat it as such. They take it to all their lessons, and they must also take it home with them. If they want to go out in the evening, they must arrange for a babysitter. This carries on for about a week, and the students also do various in-class activities involving their babies.

The idea behind this approach is to encourage responsibility, and to help older students understand exactly what becoming a parent means. Some schools also do this activity with eggs – raw or hard-boiled, depending on your kids!

Creating Fantastic Displays

Displays are a fantastic way to help your students get the most out of the time they spend in your classroom. They also help to brighten up the room for you – and if you're spending most of your working life in that room, this can only be a good thing. The National Agreement means that teachers in England and Wales can delegate jobs such as putting up displays to support staff. But to my mind, displays are one of the more interesting and creative aspects of the job, and I certainly still want to get involved in creating them.

Displays should reflect the work that's currently going on in your classroom, rather than being viewed as a kind of 'wallpaper'. Don't feel that you need to cover your walls as soon as the term begins. Take your time over putting up displays, and only display work that really merits the attention or contributes to learning during lessons. Make sure that you change your displays regularly during the year, for instance tying them into seasonal events such as Fireworks Night, Christmas or Easter.

Exploring how displays contribute to learning

Displays not only make your classroom a brighter and more interesting place to spend time, they can also contribute to knowledge in a multitude of ways. Displays help you to motivate and reward the efforts of your students – to celebrate the discovery taking place in your classroom.

Displays can help your students to learn by:

- Giving them a strong sense of motivation, through seeing their work on the walls.
- Encouraging them to feel a sense of pride and achievement in their work.
- Seeing what their peers are doing, and learning from each other's work.
- Giving them something concrete to aim for by seeing what their peers are achieving.
- Contributing to, or forming part of, the discovery going on in your classroom.

A great way to get your students really involved is to encourage them to help design and put up displays themselves. This may happen as part of a lesson or as a lunchtime activity.

No matter how tempting, don't just display the work that looks 'pretty' or the work of your most able students. Remember to celebrate the achievements of your less able students too, perhaps redrafting the work or helping them correct errors as necessary.

Understanding what makes a good display

Just as you can get creative and imaginative with what goes on in your lessons, so you can take interesting and unusual approaches towards your displays. This helps you ensure that the students take notice of, and respond to, the displays that go up on your walls.

A good display is:

- ✔ Bright, colourful and engaging – visually attractive so that it catches the eye.

- ✔ Interactive, encouraging the students to respond and interact with it in some way (see the nearby sidebar 'Ideas for interactive displays' for some suggestions on how to do this).

- ✔ Three dimensional, for example with a table in front of the display to show objects, books and materials for the children to explore.

- ✔ Topical and seasonal – changing over the course of time to match what's 'current'.

A good display gives your students the sense that you care about them and their work, and that you're happy to celebrate what they're doing in class.

You may feel that your students overlook and ignore your displays. Sadly, in some schools or situations they may even damage or vandalise them. Try not to let this put you off making interesting displays. Aim to 'tidy up' your displays regularly so that they stay neat. Persevere with displaying your students' work, even if at first they don't seem to appreciate your efforts.

Finding interesting places for displays

You traditionally find displays on the walls of a classroom: pictures or pieces of work attached to boards around the room. However, with a bit of imagination you can find many different places to put your displays. And the more unusual the place, often the more your students interact with the display.

Ideas for interactive displays

Students are used to plenty of interactivity in their lives outside school – in computer games, on the Internet, using the red digital button on the television. The more interactive you make your displays, the more likely your students are to interact with and gain from them. To create interactive displays, you can:

✔ Add Velcro pieces to the display, which the students can move around to create different effects, storylines, answers to questions and so on.

✔ Create lift-up flaps, with something interesting or challenging underneath.

✔ Put questions on your display, for the students to answer.

✔ Encourage your students to add information or ideas to the display over time, as a kind of 'working wall'.

✔ Put a few packs of Post-it® notes beside the display and ask the students to add their thoughts or ideas.

✔ Incorporate hidden symbols or clues for the students to locate.

You can:

✔ Create a washing line to go from one side of your room to the other, hanging work from it with pegs.

✔ Put up a tent and encourage the children to enter to see the display that's inside.

✔ Add some pictures to the windows of your room, using tissue paper or cellophane so that the light shines through to create interesting effects.

✔ Stick some shapes or graphics on the floor, for your students to step or sit on.

As with your lessons, the more surprising or interesting the display, the more your students notice and gain from it.

Getting Assessment Right

Assessment plays a key role in your students' progress, both in the classroom and beyond it. Assessment feeds back into the work that your students do, so that they constantly progress rather than standing still or going backwards. Assessment includes marking your students' work, but it's also about more than that. On a whole-school basis, assessment also includes tests, exams, analysing data, feeding back information, target setting, projected grades and so on.

When you assess really effectively, it has many benefits for you and your class:

- ✔ It allows both you and your students to see how well they're doing in their work and in relation to each other.

- ✔ It lets you check their progress in relation to any statutory targets or standards.

- ✔ It helps your students understand how they're getting on in the various subjects and within different skill areas.

- ✔ It lets your students understand their progress in relation to their peers.

- ✔ It encourages students to check, evaluate, understand and improve their own work.

- ✔ It helps you and your students to set realistic and personalised targets for future progress.

- ✔ It acts as a motivating factor – it pushes your students to push themselves.

- ✔ Parents and carers do like to see their children's work being, or at least 'looking', marked.

You need to be careful, though, in order to get assessment right. You have to ensure that your students get something really valuable out of the effort you spend on assessing their work. Otherwise, you're effectively wasting your time when doing it. As you think about student assessment, consider the following issues:

- ✔ **The type of assessment should be meaningful.** Sometimes assessment is a token gesture, for instance adding ticks to an exercise book so that it 'looks' like you've assessed it. A series of ticks (or crosses) does not have much real impact on the work your students do in the future. Whenever possible, aim to make your assessment more detailed and include feedback and targets for future improvement.

- ✔ **Assessment can be hugely time consuming.** You have to decide how much time you're willing to spend on it. Chapter 14 offers advice on ways to mark papers more efficiently.

- ✔ **Assessment can be counter productive.** Some forms of assessment are soul destroying for your weaker students, and can demotivate them to the point where they start to misbehave or lose interest in their work. Take care to balance the need for detailed assessment with the equally pressing need to maintain your students' motivation.

When you do spend time on assessing your students' work in detail, make sure that they actually look at and respond to what you've written, so that it has an ongoing impact on the quality of their work. Spend time in class on a brief recap of how you've marked, and give your students time to read over your comments and ask any questions.

Different kinds of assessment

Assessment comes in many different shapes, forms and sizes. It ranges from computerised, whole-school or whole-year-group target setting to brief and informal encounters between teacher and student during a lesson.

You may find yourself using the following techniques:

- ✔ **Informal assessment:** During the course of your lessons, you gain a sense of how your students are doing, through question-and-answer sessions, through their responses in discussion tasks, through taking a quick glance at their books. While you don't write anything down, getting to know your students in this informal way helps you set work that's appropriate to their needs.

- ✔ **Formal assessment:** You set a piece of work, such as an essay or story, that you assess and grade across the class. Or you give a test or mock exam, to see how much your students know and have retained on a topic. You record these marks for future reference.

- ✔ **Formative assessment:** You use assessment to develop and improve the work your students are currently doing. The assessment *informs* the learning and plays a part in improving it. This kind of assessment is now commonly referred to as Assessment for Learning. Formative assessment often also informs your planning.

- ✔ **Summative assessment:** You assess some work at the end of a topic or time period, to see how much your students have learned or how well they have progressed. You make an assessment *of* the learning in a formalised way, often via a test.

Toward the end of the school year, many students undertake school exams, particularly in secondary school. These exams are useful practice for students and are valuable for you as well, to check how far your students have progressed. Often, you'll find impending school exams coincide with a sudden boost in student motivation levels.

Some students don't fare well in exams. Nerves can mean that a student who's normally successful doesn't produce work that reflects her actual abilities. Teach your students how to approach exams, and how to control their nerves, as part of your preparation for any summative and formalised assessments.

The balancing act of marking

You can use various different approaches to mark your students' work. You may choose:

✔ **Close marking:** With this approach you mark in great detail, correcting each and every error, and writing in-depth comments on the work. This can be a great method for helping your students to improve their learning. But be warned: it's extremely time consuming, and can also be demoralising for your weaker students when they get a sea of red ink on their work.

✔ **'Tick and flick':** This approach involves putting a tick or cross on each answer, paragraph or page, and perhaps a brief comment or an overall mark at the end of the work. It typically has little value beyond making the books 'look' marked.

✔ **A mark with brief comments:** This is similar to 'tick and flick', except that you give short comments in addition to your ticks and crosses. You may show where a student's working out has gone wrong, or write a brief word or two of praise for an approach that's worked well. This style of marking helps students develop their work to an extent, but isn't as useful to students as the detailed marking explained below.

✔ **Marking for specific errors or areas:** With this technique, you mark for a particular area of potential weakness (such as spelling or punctuation) or a specific area (for example giving detailed explanations of an experiment). You explain this beforehand to the students so that they can focus on developing that particular skill or aspect of their work. You can differentiate your targets according to the weaknesses or strengths of your individual students.

As a teacher, marking is one of the trickiest balancing acts you have to perform. If you want to, you can spend hours every night marking your students' work and still have more marking left to do. When you're thinking about how, what and when to mark work, ask yourself:

✔ **What do I want my students to get out of the marking I do?** Sometimes, you just want them (and their parents or the inspectors) to feel that their work has been seen and marked, but if your aim is for them to *learn* something from the marking, you need to spend more time on it.

✔ **How much time can I realistically afford to give to this part of my work?** You can't mark every piece of work in great detail – there just aren't enough hours in the day. Work out which classes or subjects would benefit from a detailed approach. Identify a few key pieces each term to mark more fully.

✔ **What kind of value do my students get in relation to the time I spend on it?** Often, you correct the same spelling mistakes over and over again. Clearly, your corrections aren't having an impact, so try to look for other approaches, such as spelling tests and writing out mis-spelt words) that may have more impact.

✔ **How can I encourage my students to read, respond to and gain from the marking I do?** Set aside some class time for your students to read through, and respond to, your comments or amendments. If they've made a spelling mistake, ask them to write out the correct answer three times in the back of their books. If they've made an error of factual information, ask them to find out the correct answer and feed it back to you. Ensure that your students actually *learn* from the marking you've done.

✔ **What kind of approaches best suit my students' needs, and my own?** If your students are poorly motivated, you may be better sticking with constructive approaches, identifying what they've done well. If you're busy at certain points in the term, pull back a bit on the marking.

✔ **How can I record and use the results or data I get from my marking?** A mark book is a good place to keep a set of centralised results. Incorporating your marks into a teacher's planner keeps all your important information in one place.

Part III
Managing a Class

'I see Mrs Fimble has got her new
support staff.'

In this part . . .

You can't teach your class if you can't get the students to pay attention, to behave themselves. And worse than that, if your students are misbehaving, you *feel* awful as well. What you want to do is get on with teaching – find out in this part exactly how.

You're setting your stall out for your class. Organising routines, structures, expectations, rewards and sanctions that allow you to get on with delivering your lessons. And you need to learn how to handle more challenging situations and students as well. I reveal all the strategies and techniques you need to build better behaviour in this part of the book.

Chapter 7

Structuring Your Teaching and Your Teaching Space

In This Chapter

▶ Creating routines to help you manage learning and behaviour

▶ Discovering how to manage lesson time in the most effective way

▶ Exploring different methods for creating and working with groups

▶ Examining how to use the classroom space to improve students' knowledge and behaviour

*Y*our key job as a teacher is, of course, to teach, and to get your students to gain knowledge. But in order to get to the point where you can get on with doing the teaching and learning, you need to put lots of structures in place for your class. Your objective's to minimise any potential distractions, so that when you start teaching no disruptions occur. One of the key ways to do this is by creating routines and structures – the background rules and patterns by which your classroom runs.

The way your students come into and leave your space, and the way you ask them to work while they're with you, has a powerful influence on the kind of learning that takes place. It also has a strong impact (either positive or negative) on their behaviour. Imagine you're a cat: you want your students to feel that this is *your* territory, and they should be conscious of how they act while they're in it.

Teaching spaces come in all shapes and sizes. As well as controlling how your students use the space, the space itself can either improve, or damage, the chances of your students working effectively. You probably have little or no say over *where* you teach; what you can do, though, is make the most of the space you do have, and minimise the impact of any potential downsides.

Establishing Your Routines

When you meet a new class, one of your first tasks is to establish the routines you want the students to follow. These routines give a sense of structure and pattern to your lessons and your days. Routines go hand in hand with the expectations I look at in Chapter 8. As time goes on, your students assimilate the routines you've set, until following them's second nature.

You establish your routines by:

- ✔ Explaining to the class what they are, how they should follow them and what happens if they don't.

- ✔ Practising them together, so that the students understand what to do, and how to do it, for instance working on making a good straight line outside the classroom before they enter.

- ✔ Praising and rewarding the students when they follow the routines correctly and sanctioning those students who don't, or won't, do as you ask.

- ✔ Encouraging parents to help in getting your children into your routines, especially with the younger end of the primary age group.

After you've got your routines in place, you need to go over them time and time again, until the students understand exactly what you expect them to do. Make sure you display a set of rules in your classroom and preferably stick another set into your students' diaries. You can then refer to these whenever you have to give reminders about behaviour or hand out sanctions.

Your aim is to get your students so used to your routines that they follow them without even thinking. Get them 'trained up' in the structures you use, so that doing these things becomes second nature every time they visit your classroom. The routines become a physical memory – a set of movements the students perform in a subconscious way. I've had first-hand experience of how this happens, when working as a supply teacher. Sometimes the students automatically go to line up in order outside the classroom, or place their books and pens on the desk in a particular way. Even though their usual teacher isn't there, they're so well trained (some may say 'brainwashed'!) that they repeat the movements despite his absence.

Understanding why routines are so vital

You live your life by routines – everyone does, whether they're aware of it or not. You get up at a certain time (especially on work days), eat at a particular place in your home, leave for work at a specific time. You may be the kind of person who likes a highly structured approach to life, or you may be a bit more flexible and adaptable. But even the most free-spirited people have at least some measure of routine in their lives.

Young people actually welcome and enjoy routines. And the younger they are, the more they need these routines. Every parent knows that, if you want to get a young child to bed without too much fuss, you need to follow an evening routine that remains the same from day to day. If you're a primary teacher, you may have spotted that those children who concentrate and behave best in your lessons have a structured life outside of school. And those children who cause you the most problems are often those who don't have a steady or stable routine to their home life.

Routines are vital, and useful, in schools for a variety of reasons:

- ✔ You're less stressed – you don't have to explain over and over again to your students what you want them to do.

- ✔ Your students have a sense of security, clarity and continuity – they know what's going to happen, and what you expect of them in lessons. This feeling of security is especially useful for your most challenging or disadvantaged students, because it helps them feel safe.

- ✔ Clear routines and structures often lead to much better student behaviour.

- ✔ Routines are especially important for those students who have special needs – they thrive on a sense of structure.

- ✔ Routines ensure the physical safety of your students. You face less chance of dangerous behaviour, for instance 'bunching' of large groups of students, messing around with equipment and so on.

- ✔ Your routines train your students for when they leave school and start work. They learn the importance of arriving on time, wearing the correct clothing and so on.

- ✔ When applied across a school, routines help develop an overall ethos of discipline and hard work, and a sense that all staff are consistent. This means that the students perceive their school and their teachers as being fair and reasonable.

Of course, you also want your students to be able to cope with change: an unexpected teacher absence, or a day when the timetable has to be adapted. Your students need to understand that certain behaviours and approaches are required at all times in a school, no matter who the teacher or what the lesson. By creating clear routines and expectations, and making it clear that these always apply, you can achieve a sense of consistency even when the day doesn't quite run as normal.

Sometimes you know you're going to be absent ahead of time, for instance if you're attending a training course. Before you go, talk with your class about how they should stick to their usual routines, even though you're not physically present in the classroom. And warn them that you're going to ask for feedback on your return. You may get a teaching assistant to explain the routines to the cover teacher. You can also ask the teacher who looks after your class to leave a note saying how well (or not) the students did.

Creating routines that work for you

Routines are only useful if they actually work *for* you, rather than against you. If the students fight tooth and nail against a particular structure, or if circumstances conspire against you applying it, consider adapting the structure so that it works to everyone's advantage. For instance, let's say you want to insist that your class lines up before entering your classroom, because you like an orderly start to lessons. However, because of the limited space outside you find your students getting into arguments because they're crushed together. By insisting on the line, you're causing yourself unnecessary stress. Instead, ask that students come into the room and stand behind a chair until they're invited by you to sit. You retain the sense of an orderly beginning to class time, but you change it so that it works better for your situation. Adapt your approaches to your individual situation circumstances until you find something that works, but remember – what works well in one school environment may not be effective in another.

Just as you adapt your routines to your circumstances, so no one set of routines works for every teacher. Adapt your routines to suit:

- **The teaching style you want to project:** If you're after a 'strict' impression, you're best to go for the traditional approaches, such as lining the class up outside the room, making the students stand behind their seats until you invite them to sit down and using a strictly observed seating plan. If you prefer a more informal style, the students can filter in as they arrive and sit where they wish.

- **The kind of person you are:** Some teachers have a personality that lends itself to an authoritarian, old-school style and routines. If you're a big, beefy, mature, six-foot deputy head who teaches PE, you can get away with being very strict and structured in your lessons. If you're a young, small, soft-spoken, newly qualified Drama teacher, doing that's probably not going to work for you.

- **The size of class you teach:** The larger the group, the more important to be picky about your routines. With a class of thirty, safety considerations demand a very orderly start and finish to lessons. With a class half that size, you can (if appropriate) be more relaxed.

- **The subject or subjects you're teaching the class:** Some subjects need a highly structured approach, because of both safety and time constraints. In a PE lesson, you need to create a routine where the students get changed and into the gym or hall as quickly as possible, so they have plenty of time for the lesson. Similarly, if you're using potentially dangerous materials or equipment in the lesson, you need to be sure that the appropriate structures are in place.

✔ **The age of students you teach:** Some age groups respond best to a very highly ordered approach; others find the same amount of structure constricting. Young students really enjoy having a very clear day-to-day routine. Older students (say, 14 years old and above) may perceive you as patronising if you use a lot of traditional structures. This may mean you get yourself into unnecessary confrontations.

✔ **The type of students you teach:** No 'one size fits all' when it comes to the students you teach. Some respond best to lots of structure and routine, while others kick against it right from the word go. Of course, that doesn't mean you should give up on the essentials – certain non negotiables exist in every situation, such as listening to what others say in a respectful manner, or entering and leaving the classroom in an ordered way.

Work out how much structure is beneficial for your students, and if they're particularly challenging, bring in routines gradually. If you're new to your school, ask around among the well-respected and more experienced teachers to gain their advice on what works best in your particular situation.

✔ **The kind of behaviour issues you face:** If your only behaviour concern is low-level misbehaviour, you may prefer to limit the amount of structures you use. With the worst-behaved classes, lots of routines can sometimes help you manage behaviour. And sometimes, too many structures actually make the situation worse. You need to decide which routines are really going to make a difference with a particular group and actually contribute to better learning taking place.

✔ **The type of school or setting:** The routines you use vary according to whether your setting is nursery, primary, secondary, FE and so on (the next section explains how to set up age-appropriate routines). They also depend on the values and ethos you're asked to embody. For instance, independent schools often ask for a very traditional approach to classroom structures.

Look around your school to see how other teachers approach routine setting. You don't have to copy them to the letter, but this gives you an overall feel for what can work.

✔ **The teaching space in which you work:** If you teach in a cramped classroom, you need to adapt your routines to ensure that the students make the most of the available space. On the other hand, if you work in a very open environment, such as a hall, gym or studio, you must incorporate structures that encourage self-discipline and safe approaches.

✔ **The timetable you follow:** If you need to move your class from one place to another, for instance to assembly, consider the kind of routines you have in place. Similarly, take care with your timing and routines for the start and end of lessons, particularly when the students are going to or coming back from a break.

In an ordered and disciplined school environment with well-motivated students, the overall ethos can allow for a traditional approach. However, you may find a more casual approach is possible and indeed preferable. You've got to use your professional judgement to decide what's best.

Similarly, in a school where behaviour is appalling, you may be setting yourself up for huge amounts of conflict if you insist on certain old-fashioned routines that aren't entirely necessary. On the other hand, sometimes the most difficult students respond really well to highly structured routines within their lessons. Work out what your priorities are and what's going to make the biggest difference in your situation, then focus your efforts in these areas.

Don't lock yourself into a one-size-fits-all routine. Just because a routine works for one class or at one school, doesn't mean that it suits others. At secondary level, you see lots of different classes and age groups over the course of the week. Your routine can even vary to suit each one: a traditional, strict routine with the youngest; a more relaxed and negotiated one with the oldest. A good rule of thumb is to be as strict as you can get away with.

Although you need to set up your routines at the start of the school year, before you've really got to know your class, you can always adapt them slightly as time goes on.

Creating routines to suit different age groups

The routines you establish cover many different aspects of your classroom practice. You need to be specific about:

- ✔ How the students come into the teaching space
- ✔ What the students should do once they're in the classroom
- ✔ Where the students sit within the teaching space
- ✔ The point in the lesson when you register the students
- ✔ How and when they can move around the classroom during a lesson
- ✔ What they should do if they need to leave the room for any reason
- ✔ How resources and equipment are stored, accessed and cleared away
- ✔ How books, homework, resources and so on are collected in
- ✔ The way the lesson or session ends
- ✔ How and when the students leave the room

In a primary school, where you spend all or most of your time with your class, you can get the children trained in these routines within the first couple of weeks. Doing so takes a bit longer in a secondary school, where you may see each class only once or twice a week, with a slightly different routine for each one. The routines you use depend on the age group with which you're working. The following sections give sample routines for both primary and secondary school.

Perhaps this all seems a bit overly controlling and rigid to you. But honestly, if you get the right kind of routines in place and stick by them, you can get on with the main job. And that is, of course, your teaching!

A sample primary school routine

The younger the children, the more they need and appreciate routines. Just as a toddler benefits from a fairly rigid and highly structured bedtime routine, so the very youngest students enjoy plenty of structure within their school day. For instance, your routine in the first few years of primary school may look something like this:

- ✓ **How they should come into the teaching space:** When the students arrive with their parents, they hang up their bags and coats, put any lunch boxes or drinks in a trolley and then enter the room with their book bags. They put their book bags in their named trays.

  While you're waiting for everyone to arrive, you can listen to some readers and have a quick chat with any parents who need to see you.

- ✓ **What they should do once in the classroom:** You've already set up some activities at different tables, and the children choose an activity where spaces are free. They get on with this while you're waiting for the school day to start officially.

- ✓ **Where they should sit:** When the school bell goes, the students come to sit on the carpet, according to the seating plan that you set up in the first week. Your seating plan ensures that any restless or difficult children sit at the front, close to your chair.

- ✓ **When you register them:** As soon as the children are quiet and still, you register them.

- ✓ **How and when they can move around the classroom during a lesson:** After a short session of whole-class teaching, the children go to sit in their pre-set groups to work on some activities. They know that they mustn't leave their seats without raising a hand to get permission.

- ✓ **What they should do if they need to leave the room:** If any children need to leave the room during class time (for instance, to go to the toilet or visit the office), they know they must first ask your permission. You have a set of different-coloured bands to indicate the reason they're out of your room – only one band of each colour, so only one child can leave the room for each purpose at a time.

✔ **How resources and equipment are stored, accessed and cleared away:** Each child has a tray in which he stores any individual resources. They know the location of their own trays. A small group of volunteers, chosen for their sensible behaviour, gives out and clears away any equipment or resources during the day. Your equipment and resources are kept in drawers, each clearly labelled with a picture and word. You leave five minutes between lessons for clearing up.

✔ **How books, homework, resources and so on are collected in.** If books need to be collected in, the children place them in a pile in the centre of the table. If you have work to mark, the children place their books open at this page, to save you time hunting for the right spot in each book. One child from each table collects the books and brings them to you. You collect homework from book bags during the day.

✔ **The way the lesson or session ends:** When you're approaching break time, you settle the children in their seats. When everyone's quiet, you ask the best table to line up first. When everyone's lined up quietly, you allow them to go to break. At the end of the day, the children gather their things, put their chairs up on the tables and wait for you to dismiss them.

✔ **How and when the students leave the room:** When the bell rings, you allow the most sensible, best-behaved or hardest-working children to go first. You wait outside with them until you're sure that all the parents or carers have collected their children.

The younger the students are, the more often you have to explain the structures you wish them to follow. If your students aren't following a routine properly, you must keep reminding them and practising until they do. Alternatively, consider whether the routine itself is the problem. Perhaps you need to adapt the routine to better suit the class.

A sample secondary school routine

In a secondary school, your routine may run something like this:

✔ **How they should come into the teaching space:** You wait at the door while the students line up outside the classroom. When they're quiet, you allow them in one by one. You take any students who aren't in correct uniform to one side and deal with them quietly before they come into the room. While doing this, you keep half an eye on what's going on inside your classroom.

✔ **What they should do once in the classroom:** The students go straight to their desks, get out their books and pens ready for an equipment check and place their bags under their seats. At this point they copy the lesson title and objectives from the board, or complete the starter activity that's waiting on their desks.

✔ **Where they should sit:** The students sit according to the seating plan you instigated in the first lesson.

✔ **When you register them:** When the students are settled, you wait for them to fall silent and then take the register.

✔ **How and when they can move around the classroom during a lesson:** The students know that they mustn't leave their seats during the lesson without your express permission. If they do, they know that they get a couple of warnings, then a sanction.

✔ **What they should do if they need to leave the room:** Unless they have a medical condition that requires additional toilet trips, the students understand that they can't leave the room during lessons. If you need a volunteer, for instance to go to the office, you send the student with a note in his diary.

✔ **How resources and equipment are stored, accessed and cleared away:** Resources and equipment are stored in a clearly labelled central cupboard. You choose a group of monitors to give out and clear away resources. This group changes every few lessons. The job of monitor goes to the best-behaved students, as a reward. Once a term, a group of volunteers clear out any resources that you no longer use.

✔ **How books, homework, resources and so on are collected in:** When the class is on task during the lesson, you go round to collect in homework. The students put their homework out on the desks; those who haven't done the homework put their diaries out instead, so that you can write in a detention. As you go around to collect homework, you take your planner with you. You check against a student's name to see that he was present in the lesson when the homework was set. If you need to collect books for marking, the students place these in a pile in the centre of their desks, again open at the relevant page, and student volunteers gather them in.

✔ **The way the lesson or session ends:** You get the class to clear away five minutes before the bell goes for the end of the lesson. At this point you give a few words of praise, talk together about what they've discovered in the lesson or play a quick game of 'statues' to calm the students down before they leave. A minute before the bell goes, the students push in their chairs and stand behind them, waiting in silence to be dismissed.

✔ **How and when the students leave the room:** When the bell goes, you let the students leave a table at a time, with the 'best' table going first. If the lesson's at the end of the school day, the students put their chairs up on the desks before they wait for you to dismiss them.

If you follow this pattern or a similar one day after day, lesson after lesson, your students quickly become 'trained up' in the way you work. And after a while you don't even need to tell them what to do – they follow the routines automatically, saving you a great deal of energy.

Maintaining your routines

After you have your routines in place and the students know exactly how you want them to behave and work, life in your classroom becomes a lot easier. You don't have to harp on and on about what your students *should* be doing. You can get on with teaching them instead. But you may have to do some maintenance or make some adjustments to your routines over the course of the school year.

Even a brand new house eventually needs repairing; your routines also need some maintenance throughout the year – a bit like adding some paint to touch up the walls, or tightening a door knob that's come loose. The basic essentials (walls, doors) are all in place, but they don't stay fresh and new for long. Of course, if you build a house using quality materials in the first place, they last much longer. The same applies to your classroom routines – get them right in the first place, and you have less need to revisit them over the year.

You maintain your routines by:

- ✔ **Giving your class regular recaps about your routines, preferably** *before* **they start to go wrong:** Remind the students regularly of how they should behave during the routines. For instance, exactly how to line up outside the room at the start of lessons: in silence, in a good straight line, in correct uniform.

- ✔ **Using a lot of individual praise for those who always get it right – not just focusing on those who don't do what you ask – and incorporating whole-class rewards if the whole class manages to follow the routine exactly:** For example, if everyone hands in their homework on time, you may give them a night off work. This strategy utilises peer pressure – a very powerful motivator for your students.

- ✔ **If things aren't working, not immediately blaming the students but also questioning whether something's wrong with your routines:** Perhaps they don't match the situation or the class all that well.

- ✔ **Playing around a bit with your routines, so the students don't get bored:** For instance, you may change the way you take the register – singing it rather than saying it, or asking a student to call out the names for you.

- ✔ **Relaxing your routines slightly, as you get to know the class better, but only if students deserve it:** For example, you may allow them free choice of seating as a reward for following your routines properly.

As the holidays approach (or even just on a Friday afternoon), you may be tempted to let standards slip. You're feeling worn out, and your students are getting into 'holiday mode', ready to relax. Make sure you make a conscious decision if you do choose to relax your routines a little. Let the students know that you're only doing this because of their continuing good behaviour. And warn them that if they start to take advantage, you're back to the old ways in a flash! This way, you don't have to start again from scratch at the start of each new week or term.

Managing Your Lesson Time

Managing your lesson time effectively is trickier than you may think. I often find that, no matter how self-disciplined I aim to be, I end up having to rush through the last bit of a session. You may find that you tend to over-estimate how much you can get through in a lesson, or conversely that you don't plan enough and the students finish all the tasks well ahead of time.

Managing your lesson time effectively is vital because of the following:

- ✔ You want to have enough (but not too much) time for your students to do each individual activity or part of the lesson.

- ✔ You want to maintain that sense of structure you've worked hard to create, and keep yourself feeling calm, in control and relaxed as you teach.

- ✔ You don't want to over-run and make the students late for their next lesson, or for their break time.

- ✔ You need to avoid a hurried and harried feeling during lessons, as this can lead to issues with behaviour.

- ✔ Similarly, you want to avoid the same feeling at the end of lessons – this is what your students remember next time you teach them.

- ✔ You must leave enough time at the end of a lesson for the students to clear up, otherwise you end up doing it yourself. This is especially important for messy subjects such as Art or Cookery.

- ✔ In the secondary school, you want to be relaxed and ready for when your next class arrives.

With experience, you gain a sense of how long each part of a lesson will take, how much you can fit into a session and whether you're spending too much time on an activity early on in a lesson. But remember, even the most experienced teachers have days when they just can't get their timing right.

Predicting how long activities should take

When you plan a lesson, include some approximate timings for each activity. Don't expect to stick exactly to these, but they give you an idea of how much you can fit into the time you have available. Remember to allow time for handing out resources and for clearing up. Human nature being what it is, students hand out exciting resources much more quickly than they clear up their own mess.

Teacher talk often takes up far more lesson time than it should. Be strict with yourself about how long you talk to a class. Incorporate questions during an introduction to a lesson. Doing this takes longer, but helps keep your students involved and gains you valuable feedback about whether they understand what you've said.

Use these timings to give you a rule of thumb for how long different activities may take:

- ✔ Starter activity: 5 minutes
- ✔ Teacher introduction: 5 minutes
- ✔ Teacher introduction with student Q&A: 10 minutes
- ✔ Whole-class discussion to gather ideas: 10 minutes
- ✔ Teacher setting an activity: 5 minutes
- ✔ Paired discussion task: 5 minutes
- ✔ Group discussion task: 10–15 minutes
- ✔ Individual written task: 10 minutes
- ✔ Practical activity (including set up): 15–25 minutes
- ✔ Clearing up: 5–10 minutes

Lesson times vary, from the very short session of only half an hour, to the 'double' period of up to two hours. In a short session, aim for a maximum of three activities. In a longer session, consider breaking the time into two parts, with five minutes or so to relax in the middle.

Pacing a lesson to fill the time allotted

The time in a lesson has a tendency to 'concertina' – that is, it starts out seeming like you have an eternity to fill and then proceeds to squash up as the end of the lesson approaches. To have time left over at the end of a lesson is far better than to rush through the last few activities. You can fill up any spare time with a review or evaluation, or some feedback from your students on what they've learnt.

Beginning and ending a lesson well

The start of your lesson or day sets the scene for what's to come. If the lesson begins in an ordered, calm and structured way, your students are far more likely to behave well and learn lots. But if the opening part of your lesson or day is chaotic, tense and unplanned, you may find getting the class back under control almost impossible. If you get all this right, you should hopefully get yourself on the way to a really successful session with your students. When your students arrive, make sure that:

✔ You position yourself to make it clear that this is 'your space'.

✔ If possible, you line them up outside the room before you allow them in, particularly at secondary level.

✔ You welcome them into the room in a positive way, using their names.

✔ As they come in, make some general, affirmative comments, such as 'good to see you', or noting if someone's looking especially smart.

✔ You deal with anything that may be an issue quickly and quietly, in a low-key manner, preferably before you bring students into the classroom.

✔ You project an air of relaxed confidence.

✔ You have a clear routine for the opening part of your lesson or day.

Similarly, the end of lessons is a key time – aim to finish in a calm, structured and positive manner, rather than in a rushed and disorganised way. Again, this is what your students remember when they next meet you, so ensure that they leave with a positive feeling about your time together. If you end on a high note, your students are keen to come to your lesson again.

At the end of a lesson, or when you send the children out to break, try to:

✔ Focus on what's gone well in the lesson, and how next time around you can repeat this.

✔ If any issues have cropped up, talk about how things can improve for your next lesson together.

✔ Give out some specific praise or rewards to those who have worked and behaved well.

✔ Let those who've behaved and worked best be the first to leave.

✔ Summarise what you've all gained from the lesson, and what you're going to be doing next time round.

✔ Leave plenty of time – you can always use some 'fillers' if you have time to spare. Make sure your students don't feel that you've had to rush to get everything finished in time.

✔ Ensure that the students leave your room in the state they found it – neat, tidy and ordered, ready for the next class.

To avoid running out of time towards the end of the lesson, make sure that you:

✔ Keep a close and constant check on the time.

✔ Leave more time than you think you might need for setting up activities and clearing away at the end.

✔ Be responsive to how your students are working. If they're doing really well on an activity, see if you can cut another one out to leave more time for it.

✔ Similarly, if you set an activity and your students look perplexed by it, be willing to say 'okay that's not working, let's try something else'.

✔ Don't try to fit too much in. Far better to do a couple of activities really well in a calm and unrushed manner than to skim through lots of different tasks.

Make sure you've got a decent-sized, accurate watch on your wrist at all times. Then get yourself into the habit of looking at it regularly – at least once every five minutes or so. This sounds obvious, but you very easily get so hooked up in the lesson that you forget to keep a check on the time. If you're particularly bad at finishing on time, you may even set your watch five minutes fast, so that you always have a bit of spare time at the end.

Working with Groups

When you teach from the front of the room and deliver a lesson to the whole class, you feel safe and controlled. The moment you set the children off on their own, you lose that element of tight control. But group work is an essential part of your students' learning experience. You need to discover the best ways to get them working in groups, so that they get the most out of this activity. You also need to consider the most effective ways of organising groups and the kind of activities that do most to boost their discovery.

Your students need to *learn* how to work in groups – they certainly aren't perfect at it at first. In fact, remember that group work's a fairly artificial construct, mainly found in classrooms rather than in the 'real world' outside the school gates. Although some jobs do require people to work in groups, those involved tend to have a leader or director of some kind who delegates the jobs. In schools, you're aiming for the kind of cooperative group activity that's actually very hard to achieve.

Understanding why group work matters

Obviously, group work is important because it's a key statutory element of many different subjects. But it's about much more than that. Group work matters because it teaches your students a range of key skills, ones that improve their work and behaviour whatever activity they're doing in the classroom.

The skills your students gain from group work include:

- ✔ Cooperation – working together with others regardless of personal feelings about them.

- ✔ Understanding a variety of views on a subject or topic, and being able to accept that not everyone thinks the same.

- ✔ Taking turns and letting everyone play an equal part in an activity.

- ✔ Discussing ideas as a group, bouncing thoughts around and connecting disparate suggestions.

- ✔ Gaining from each other's skills, ideas and approaches.

When your students manage to work cooperatively in groups, they can discover a huge amount from the activity. Group work's also a great way to boost relationships within a class, and between students who don't normally talk or work with each other.

Organising your groups

You can group your students in various ways, partly according to the type of task you've set, and also according to the kind of outcomes you want to achieve. When you plan to do some group work, consider the kind of group that works best for the particular activity you're setting. You can group students according to ability, group them randomly or let the students group themselves.

However you decide to organise your groups, make sure that you make a conscious decision based on the type of task you're setting. If you don't specify, the students go ahead and create a group with their friends.

 Insist, right from the start, that your students work with anybody and every-body. This pre-empts complaints of: 'I can't work with him/her!' If you've already set up the expectation that they work cooperatively whatever the grouping, you can ignore any complaints. If you start mixing groups around according to the whims of your students, you're effectively handing over control of the groups to them.

 I always insist from the beginning that students be willing to work with members of either gender. In fact, I often start off by doing some paired work that deliberately uses boy/girl partners. If you do this right from the start, your students don't think to question it. If you always allow your students to choose their own groupings, they inevitably get into single-sex groups. Avoid this by making your expectations clear from the start.

Ability groups

One way to group the students is according to their ability in the subject. That way, you can focus your resources (for instance a member of support staff) to work with a target group whose members most need help.

You can also set the group up so that students of all different ability levels work together. Remember that ability isn't just about academic achievement – some students are very able at speaking out and giving ideas. These students aren't necessarily the most able at tasks such as writing.

If you're planning to used single- or mixed-ability groups, you need to organise these yourself before the lesson, based on your knowledge of the students' abilities and personalities. Where feasible, make sure that your groupings:

- Don't contain students you know will 'clash' instantly.
- Have a good mix of the confident and less-confident students.
- Avoid placing two very strong characters together.
- Help to 'pull up' those students who might benefit from working with the most able.
- Are likely to encourage the quieter, or less able, to feel comfortable about joining in.

As you get to know your students better and see them doing activities in different groupings, you get wise to which mix works best.

Friendship groups

In friendship groups, you let the students choose who to work with, depending on their social groups outside of class. This can have some benefits, as friends often work better together. However, it also has downsides: the less popular students can end up being left out of the groupings, and you run the risk of off-task, social chatter. Keeping friendship groupings as a treat or a reward, for when you feel the class really deserves it, is a good idea.

Random groups

You can also group students using a random selection method. This can work very well as an approach, because it encourages your pupils to work with anybody and everybody. Unfortunately this method can have unintended downsides: where tensions exist between students in a random group, this can have a negative effect on behaviour and work.

You need to decide on the approach you're going to use for creating random groupings. I use the following strategy, which works with any size of class. It sounds a bit complicated, but the method's actually very straightforward once you get the hang of it. Here's what you do:

1. Count how many students you have in the class, for example 30.

2. Now divide this by the number of students you want in each group, so 6 may be 30 ÷ 6 = 5 groups.

3. Next, ask the students to count around the room up to this number, calling 'their' number out loud.

   So your students count 1, 2, 3, 4, 5 ... 1, 2, 3, 4, 5 ... and so on, until everyone has a number.

4. Ask all the 1s to raise a hand – this is group number 1 and six hands should be raised.

5. Repeat with each of the numbers in turn, so that every student in the room is aware of the number of his group.

6. Allocate a spot in the room for each group, either a specific set of desks or an area of the room if you're working in an open space.

7. On your instruction, the 1s stand up and move to their group.

8. Repeat with the numbers 2 to 5.

This also works where you have an odd number of students in the class; simply round down to the nearest number. So if you want groups of about five in a class of twenty-seven, the students count around the room up to five. You end up with three groups of five students and two groups of six.

Getting the most out of every group member

In the world of work, genuine group work is surprisingly rare. In most instances someone takes charge of the group – a director controls his actors, a manager organises his team. In school, however, you want to help your students learn to take on different roles, and to work in a cooperative way. You need to get the most out of every group member, ensuring that everyone takes part when you set a group activity.

Taking turns

For many students, one of the hardest skills involved in group work is taking turns. Some students tend to be leaders, wanting to direct and take over the group and not allowing anyone else to give their ideas. Other students prefer to sit back and let the rest do the work, or are too shy to contribute very much to the activity.

Use various ways to encourage your students to take turns. You can:

- Designate roles to the various group members, ensuring that you encourage students who don't normally contribute much to take more of a leadership role.

- Use a 'conch' – an object of some kind that a student holds during his turn to speak. Suitable objects include a conch shell (this idea originally comes from William Golding's book *Lord of the Flies*) or a 'speaking stick'.

- Set up the activity by insisting that everyone takes turns to give their ideas, with one quick suggestion from each person in turn.

- Use a timer for passing around the group, giving each student a chance to speak for the allocated time.

Of course, success also depends on how you set up the groups in the first place. Make sure that you mix up your groupings in an appropriate way, for instance putting your quieter students in a group without any 'big' personalities who may take over.

Keeping groups focused on a task

Sometimes you set the groups off on a task and within a few minutes you realise that they're not actually doing the work. Some are involved in social chat, others are just sitting there not doing anything at all. You can find many ideas for keeping individual students focused on their work in Chapter 6.

You can use various strategies to help keep your students on task during group work:

- Don't give them too long to do the activity. The longer they have, the more likely they are to spend some time off task, either at the start of the activity, before they get going, or towards the end, when they feel that they've 'finished' the work.

- Give a strong focus for the task. For instance, set it up as a competition between groups, to see who can get the most ideas in the time frame given. This creates a sense of momentum and energy.

- With longer tasks, incorporate some times when everyone stops what they're doing and gives feedback as a whole class.

Using the doughnut to share group work

The 'doughnut' approach is a very effective way of sharing ideas between groups. Allow the groups a limited amount of time to brainstorm ideas, say five minutes. During the brainstorming period one person in the group acts as scribe, writing down everyone's ideas.

At the end of the allotted time, you pause the class and get everyone's attention. Now all the scribes in the room stand up and move to the next group along, in a clockwise direction. The scribes then spend a few minutes reading out their ideas to the new group.

You can repeat this several times over, so that the scribes move through several groups, passing on ideas as they go.

As well as achieving a good focus, you also want to ensure that students record any ideas for later use. You can ask every individual in the group to make notes, or for each group to get a volunteer to act as scribe, someone who writes down the ideas as a central record of what the group has said.

Evening out the workload

As your students work within their groups, move around the teaching space to keep an eye on how much everyone is contributing to the task. Where you notice a student sitting back and doing very little, you might set him up as 'leader' for the next five minutes. If you see a student taking over and bossing a group around, you could ask him to take over as scribe – it's hard for students to simultaneously write down ideas and boss others around!

Grading group work

When you want or need to assess a piece of group work, think ahead of time about the approach you'll take. Consider whether you should allocate two marks – one overall grade for the group as a whole and individual grades for each student within the group. Much depends on the type of subject you're teaching and the type of task you've set. Where appropriate, get your students to write an evaluation or feedback on how they approached the task, as this gives you an additional insight into what took place.

When grading a group task, think about the kind of skills you want to see. Depending on the age of the students and the subject you're teaching, your focus might be on:

✔ Working cooperatively

✔ Taking turns

✔ Contributing good ideas

✔ Understanding a range of viewpoints

✔ Creating a good finished product together

You may find it surprisingly hard to give accurate marks for group work; you can't be there watching over every member of your class to see how much or how little they contribute. If assessed group tasks play a key role in the subject you're teaching, for instance in Drama, getting video footage of the class as they work works well. This gives you the chance to look back at what went on during the lessons.

Setting Up Your Space

You have a wonderful feeling when you first get your very own classroom: a space of your own that you can set up as you like. But with that space of your own come a whole host of different options and questions that you need to consider.

Schools tend to maintain the status quo. Classrooms often stay looking exactly the same for many years. The desks remain in the same layout, facing the same way. Any new teachers who come into the space stick with what's already there. Perhaps they're nervous about making any radical changes; perhaps they don't even think of change as a possibility. And when a classroom looks exactly the same as it always has, the students are tempted to perceive the teacher as part of the 'same old same old'.

Of course, some spaces are almost impossible to rearrange – physical impediments stop you making any kind of changes. But often, the problem isn't that you *can't* change the space, it's that you don't feel comfortable about changing it.

When the students enter their classroom for the first time, if it looks different to how it used to be, this alters their perceptions of the space, and of what you're going to do within it. This is especially so if they're familiar with the space from a previous year at the school. With a tricky class or year group, or in a subject where the students lack motivation, change can be a great way to get them rethinking their attitude.

Before your students arrive at the start of the year, take a long, hard look at your teaching space and ask yourself the following:

✔ Is this space exactly how I want it to be?

✔ Do I want to make any changes?

✔ Are these changes feasible?

✔ Do I need to take into account any fixed elements (columns, radiators, whiteboards)?

✔ Where's the best spot for me to stand in order to teach the whole class?

✔ When the students are doing group work, am I going to be able to get to each individual easily?

✔ What's the best place for me to store resources and materials?

✔ Are the desks in the best possible layout; if not, is space available to change them around?

Some teachers, particularly in a secondary school, don't have a classroom of their own. This can lead to issues with personalising the room to suit your own needs. You also have to deal with lugging equipment around the school. Wherever possible, ask for a wall for displays and some storage space in each classroom you teach in.

I was once given a great piece of advice that helps you understand how your students perceive and experience the space, and you within it, while you're teaching. Before the students arrive, go around the space and sit in each of the chairs for a moment. When you do this, you often notice little problems or snags. For instance, a student sitting in particular spot isn't able to see the board, another student may bang his leg against a hot radiator. Try out this approach in your own classroom – the results may surprise you. You certainly gain an insight into how your students feel while they're watching you teach.

Understanding the importance of layout

The way you lay out the desks affects the kind, and quality, of work that goes on in your classroom. No one 'right' way exists to set up your room; as with so many things in teaching, you need to adapt your approaches to suit your situation. Find the classroom layout that works best for you and for your students.

The layout you choose depends on many factors, including:

✔ The age of the children you teach – most lower primary teachers tend to group their desks together.

✔ The type of students you teach – if student behaviour's a problem, desks in rows rather than groups often works better.

✔ The subject you teach – if your subject requires lots of discussion work, you're best to group the tables to facilitate this.

✔ The approach you prefer to take to learning – whether you like to take an old-fashioned, authoritarian approach or use a relaxed, modern style.

✔ Your own educational philosophy – whether you feel the students learn better from each other or you prefer to teach mainly from the front.

✔ What's generally accepted as the 'right thing' in your school, or by your head teacher (although you can always be brave and buck the trend!).

No harm at all in playing around with various layouts, until you find the one that best suits your class.

If you do decide to rearrange your classroom, a good idea is first to make a plan on paper. I tend to use little cut-outs of the various bits of furniture, preferably to scale. That way I can play around with the options easily, to see whether my preferred layout actually fits the classroom space. This is far preferable to lugging lots of desks and chairs around and then discovering that the arrangement doesn't work within the space. When you do come to physically rearranging the room, get some help – another teacher, a member of support staff, a caretaker or even some willing student volunteers.

Developing layouts for learning

The most effective layout in any situation is the one that works best for you, your students and their work. Of course, certain desk layouts lend themselves better to certain types of learning. Different layouts also help you manage behaviour – a vital factor in actually getting your students to learn.

Try these ideas:

✔ **Desks in groups:** This layout is very useful for collaborative learning. It makes it easy for the students to do discussion work. Handing out resources is often easier, because you only need one set for each group of tables. Downsides do exist, though. Your students may view this layout as indicating a more informal style of teaching, and consequently their behaviour may reflect this. Ensuring that each and every student can see the board and that you have everyone's attention when you address the class is also tricky.

✔ **Desks in rows:** This layout indicates a more formal, old-school style of lesson or teacher. The students can all see the board and checking that everyone's paying attention is easier. The layout's useful for individual and paired work, but not so good for group discussions. Students tend to behave better when the desks are set out in rows, because they sense a teacher with a more formal approach. Physically getting to every student in the class can be harder, however.

✔ **Desks in a 'U' shape:** If your space allows, this is a very useful halfway house between the two layouts discussed above. The students can all see you and the board easily. They have less chance of getting away with not paying attention, as you can see all their faces. This layout is especially useful for whole-class discussions and activities like debates.

Make sure that the layout you choose suits the class or classes you're teaching. If you teach lots of different year groups in the same room, at secondary level, you have to pick the one that best suits the majority of your classes.

You don't have to stick to the same classroom layout all the time. Rearranging the chairs and desks for a single lesson is perfectly feasible. Do make sure that you put them back in their previous arrangement at the end, especially if the teaching space isn't solely yours. Factor in some time at the start and end of the lesson for rearranging the layout. Get your students to do all or most of the furniture moving. Of course, you can dispense with desks and chairs entirely once in a while, for some impromptu movement or drama work.

Managing the learners in the space

As well as moving the furniture around into your favoured layout, you must also manage what your students do within the space. This is all part of giving them the sense that you're in control of your classroom. The way you manage the students within the room has a strong impact on the kind of behaviour and work that go on.

You need to consider:

- ✔ **Where the students sit in relation to you:** You can keep a close eye on those at the front, and they have less chance of getting distracted by others. Choose a spot at the front for any students who tend to misbehave.

- ✔ **Where the students sit in relation to each other:** A seating plan (flip to 'Using a seating plan', later in this chapter) helps you overcome the majority of tensions and problems that can arise between individuals.

- ✔ **The personal needs of your students:** Remember that any students who have difficulties with their sight or hearing need to sit close to the front. From this position they can see the board or hear your voice more easily.

- ✔ **The students' preference:** Given the choice, many students choose to sit at the back of the room, or close to their friends. Be particularly aware of your 'rebels' – if you give them free choice of seating, they are most likely to hide at the back and mess around.

Again, nothing stops you from moving students around from lesson to lesson, or even within a lesson. You may even pop a chair at your own desk for your very worst-behaved or most distracted student.

Using a seating plan

With the vast majority of my classes, I use a seating plan from the very first lesson. This ensures that I, rather than the students, control where everyone sits. You can use various approaches to organise your seating plan, depending on the type of class you have.

You can:

- ✔ Sit the students in alphabetical order – you can use the 'excuse' of getting to know their names.
- ✔ Sit the students in boy/girl order – this often helps eliminate any unnecessary chatter.
- ✔ Sit the students in an order of your choice, based on what you know about their individual needs and behaviour.

As well as working out how to order the seating plan, you also need to consider how you instigate the plan in the first lesson. What you want to avoid is a chaotic start to your first session with the class.

You can:

- ✔ Put a seating plan layout on the wall before the first lesson, and ask the students to find their correct seat using this.
- ✔ Line the students up outside the room in the order you want them to sit, before letting them into the room one by one to go to the relevant seat.
- ✔ Ask the students to sit boy/girl in any pair of seats, and then draw up the seating plan during the lesson.

When you're the one saying who goes where, this sends a powerful message about the levels of control and structure within your lessons.

Establishing a 'silent spot'

You do yourself a big favour if you establish a 'silent spot' in your classroom – a position where you stand when you want to address the class. Keep coming back to the same spot every time you wish to speak to the class, and your students should automatically fall silent when you stand there.

Your silent spot is probably at the front of your room – a place where all the students can see you easily. My spot tends to be just to the right of my board. Some primary teachers sit down in the seat beside the carpet area, to indicate that all the children should gather on the carpet.

The teacher in the space

The way you move within and around your room has a powerful effect on how your students behave and learn. The idea is to establish the space as your territory, while at the same time making sure that the students feel happy to be there, safe and secure and ready to work. In Chapter 3 you find lots of advice about how to use your body to control your students and your teaching space.

You should:

- Move around the space as you teach to show that it's 'yours' and to maintain your students' interest.
- Teach from different positions in the room – the back as well as the front, the sides of the room too.
- Ensure that you 'visit' each of the students during the course of a lesson, for instance moving around the room once you've set a group or individual task.
- Move towards a student when he answers a question – this helps to show you're interested in his contribution.
- Move towards a student if you notice any minor misbehaviour; this is often enough to stop the problem immediately.
- If a further intervention's required, place a hand on his desk.
- When teaching, use expansive hand gestures and body movements to interest the class.
- When dealing with misbehaviour, keep your movements small and low key, so you don't draw attention to the issue.

The more you move around your teaching space, the more your students feel that you have ownership of your classroom. And if they perceive you as being in command of the space and how it's used, they're likely to behave and work much better for you.

Most people have a dominant side: if you're right handed this is probably your right side, and vice versa if you're left handed. You tend to teach to the side of the room that's on your dominant side. So if you're right handed, you have a tendency to focus on the students sitting to your right. Make a concerted effort to teach to both sides of the room, and be particularly conscious of focusing at least half of your teaching to your non-dominant side.

You can find lots more advice and tips about getting silent attention from a class in Chapter 8.

Chapter 8

Building Better Behaviour

*W*hen you're in charge and in control of a class, it feels great. The students do as you ask, they learn loads and (if you're honest) it's a great boost to your ego. But getting better behaviour is *never* about making the teacher feel good. Getting better behaviour is only ever about allowing you to get on with teaching, so that your students can get on with learning.

In this chapter you find out how to get, and maintain, better behaviour in your classroom. You discover how to set clear and reasonable expectations, so that your students understand how you want them to behave. You also find out how to make the most of your best points and overcome your weaknesses.

Establishing Your Expectations

When you meet a class, the very first thing you do is establish your expectations, the list of rules or standards by which you run your classroom. This is absolutely essential for getting better behaviour. Setting your expectations says to your students, 'This is how you must work and this is how you must behave.' But what exactly are expectations, why is establishing them so important and how do you go about doing it?

Your expectations are the way you expect everyone:

- ✔ To behave
- ✔ To work and learn
- ✔ To treat each other

✔ To treat you

✔ To treat the classroom and everything in it

You can enlist the help of your class in creating your rules. Doing so is more time consuming, but helps build the feeling of working as a team. You can find more about building bonds with a class in Chapter 11.

If you're only spending a very short time with a class (a single lesson perhaps as a supply teacher) you need to keep your discussion of expectations brief and simple. But even so, you must still set out your stall – *this* is how I want you to behave while you're with me – because if you don't, you have no right to complain when they start to push at the boundaries.

A few general principles apply to establishing expectations in most situations, as the following sections explain.

Defining what's inside the box

Setting boundaries and expectations is like giving your students a box. Effectively you say, 'Inside this box, everything is allowed, but if you try to push outside the box, I will stop you.' It's about letting your students feel safe, secure and in a good frame of mind to work. Most students actually *want* you to limit the options for behaviour in this way, so they can get on with learning.

As you define what your own expectations are, here's a sampling of behaviours that are unwelcome and 'outside the box':

✔ Using inappropriate language

✔ Being rude

✔ Refusing to cooperate

✔ Tipping on chairs

✔ Throwing things

✔ Shouting

And here are some that are welcome and 'inside the box':

✔ Being kind

✔ Helping others

✔ Speaking politely

✔ Listening carefully

✔ Taking responsibility for your own learning

✔ Doing as you're asked the first time you're asked

You want to encourage your students to 'think outside the box' in their learning, to get involved in lots of creative, lateral thinking. But in their behaviour, you want them inside that box, with all the boundaries and limits firmly in place.

Different teachers establish their expectations in different ways. The approach you use depends on your teaching style (more on this in Chapter 2). It also depends on who and what you're teaching – for instance, young children, teenagers, adults, arts and practical subjects may all need different approaches. If you're working with students who have special needs, you'll need to vary the techniques you use as well.

Your expectations must apply to the way *you* behave, as well as the way your students behave. You can't set up a series of rules that only apply to your students – they will rightly see this as unfair. You are a role model for the class: if you behave properly, they are more likely to behave properly as well. This means you can't shout, be rude, be disrespectful or talk over them. Whatever you tell them they must do, you must aim to do as well.

Picking the right time

The sooner you establish your expectations, the sooner everyone can follow them. Don't wait until someone misbehaves before saying, 'I didn't want you to do that'. That puts you in a position of weakness, rather than strength. You must establish your expectations from the word 'go' because doing so:

✔ Shows that you're a teacher who knows what's what – you're in control of the classroom and everything and everyone inside it.

✔ Lets the students in on the secret of how you want them to behave and work. If you don't tell them, they experiment until they find out. And this means they push at the limits until you say 'stop!'.

✔ Establishes a relationship of mutual respect – you let your students know where they stand and the rules they must follow to help everyone get along.

✔ Makes your life a whole lot easier. Establish your expectations right from the start so you can get on with the job of teaching your students.

✔ 'Sets out your stall' and shows the students what's going to happen during your time together. You're telling them what kind of teacher you are.

After you've set up your initial expectations of a class, you can 'drip feed' more rules in as you go along, for instance when you do a new type of activity (such as group work) with a class.

Get the expectations sorted *before* any new activity begins, rather than waiting for things to go wrong and then jumping in. For instance, the first time you take a class outdoors for a lesson, explain your expectations before you set off.

Sharing your expectations with your class

Your school or setting has a set of general rules for everyone to follow. Introduce your own expectations to build on the general rules of the establishment where you work. After you've established your expectations, keep referring back to them regularly to make sure they form an integral part of your classroom routine. When you're sharing your expectations with the class:

- ✔ **Don't overload them.** Don't list vast numbers of expectations in your first lesson. Your students will switch off after the first three or four. They certainly won't remember a list of ten or more demands. Stick to the key expectations first, then introduce more in future lessons.

- ✔ **Make positive statements of what you want.** Frame your expectations as positive 'I want . . .' statements, rather than negative 'I don't want . . .' ones. This sets up a positive feeling – everyone can aim for something good, rather than avoiding something bad. 'I want everyone to behave respectfully towards each other' is better than 'Don't be rude'.

- ✔ **Be specific about what you want.** Avoid vague statements like 'be quiet'. Tell your students *exactly* what you want: 'I want you to listen silently and pay full attention when someone is talking to the class.'

- ✔ **Let your students know exactly what happens if they do/don't meet your expectations.** This helps your students feel secure and confident. Have plenty of rewards in mind for students who follow your expectations exactly; know what the sanctions are for those students who refuse to do as you've asked. You can find out lots more about using rewards and sanctions in Chapter 9.

Helping students mind the rules of the road

The expectations you set are your classroom 'rules of the road'. If you want your students to follow them, you need to ensure that the rules seem fair, reasonable and sensible. People tend to follow rules if they:

- ✔ View them as reasonable, equitable and fair.

- ✔ Realise they're in place for a good reason.

- ✔ Understand what the rules are and why they're important.

- ✔ Apply to everyone, and not just to some.

- ✔ Are likely to get caught if they break them!

That last one is vital. If you think you can get away with speeding, you're more likely to do it. But if the speed camera is there, and you know you'll get fined if it flashes you, then you slow down so you don't get caught. Exactly the same applies to your students. If they think they can get away with doing something naughty, they'll probably do it. But if they know you're going to crack down on them, they probably won't. See Chapter 9 for more information about the effective use of sanctions.

Children always try to push at the boundaries – doing so is part of the job description. The role of adults is to show them where the boundaries are, and to show why they shouldn't go past them. These adults may be their parents, although sadly some parents find establishing appropriate boundaries with their children rather difficult. (If you're a parent as well as a teacher, Sue Atkins' *Raising Happy Children For Dummies* offers an excellent starting point for understanding this.)

And to keep these rules ever-present in your students' minds:

- ✔ **Refer back to them regularly.** Go back over your expectations time and time again. Note out loud when a student does what you've asked: 'Well done, Sandy, you're listening really carefully.' Refer back to your expectations at least five times in the first lesson, and at least twice every lesson after that.

- ✔ **Reinforce them through your own behaviour.** If you've asked your students to listen in silence, don't talk over them. Doing this shows that you didn't mean what you said. If you've asked students to be responsible for their own learning, don't 'nanny' them and do the work for them. Clarify and reinforce your expectations through the way that you behave – day in, day out.

- ✔ **Give a visual back-up.** Create a list of class rules to go on your classroom wall. Make a list to go inside the students' exercise books or diaries. This boosts the importance of expectations, and is a useful reminder that you can refer to as you teach.

The younger a child is, the less she may understand why a rule exists and why she shouldn't break it. Consequently, the more likely she is to try to push at or go beyond the boundary. This is one of the key lessons of life. Some children take longer to learn it than others (and some never do, particularly those with very high-level special needs). An important aspect of your role is to teach your students about acceptable behaviour, why it's important and the consequences of behaving in the wrong way.

How to draw the line

I once heard a wonderful suggestion for establishing expectations and setting boundaries. The teacher who told me this story worked with FE students (16 plus). With older students, who understand more about boundaries and rules, you can use slightly different approaches.

The teacher explained to me that, on first meeting a class, he drew a line on the board and asked the class, 'What's that?'

After a while, some bright spark said, 'It's a line, Sir.'

'That's right,' he said, giving the class a bit of a glare. 'So just make sure you don't step over it.'

Don't be surprised if, at first, you get more 'outside the box' behaviour than you want. This is all about your students testing you to see where your limits are, and how you enforce them.

Making a Class Come to You

To get good behaviour, you must establish a high-confidence, high-control persona, like the one Chapter 2 describes. Calling out repeatedly to a class to listen is bound to dent your image. The absolute ideal is that a class comes to you – that you simply stand there in front of them, ready to teach, and they fall silent of their own accord.

Unless you teach in a setting where behaviour is incredibly good, having a class come to you of its own accord is not a regular experience. This may happen in the first lesson, while the students are getting to know you, but after that it may not happen again until you're half way through the academic year. By then, you've had to put loads of strategies in place to get the desired result.

Getting silent attention

You must be able to get silent attention from your class, because without it you can't talk to them or teach them effectively. Not that you're going to talk *at* them for any longer than is strictly necessary, but when you *do* have to address them, they really must be able to listen properly. You learn how to get your students to give you this silent attention with time and experience. Doing so is rarely easy.

In the palm of your hand

Quite early on in my career, I had the fantastic experience of teaching a class who came to me of their own accord. Perhaps this came from the mix of students, or the subject I was teaching (Drama). Maybe the relationship I built up with the students was a factor (we had worked on school shows together in the past). Whatever the reason, every lesson they entered the room, took off their shoes, sat down in a circle and waited for me to begin.

Having a class in the palm of your hand is a marvellous experience. We got on with learning, with no time wasted on waiting for their attention, or on dealing with misbehaviour. I was able to be experimental in the approaches I used, safe in the knowledge that they wouldn't push at the boundaries. They were too keen to just get on with doing the drama.

In one lesson, a student came up to me and asked, 'How do you do it, Miss? Why do we come in and just sit silently and wait for you to start?' I was loath to put a name to it, on the basis that I may frighten the magic away. 'I think you just love the subject,' I said, but I knew in my heart the reason was an awful lot more complicated than that.

Talking over a class is very tempting, particularly when getting all of them to be silent at once is hard. This is a big error, though, because it's the first step on a very slippery downward slope. The first time you do it, it doesn't seem so bad. But soon your students talk a little bit more, then a bit more, until you can't get them to pay any kind of attention at all.

You must get your students to give you their silent attention because:

✔ It allows you to get on with explaining a topic or setting work.

✔ It means that everyone can hear what you're saying.

✔ If you don't get silent attention and decide to talk over a class, you're sending the message that what you say doesn't matter.

✔ Every time you talk over your students, getting them to pay attention in the future becomes that bit harder.

You can get a class to give you their silent attention in various ways. As with most things in teaching, different strategies work best with different classes, or in different situations or schools.

Where possible, use a non-verbal intervention to get silence, rather than a verbal one. If you get a class to fall silent without even opening your mouth, this suggests that you have some kind of special power over them. Ideally, you want the students to be unsure of exactly *why* they went quiet, to be unsure of what you actually *did* to get them silent. To make things almost look as though you did nothing at all!

Start with low-level interventions before moving on to higher-level techniques if these don't succeed. Here are ten different techniques that you can try, on a rising scale of the strength (or wackiness) of the intervention:

1. **Stand with arms folded, looking calm and relaxed, and wait for the class to come to you of their own accord.**

2. **Clap your hands three times and then say, 'Right everyone, let's get started.'**

3. **Use a noise, such as a shaker or tambourine, to cut through the chat (this works well with primary-aged children).**

4. **Give verbal praise to those students who are sitting in silence, for instance saying, 'Well done, you obviously want to go to break on time.'**

5. **Click a rhythm, for the class to click back to you (this works particularly well with young students).**

6. **Count down from five to zero, perhaps with a counter on your electronic whiteboard to give a visual back-up.**

7. **Write the names of silent students on the board, with a smiley face beside them for younger children.** This is better than highlighting those who aren't willing to be silent – you don't want to give your attention to the miscreants.

8. **Draw a large circle on the board, then look pointedly at your watch and begin to add minutes to the circle.** When a student asks, 'What are you doing?' reply, 'I'm counting how much time you're wasting, so I can waste that amount of your time in return.' This tactic is especially effective for older students who hate to miss their breaks.

9. **Write a message to the class on the board – something like, 'I want everyone to be silent now so that we can get on with doing the lesson and so I don't have to keep you in at break.'** By the time you're half way through writing that, most students fall silent to see what you're doing.

10. **Make a dramatic intervention – for instance, pretend to bang your head on a desk and cry out, 'Why won't they be silent, I just can't take it!'** You've got to be a bit of a drama queen (or king) to make this work, but it adds a good sense of kookiness to your classroom, and always raises a laugh from the kids.

The techniques you use depend on your teaching style (for more on this go to Chapter 2) and on the subject you teach. For instance, I met an Art teacher who had a set of fairy lights around her board, which she flicked on when she wanted the students' attention. This imaginative approach very much suits a creative subject like Art.

With some really challenging classes, getting silent attention at the start of a lesson is practically impossible, at least until the students get to know you. In these situations, find alternative ways to start the lesson. You can have a quick starter activity on the desks for when the class arrives, for example. When they've settled down, it should be easier to get everyone silent and focused for any short but essential teacher input.

Maintaining focus

Making a class come to you isn't as simple as getting a class silent so that you can address them: you've got to *keep* them silent for long enough to say what you need to say. You may need to pass on information about a subject, give instructions or explain a new topic. You must ensure that your students are focused and actively listening the whole time you speak.

You can use various strategies to help your students maintain their focus:

- ✔ **Keep what you say brief and to the point.** Don't lecture your students for long periods, particularly the young ones. After a while they switch off and cease to take in what you're saying. (See Chapter 3 for more advice on concentration spans.)

- ✔ **Get them involved.** Ask questions while you talk, and take an active interest in the answers that your students give.

- ✔ **Get them active.** Ask your students to *do* something while you speak, for instance take notes or write down key words.

- ✔ **Use lots of praise.** While you talk, comment on how well your students are listening (if they are).

- ✔ **Use visual back-up.** Incorporate visual aids while you speak: notes on the board, diagrams on a whiteboard or an interesting resource.

- ✔ **Move around the space.** As you speak, move around the room and linger beside any students who seem not to be listening. Your presence should encourage them to pay attention.

- ✔ **Don't flog a dead horse.** If your students switch off, change tack a.s.a.p. Set a quick group discussion task, get them to start on an activity or to do a quick diagram about what you've been saying.

With time, your students become more adept at listening for longer periods. As this happens, you can gradually increase the length of time for which you talk, but only do so if really necessary.

Maximising Your Strengths

Every teacher has strengths and weaknesses. The key is to work out what your strengths are, so you can maximise them, and to figure out where your weaknesses lie, so you can keep them in check. To maximise your strengths, become ever more aware of what makes you 'tick' as a teacher. Perhaps you have a particularly powerful personality – a charismatic persona that hooks your students in. Maybe you're especially good at establishing empathy with a class. Whatever your best qualities are, make the most of them to get better behaviour and stronger relationships.

The power of personality

You can't do an awful lot to change your personality. If you're an outgoing, gregarious type, you're not going to turn overnight into a shy, retiring daisy. Similarly, if you're quiet and shy, building up your confidence is going to be a challenge. The secret is to identify how the power of your own personality can help you as a teacher.

Maybe you use a quiet, low-key approach to get great results. Perhaps you're a drama queen, who gives a flourish and a sense of theatre to your classroom. Maybe you take a humorous, comic approach that gets everyone laughing and learning. You need to develop a teaching style that works for you and your students. You can find out lots more about teaching styles in Chapter 2.

To identify how different teachers use their own personality traits effectively or not, think back to when you were at school:

1. Picture one of your best teachers. What kind of personality did she have? How did she use it to her advantage? How did it contribute to the effectiveness of her teaching? Did everyone feel the same way about this teacher? And if not, why not?

2. Now picture a teacher you just didn't get on with. Was it something about her personality that meant you didn't click? Which aspects of her inner self came out in her teaching? How did these negative areas affect your perceptions of her? How did other students at your school view this teacher?

3. Finally, think about how these positive and negative memories relate to you, your personality and your teaching. Think of one student you get on really well with. Can you identify those aspects of personality that make you 'click' together? Now think of one student you always seem to 'clash' with. Is there something about your personality that this student might find hard to handle?

No one personality type makes a perfect teacher. Some people do seem to have 'it' – a kind of charisma that is hard to define, but which makes them naturals at the job. Thankfully for the rest of us, you can do lots of things to employ the power of your particular personality.

The lively and enthusiastic type

Those teachers who take a lively, enthusiastic and high-energy approach often get good behaviour in their lessons. All that passion and inspirational drive seems to pull the students along in its wake.

The strict authoritarian

Some teachers take a very strict, authoritarian approach. These teachers are often physically imposing, with a loud voice and a powerful manner. This style can work in some situations, but often the students are behaving themselves for fear of what may happen if they don't.

The style that 'strict and scary' teachers use can be high impact in terms of results, but it's incredibly hard work to sustain. In the long term, all that shouting can do serious damage to your voice. Experienced members of staff, those in a promoted post or those with an ongoing reputation in a school often use this style. If you're an inexperienced teacher you can get yourself into some serious confrontations if you try being scary. Your hostile manner may attract hostile reactions in return as the students mirror your approach.

The 'quiet but deadly' type

If you're naturally quiet, self-contained and modest, and lively/aggressive doesn't work for you, a 'quiet but deadly' approach can pay dividends. To use this approach to its best effect, you need to:

- ✔ Talk at or below a conversational level most of the time.

- ✔ Stay calm and self-controlled, like a pot simmering on a stove.

- ✔ If misbehaviour merits it, 'turn on a penny' and let your students know what you think of them (but still in a calm, controlled manner).

- ✔ Immediately afterwards, drop straight back into your usual, quiet style.

The great thing about this approach is that your students are never quite sure when you're going to turn. They tread carefully, for fear that one day you may really bite! As the saying goes, 'Walk quietly, but carry a big stick.' You can find more about this approach in Chapter 18.

Creating a powerful relationship

If your students have a strong and positive relationship with you, they're almost honour bound to work and behave well for you. This is not the same kind of relationship that you have with a friend or a family member, though. Instead, you find ways to bond with a class. Your students don't have to like you (although that can help); their feeling that you relate to them, and that they can relate to you, is what's important.

To create a powerful relationship you need to:

- ✔ **Build a sense of teamwork.** Create the sense that you work *together* with your class, rather than force them to do as you ask. Adopt a 'we' rather than a 'them and us' mentality. Use language that reinforces this – 'we are going to', 'what do you think we should do next?'.

- ✔ **Make skilful use of verbal and non-verbal communication.** Use your voice and your body to build a strong relationship with your class. Talk to them in a respectful, relaxed and open manner. Think about how you move around them in the space – use assertive but not aggressive body language. You can find lots of ideas for developing your communication skills in Chapter 3.

- ✔ **See your students as people, and not just as pupils.** Do this in lots of ways: notice when a student has a new hair cut, or ask after her when she's been off sick. Acknowledge your students outside of the teaching situation – say 'hello' to them when you pass in the corridor. Get involved in extra-curricular activities if you can (take a look at Chapter 15).

- ✔ **Treat them as you'd have them treat you.** In teaching, you often find that you get what you give. If you treat your students with respect, hopefully they should offer you the same in return. The aim is for you to achieve an atmosphere of mutual respect. This might not happen instantly, but keep up your side of the bargain and eventually you should win over your students.

- ✔ **Understand what makes them tick.** Ask your students about their interests and, wherever possible, incorporate these into your lessons. Find out the latest craze and base some lessons around it. Discover what hobbies and sports they love, and use these to introduce a topic. Show an interest in finding out about every aspect of your students' lives.

A powerful relationship takes time to establish, so don't expect to bond with your students overnight. But with time and effort, you can create a sense of working as a team.

Establishing empathy

Establishing empathy is a key skill in encouraging good behaviour and building positive relationships. An empathetic person understands or even feels what others are going through. Empathy is about acknowledging that the way you behave affects other people, that you can make others feel good or happy but also bad or unhappy. For some very sensitive people, empathy is about being so in tune with others that they actually experience those feelings themselves. Developing a sense of empathy is a key factor in regulating behaviour. If I understand that I can affect you through the way I behave and that my behaviour makes you feel pain or unhappiness, I have a duty not to behave in that way.

You may find that some of your students don't have a fully developed sense of empathy. They find it hard to understand that other people also have feelings. This is often to do with parenting problems in the early years of their lives, perhaps due to a carer who was emotionally unresponsive. Students who lack empathy misbehave because they fail to see why they shouldn't behave exactly as they wish. They just don't understand how their behaviour makes other people feel. Their behaviour is about 'me, me, me' rather than 'you'.

You must establish empathy with your students, and encourage them to feel empathy towards you and towards each other. This helps you bond and create strong and positive relationships. It also encourages better behaviour. To establish empathy:

- ✔ **Express your emotional responses to misbehaviour.** You don't have to break down in tears if a student misbehaves; instead, state clearly how the misbehaviour makes you feel. Say something like, 'It makes me feel disappointed when you do that, because I know that you're really a very good and hard-working student.'

- ✔ **Use non-verbal cues to 'click' with students.** Make eye contact with each and every one of your students, so that they feel you connect with them. Move towards a student when she answers a question, to help her feel included.

- ✔ **'Mirror' a student's behaviour.** Save this technique for when you have established a relationship with a class or individual. The idea is to show a student how her behaviour appears, by mirroring it, performing it to her so she can see how she appears to others. You may want to show her how she looks when she is in a stroppy mood or when she speaks abruptly.

> ✔ **Explore emotions with the class.** Get your class to talk about their feelings on a regular basis. Do this during circle time with a younger group, or in a PSHE lesson with older students. You'll also find opportunities to discuss issues such as prejudice and understanding different viewpoints in subjects such as English or History. Encourage your students to express how they feel in a variety of situations and to talk about how others might feel as well.

The more you establish empathy, the better relationships you develop with your students, and the better behaviour you get from them as a class.

Overcoming Your Obstacles

Just as you want to maximise your strengths, so you have obstacles to overcome. Many of the weaknesses described below afflict most teachers at some point in their careers. For instance, staying calm when faced with a class of misbehaving students is extremely hard. Unless you have the patience of a saint, you have days when you can't contain your irritation.

Your students are aware (either consciously or subconsciously) of which buttons to press to get you going. They know how to get you wound up, and how to turn you into a shivering bundle of nerves. Take charge of sorting out your weak areas and regain control from your class.

Dealing with nerves

I regularly train and work with large groups of teachers. When I ask who feels nervous or sick at the start of the school year, many hands go up, even those of the most experienced staff. This nervousness is entirely natural – you stand alone in front of a large number of students, who may or may not be willing to do as you ask. You experience something like actors' 'first-night nerves'.

If you find yourself feeling very nervous before facing a class:

✔ Take some deep breaths in and out, to avoid hyperventilating.

✔ Look for the positive, rather than focusing on the negative.

✔ Try not to overreact when something goes wrong – learn to laugh and to shrug off minor incidents.

✔ Remind yourself that, even in the most difficult classes, many students want to learn.

✔ Remember that nerves give you a boost of adrenaline: this helps you deal with any problems that crop up.

✔ Get support in whatever forms it's offered – if you're teaching a difficult class, ask a more senior teacher to stand in while you begin the lesson. See if you can get together with another teacher to do some team teaching of the trickiest classes.

✔ Remind yourself that, whatever happens in the lesson, this is not the whole world. You have a life outside of teaching.

The longer you teach, and the more classes you work with, the less nerves will bother you. But a little bit of nervousness at the start of the year is nothing to fear.

Teaching is like riding a bike. Once you learn how, you never really forget. You go for years and years without sitting on a bicycle, then one day you get on one. And off you go, pedalling with no wobbles or worries. The same applies to teaching – once you've done it, you always know how.

Staying calm

I'm sure you've heard of the 'fight or flight' response. That ancient instinct kept primitive human beings safe from harm, and helped them catch the occasional woolly mammoth for their dinner. When you see or sense a threat, your body produces a rush of adrenaline that is designed to help you either fight off the danger or flee from harm.

As a teacher, you come across many 'threats' in the course of a day. A student attacks your lesson by misbehaving; another student threatens your status in the class by taking you on in a verbal battle of wits. The problem is, every time this happens, that ancient instinct kicks in. You get a rush of adrenaline and your body wants to do something with it. Have you ever felt the urge to flee the classroom, that you just can't take any more? That's the flight bit of the response in action. And have you ever felt the urge to fight back, to take on a student by giving her a dressing down? That's the fight bit at work.

You have to learn how to stay calm and to sublimate that adrenaline rush. Every time you let the fight response take hold and scream your lungs out at a class, you do a bit more damage to your relationship. You also put a dent in the teacher character you have created (turn back to Chapter 2).

You need to learn to keep your cool because this ability:

✔ Helps you deal with problems in the classroom more effectively, in a rational rather than an emotional manner.

✔ Stops minor behaviour issues from escalating into more serious arguments.

✔ Provides a great role model for your students – you show them how they can behave when they're cross or frustrated.

✔ Shows your students that you're in control of yourself and your emotions.

✔ Helps you take care of your voice by avoiding shouting.

✔ Means students see no mileage in trying to wind you up, so they probably won't bother.

✔ Helps you avoid making an embarrassing spectacle of yourself when you're in a temper.

✔ Limits the amount of stress in your working life.

Preparing yourself for teeth-gnashing triggers

You face the possibility of losing your cool in a variety of situations. For instance, if:

✔ A student point blank refuses to follow an instruction.

✔ A student is extremely rude or aggressive towards you.

✔ Several students in a class refuse to listen.

✔ An entire class messes around when you are trying to teach.

✔ You ask a student to put her mobile phone away; she ignores you and carries on sending texts.

Consider how you may react in each of these situations. Which ones do you find hardest to deal with? Identify your triggers so you can work out ahead of time how to respond in a calm and rational way.

Teachers do many different things to keep themselves calm. Find a variety of approaches that work for you, and make sure you remember to use them when you feel your temper rising. You can take a few deep breaths, you may count to ten in your head, you can go over to the door and look out to remind yourself of the world beyond the classroom. As with so many things in teaching, whatever works for you is the best method to use.

Knowing what to do when you lose it

I've met a few teachers who are naturally calm, who can keep their cool no matter what the provocation. They're rare, though, and you will probably find yourself losing your temper from time to time.

Accept that you probably will shout from time to time. But afterwards – when you've calmed down, or in the next lesson – make a point of apologising. Explain that what you did was wrong and say sorry. You may want to talk with your students about why it happened – did they contribute to you losing your rag? This does *not* lower your status in front of the class; it does the opposite. Your students think far more of you if you 'fess up to your mistakes than if you pretend to be perfect.

Being consistent

Consistency is about equality – about keeping the same standards, for all your students, all of the time. If you're consistent you're saying 'all students are equal' and 'the standards apply to everyone'. Here's the theory:

- ✔ You apply the same rules in the same way to all the students in your class, giving out the same punishments if they misbehave. This shows the students that the same standards apply to everyone (and this should really include all the staff as well).

- ✔ You apply the same standards to your class every time you meet them, again applying the same sanctions if they fail to comply. If everyone knows that behaviour x leads to sanction y, you can apply the sanction and get on with teaching.

- ✔ All the staff right across the school administer the exact same rules and standards, with the same punishments for any infractions. Showing a united front demonstrates that staff support each other. You avoid the situation where some relaxed teachers let the students get away with murder, making the strict ones look like they're really mean.

So a student who's not wearing a tie should, in theory, receive the same response from any member of staff who spots her. Not 'where's your tie?' from one, pretending not to notice from another and an instant sanction from a third.

Of course, you can't make the other staff at your school be consistent – that's the job of a strong senior management team – but what you can do is focus on being consistent yourself. Wherever possible, enforce the school rules as they're set out, with every student, inside lessons and outside. Play your part in maintaining a positive, fair school ethos and in supporting your fellow members of staff.

Consistency – from you and the whole school staff – is important because then all the students know where they stand. They know what is and isn't allowed, no matter which member of staff they encounter. And consistency is fair!

The thing is, though, you're not a robot. And neither, for that matter, are your students. Even though you know consistency is important, being consistent all the time is really hard. You may be too tired to hassle your students about minor uniform infringements; you may have a really difficult student who freaks out if you punish her. Try to be consistent most of the time, and you find your students accept the occasional lapse.

Sometimes, a little bit of flexibility is the best thing. Differentiate your behaviour management approaches, just as you differentiate your lessons. This doesn't mean you've got different standards, you're just applying them in a slightly different way. For instance, say you teach a disaffected group of older teenagers who really don't want to do any work. Rather than apply the 'work to the best of your ability at all times' rule, you barter a bit with them. If they work really hard for fifteen minutes, you let them have a couple of minutes to relax. Or you work with a student who has a serious behavioural disorder and becomes confrontational at the slightest problem. She arrives with her trainers on, rather than her shoes, and she's clearly in a seriously bad mood. Rather than immediately applying the 'correct uniform at all times' rule, you decide to deal with the trainer issue later, once she's settled down.

Maintaining a distance

A delicate balance exists between building a strong relationship with your students (refer to 'Creating a powerful relationship', earlier in this chapter), and getting too close and friendly with them. Many new teachers find themselves drawn into a buddy-style relationship, especially with older students. This works wonders at first. But after a while, the students start to push at the boundaries. And cracking down on someone who thinks you're their friend is awfully hard.

You should also be aware of the dangers of being too friendly with your students in terms of the law and your duties as a professional. For your own sake, and for the sake of your career, you need to keep a safe distance between you and your students.

Heed this advice to maintain a sensible distance:

- ✔ Don't let students slip into using your first name, even if you're working with them on extracurricular activities. It might be just semantics, but it does make a difference to their perception of your relationship.

- ✔ Avoid mirroring the language your students use. This can happen without you realising, especially if you feel close to them. Stick to standard English, and avoid slang and colloquialisms.

- ✔ Keep well out of your students' private space. This extends to about a foot around a person. However, you might want to relax this rule a bit with a young child who is very upset.

- ✔ Don't butt in on private, social conversations, either in the classroom, the corridors or the playground. You might be privy to something that you're better off not hearing!

Liking some more than others

An unspoken truth in teaching is that you like some students more than others.

Think of a student who gets on your nerves – this is Student A. Now think of a student you really like – this is Student B. Imagine these students are in the same class. You look across the classroom and notice Student B talking to her neighbour. 'Shush, sweetie,' you say. Now you notice that Student A is talking as well. 'You're talking again!' you shout. 'Why are you always talking in my lessons?!' Do you recognise yourself in that? I certainly do.

No one wants to admit it, but in teaching you get on with some students better than others. The secret is not to let your personal feelings dictate the way you respond. And that's hard.

You're not your students' friend, and they don't *want* you to be their friend. You're not their mum or dad, and they don't *want* you to be a parental figure (although some of them may accidentally call you 'mum' or 'dad', much to their eternal embarrassment). You're their teacher, and they want a degree of formality, a slight sense of distance from you. Think about that 'teacher character' that I talk about in Chapter 2 – that's what they want you to be. And if you manage to achieve this, when you do happen to give them a tiny insight into your 'true' self, they're delighted and enthralled.

Staying on track

Students are brilliant at deflecting teachers, at distracting them from the main purpose of what they're doing. You know the scenario: you ask Jenny to get on with her work, and she immediately launches into a tirade about how you're picking on her and how her friend stole her pen and won't give it back. Before long, you've completely forgotten the original purpose of the discussion, which was to encourage Jenny to get on with the task.

To keep yourself on track:

- ✔ **Refuse to get drawn into debates and arguments.** Make a statement about what you want, and stick to it.

- ✔ **Develop selective hearing.** If a student moans or tries to pass the buck, pretend you haven't heard.

- ✔ **Use lots of repetition.** Let the student have her say, then repeat your original request.

> ✔ **Offer 'the choice'.** Give the student a choice: do this now, or accept a sanction. You can find lots more about using the choice in Chapter 9.

Some students try anything and everything to avoid doing their work. Don't let them push you off track.

Avoiding aggression

You can come across some very aggressive students in your time as a teacher. And when someone screams in your face, you may have difficulty in not becoming aggressive in return. When you lose your temper, your stress level rises and you ruin that cool, calm persona you've worked so hard to create. Avoid aggression by refusing to be drawn into arguments with your students. You'll find lots of advice on dealing with aggressive students in Chapter 10.

The thing with aggression is that anger breeds anger. A bit like adding oxygen to a fire, aggression only makes things worse. If you react angrily to an angry student, you give her just the ammunition she needs to keep the quarrel going. Any student who's extremely abusive to a teacher must have some pretty horrible things going on in her life. You don't have to excuse her behaviour, but you can try to understand it.

If a student gets really aggressive, and you feel that the situation is spiralling out of control, don't be afraid to call for help. Most schools and settings have a system whereby a senior member of staff is available in the case of serious incidents. Find out what the system is, and use it as you need.

Sometimes you want to keep a student behind after a lesson to deal with an incident of misbehaviour, but the student doesn't plan on staying to talk to you. Never block a student who's hell bent on leaving the room. If you do, an aggressive student can become violent and you can get into serious trouble. Chase up the incident later. Put your own safety and that of other students first at all times.

Finding Strategies that Work for You

The only good strategy is one that works. I've taught in many different schools, locations and age groups. And I've been amazed that a strategy that worked brilliantly in one place is no use at all in another. Find out which strategies actually work for you, in your setting, in your situation and with your students. Then use them.

Matching the strategies to the situation

The situation in which you teach has a huge impact on the strategies that are going to work. So take a look around your place of work and the people in it. What kind of students are they? What's their background? What sort of area do they live in? What are their parents or carers like? Your goal isn't to make judgements about what's right or wrong; it's about finding out which approaches get results.

To find the right strategies to use, you need to:

- ✔ Work out how firm/strict you can be without tipping over into lots of confrontations.

- ✔ Figure out the best way to get the most work from your students.

- ✔ Ask yourself how much support you're going to get from those above, and how this affects the strategies you can use.

- ✔ Decide how you can create a positive atmosphere, and positive behaviour, in your classroom.

In a really tough school, where behaviour is generally out of control, don't give up if the strategies you try don't work at first. Aim to make your own classroom an 'oasis' of calm and hard work – this takes time but it's possible to achieve.

Ask around to see what works for other staff at your school, and whenever possible, ask to watch other teachers in action, especially those who've been working at your school for some time. These teachers have had time to work out which strategies are most effective in this specific setting. Look for how they start and finish their lessons, and how much work they manage to get out of their students. Consider also the kind of balance they go for between being firm and using a more friendly approach.

Matching the strategies to your style

The thing about teaching styles (more on this in Chapter 2) is that the students come to expect certain things from you. If you've decided on an authoritarian style, you can't suddenly turn into the classroom comedian. Similarly, if you use a relaxed style, cracking down when necessary is that much harder.

If your style errs on the firm side, pick out the strategies that reinforce the impression of a strict teacher. If your style tends towards the laid-back end of the spectrum, find the strategies that sit well with this approach. If a strategy 'feels' right for you it probably is, and if it feels 'wrong' or unnatural, then just don't use it.

Practical strategies for managing behaviour

Here are some useful and practical strategies for managing misbehaviour. These approaches also help you get better behaviour from your students. You can also discover many more techniques in Chapters 9, 10 and 17.

- ✔ **Always follow through.** You've got to mean what you say in the classroom. If you threaten terrible things but never do them, your students soon suss that you're bluffing.

- ✔ **Don't give attention to the attention seeker.** You know the one: she just can't keep quiet, she always has to butt in or make a joke to get the class laughing. The more you pay her attention, the more she misbehaves. So use the 'tactical ignore'. Make a conscious decision to ignore what she's doing, unless that's really interfering with your ability to teach the lesson, or unless her behaviour's good. And if she's being good, praise her to the max.

- ✔ **Keep it private.** When you have to talk to a student about her behaviour, keep your conversation private from the rest of the class. If you shout across the room, her entire peer group are waiting to see how the situation develops. Instead, move beside her, crouch down and have a quiet chat.

- ✔ **Keep a sense of perspective.** If you're feeling emotional or stressed, you may be tempted to react instantly to every minor incident as though it's the end of the world. A good rule of thumb is to respond only when misbehaviour is immediately interfering with your ability to teach the class. Deal with anything else once the students are settled to their work. Give a quick warning, 'I'll talk to you in a moment', and a quick glare, but focus mainly on delivering your lesson.

- ✔ **Use 'the choice'.** The idea behind this strategy is that you can't actually *force* a student to behave. She has to make the choice to behave well, but she should understand that wrong choices have consequences. So you say, 'You have a choice, be quiet now or you force me to keep you in at break.' Chapter 9 has lots more detail about this technique. By using the choice, you encourage your students to take responsibility for their own behaviour and learning.

The secret to good behaviour management is to have an entire backpack full of strategies that you *can* use, and to dip in and pull out the relevant one at just the right moment.

Chapter 9

Creating a Positive Classroom Atmosphere

In This Chapter

▶ Exploring why creating a positive feeling in your classroom is important

▶ Finding out how to establish and maintain a good atmosphere

▶ Discovering how to make the most effective use of rewards

▶ Examining which sanctions work, and how you can apply them to get the best results

Your classroom is your kingdom. And you and your students must work together to make it a great place in which to learn. Sometimes your students do this naturally, as a matter of course. Other times you have to work hard to establish and maintain a good, positive feeling in your classroom. No matter how 'easy' or 'difficult' the class, you need to use motivators (rewards) and punishments (sanctions) to keep your students on track with work and behaviour. And once you've managed to create that good feeling in your room, you can get on with teaching – and that's what you're there to do.

 Even in the most challenging school, you can still make your own classroom an oasis of peace, calm and learning. When you shut your door, you shut out any worries, problems and negative issues that pervade the rest of the school. Creating this oasis can take a great deal of time and effort, especially if your students feel that the school isn't a caring or fun place to be. But you can, and in this chapter are lots of ways to do it.

Understanding Why Positivity Is Important

You agree, I'm sure, that people need to feel positive about being in their workplace. When you feel good, happy and relaxed at school, you maintain your enthusiasm and keep your energy levels up. Exactly the same applies to your students – make sure they *enjoy* being in your lessons and you encounter far fewer problems. But a positive approach has benefits beyond your own emotional wellbeing.

Positivity is also important because of the following:

- ✔ **It's good for building teacher/student relationships.** You and your students spend a lot of time together. If either you or your students feel bad or even resentful about being there, this feeling is going to cause you problems. If you feel good about spending time together, you can focus on learning.

- ✔ **It helps your students to learn.** When your students feel happy and relaxed, they're in the best possible frame of mind to discover new things. Conversely, if they feel bored or negative, they aren't going to learn as effectively.

- ✔ **It creates a 'fresh start' feeling.** Sometimes you have to overcome your students' preconceptions about a particular subject, or about education in general. Make your classroom feel like a fresh and inviting place to be. Make the subject you're teaching seem like the best thing since sliced bread. It may not happen overnight, but keep at the task, stay relentlessly positive and you'll get there eventually.

- ✔ **It helps you stay optimistic.** Being positive means you look for the upsides in every situation. You may have times as a teacher when you feel like you just can't cope. Maintaining a positive frame of mind helps you get through these times.

- ✔ **It helps you stay calm and rational.** Your students need to see that you're in control of yourself, as well as your classroom. Look for the best, and stay relaxed and rational. This helps you deal properly with any problems that do arise.

- ✔ **It helps you sanction effectively.** It may seem odd to be talking about sanctions in a section on positive approaches. But you have to use sanctions at some point in your teaching, no matter how good the school or how well behaved the students. Taking a positive approach means you apply sanctions in a calm and considered way. And most of your students accept the sanctions you use without becoming confrontational or aggressive in return.

Creating a positive atmosphere in your classroom is a long-term project. It doesn't happen overnight, but you should have time to create a good feeling during the first few weeks of the school year.

You've all got an 'A'

Many great films have been made about teaching. These films are often not very realistic, but the best ones get you thinking about your approaches in the classroom and the techniques that may work best with your students.

I'm a big fan of *Kindergarten Cop* because it shows an inventive, imaginative way of getting young children to behave themselves. But one of my all-time favourites is *Dangerous Minds* starring Michelle Pfeiffer.

In this film, based on a true story, Pfeiffer starts work as a new teacher at an inner-city school in California. When she meets her class for the first time, you can see from their body language

and behaviour that they're the ultimate 'difficult' class. But rather than expecting the worst, one of the first things she says to them is that they all have an 'A'. When they question her sanity, she says something along the lines of 'Yes, you do all have an "A", it's just that it's up to you whether you hang onto it, or whether you throw it away.'

By starting out on this positive note she shows her students that she believes in them, even if no one else has done so in the past. She reminds them that they have control of their own destinies. Do the same for *your* students: make them feel positive about themselves and their lives.

Establishing a Positive Atmosphere

Creating a positive feeling in your classroom isn't about following one simple technique and then waiting for instant results. You need to do a thousand and one small things that all play a part in establishing a positive atmosphere. What works depends on you, your teaching style, your students and the kind of place you're teaching in.

No shortcut exists to establishing a positive atmosphere. In some schools the students are fairly positive toward you at the start, and your role is to maintain and boost that positive feeling. But in other schools the students test you again and again to see if you crack. Refuse to do so!

Put on a happy face

I'm sure you've noticed how a good (or bad) mood is contagious. When you get out of the right side of the bed, the day just runs that much more smoothly. Sometimes, just pretending to be in a good mood helps you put yourself in a more positive frame of mind. In your quest to establish a positive feeling in your lessons, try some or all of the following:

✔ **Smile at your students.** Do it frequently, with warmth and with feeling. Smile about what you're teaching, about how your students respond, even smile when things go wrong. It helps relax you and your class.

✔ **Use an open and friendly posture.** Keep your body relaxed and open, so your students feel welcomed and included (although not *too* relaxed, because you still need to appear in control). Avoid defensive body positions like drooping over forwards with arms folded in on yourself. Also steer clear of postures that may appear aggressive or authoritarian, such as towering over a student to tell him off.

✔ **Talk things up.** Make your lessons *sound* exciting and inventive, and preferably make sure they *are* exciting and inventive as well. Whenever you introduce something to the class (a topic, a reward, even a sanction), do so in a positive and interesting way.

You have to model the kind of behaviour, attitude and approach that you want to see from your students. If they look at you as someone they want to emulate, you're on the right track. As the saying goes, 'treat them as you want them to treat you'.

Make your students feel worthwhile

Everyone benefits from a sense of self-esteem, which boosts your confidence and helps you feel that you're valued and of value. Some students have a very negative self-image. You can play your part in bumping up their self-esteem and you do both them and yourself a favour. To do this, you can:

✔ **Talk them up.** Make clear that you see the best in every student you teach. This is easy enough with the polite, pleasant ones; it's much harder with the rude, difficult ones. Insist on maintaining your high standards and expectations no matter what your students do. Even if a student tries again and again to drag your impression of him down into the mud, refuse to let this happen. Be firm but fair about your standards, and insist that he can and will do better. Be the one who sees him as a 'golden child'.

✔ **Treat them as people.** Take an interest in the person behind the student. Treat your students as though you're working in an office – be as polite and respectful to them as you are to your co-workers. Again, this can be hard when students are disrespectful to you. But aim not to rise to the bait.

✔ **Get their names quickly, and use them frequently.** When you address a student by name, this helps the two of you connect. Until you have your students' names, they're effectively strangers to you. But after you master their names, you can use them in all sorts of ways, especially when you're being positive about their work or behaviour.

✔ **Avoid shouting and sarcasm.** I'm not going to suggest that you'll never slip up and shout or be sarcastic to your students. It does happen from time to time, especially when you're tired or stressed out. But try your absolute hardest not to, because both shouting and sarcasm damage the fragile, positive atmosphere you've worked so hard to create. Rise above the pressures of the job and aim to stay professional at all times.

As a child, events and situations seem that much more important and meaningful than they do once grown up. As an adult, you can probably shrug off someone making a rude or negative comment to you. For a child, the same flippant remark can do lasting damage to self-confidence and self-esteem. Take care to say the right things to your students; avoid the temptation to put them down or to be sarcastic.

Use rewards and sanctions appropriately

In creating a positive atmosphere, you should use plenty of rewards. Students can't help but feel positive toward someone who rewards their hard work. Using rewards is a complex business, though, and you need to get the balance right between encouraging self-motivation and rewarding a class to keep the students in line. This topic is so important, in fact, that I devote the next section to it entirely. For specific information about the type of rewards you may use and how to go about applying them, head to the section 'Getting Rewards Right', later in this chapter.

As part of your drive to create a positive atmosphere, you'll also have to use sanctions. When you use sanctions properly, they assist you in creating a calm, controlled and relaxed atmosphere within your classroom. Your students need to see that you are fair and consistent in your use of punishment, that you use it so they can get on with their work and that you see it as a last resort. If you achieve this, and if the sanctions system at your school is overseen properly by more senior staff, the majority of students will accept sanctions with good grace. See 'Setting the Scene for Sanctions' later in this chapter for more detailed advice.

We're in this together

One of the keys to getting a positive atmosphere is to create a sense of team-work and partnership between you and your students. You want them to feel that 'we're in this together' – that even when you're having a go at them, you always have their best interests at heart.

You can create a sense of partnership in many ways:

- ✔ Use inclusive language – 'we're going to discover how to . . . '.

- ✔ Encourage your students to play a part in directing their learning and deciding what to do next.

- ✔ Use rewards as a bargaining tool – if the students work really hard and do half an hour of silent writing, in return you can play a game with them for five minutes at the end of the lesson.

- ✔ Get your students to contribute their own resources and ideas to lessons, for instance bringing in examples of their favourite music to inspire writing on 'my favourite things'.

- ✔ If you work with a teaching assistant, involve him as part of your team – use him to bounce ideas off and to voice your thoughts ('aren't they all working really brilliantly today?').

If your students feel that they work in partnership with you, and that together you make up a 'team', they're much more likely to cooperate and work hard for you.

Manage your own moods

A key part of your success in creating a positive atmosphere is about managing your own moods. Teachers are subject to a range of moods, just like anyone else. The problem is that, every time you allow your own bad mood to affect the way you treat your class, you damage the 'special relationship' you've worked so hard to build up.

To manage your moods effectively, you need to:

- ✔ **Know your triggers.** Figure out what 'sets you off' and try to avoid falling prey to these triggers. If you get wound up and bad tempered when students are late, find ways to encourage them to be on time.

- ✔ **Watch your body clock.** As well as having an understanding of when your students work best, also consider which times of the day or week are best for you. And if you always lose your temper last lesson on a Thursday, don't aim to do anything too tricky at that time.

- ✔ **Watch for students who wind you up.** If you're honest, some students know which buttons to press and can wind you up with the slightest misdemeanour. Be conscious of this, and make a concerted effort not to react and to treat all students equally. Think about how and why they're winding you up, and whether you can make any changes to your approach that might minimise their desire to do so.

✔ **Be aware of the behaviours that wind you up**. Similarly, you find that certain misbehaviours get you irrationally irritated. Some teachers react to students tipping back on their chairs, others to students who make silly noises. Be aware of what winds you up, and take steps to deal with it in a rational way.

Being able to manage your moods, and keep your negative, angry side under control, are essential teaching skills to grasp. At first you may find it difficult, but with time and experience you're able to do it most of the time.

If you find that you're in a really bad mood, you have a couple of options, beyond simply taking out your negativity on your class. The choice you make depends on the students you teach. First, if yours are the kind of students who sympathise with teachers, you can just tell them that you're not feeling all that great, so can they be gentle with you today? Often, you can be surprised by how tender and sensitive young people are. Unfortunately, with some classes saying that is like waving a red rag in front of a bull. If your students are more likely to play you up than care for you, then you must take the second option. And that's to pretend you're in a good mood. Grit your teeth, slap a smile on your face and save your sobs for the staffroom.

Teachers do different things to keep themselves calm. You can find many suggestions in Chapters 8 and 18. Work out the best way for you to keep yourself calm or to regain your inner sense of serenity when it's flown out of the window. And always remember, when you get angry, you not only encourage the students to wind you up even more, you also damage the positive feeling you've worked hard to establish.

Maintaining your positive atmosphere

After you have that positive feeling up and running, you have to do a bit of maintenance over the course of the year. With most classes, after you set your standards and the students are complying, you can gradually relax a little. Make sure that your students realise that, if they begin to push at the limits, you still come down hard on them.

Some situations may put a dent in your positive atmosphere. Watch out for the following:

✔ The lesson *after* you've torn a strip off the class – they may resent you for putting them back in line.

✔ The end of term when the students get excitable and behaviour issues sometimes arise.

✔ If you're absent for some reason and a cover teacher takes the class and doesn't get on well with them.

  ✔ The type of lesson content you're having to teach (exam practice is often unpopular).

  ✔ The weather, time of the day or week or a whole host of other external or environmental factors.

  ✔ When the students turn up having had a bad experience in a previous lesson, which carries over into the current one.

If you've established a good feeling in your classroom, you're able to overcome these problems and get back on track without too much difficulty. Talk things through with your students – appeal to their sense of reason. If appropriate, let your students have their say. Sometimes this helps to clear the air so you can rebuild a more positive feeling.

Getting Rewards Right

Do you know the saying, 'use the carrot over the stick'? Positive teachers, in their positive classrooms, turn to rewards rather than sanctions most of the time. They understand that while punishments are sometimes necessary, encouragement and motivation are the best ways to get results. But they have a problem. Faced by misbehaviour, your first instinct probably isn't to hand out rewards, you're more likely to call out the sanctions that the students are earning themselves. Yet turning to rewards, rather than immediately reaching for sanctions, helps you maintain a positive atmosphere.

Mentally put yourself in a classroom situation where the students are refusing to listen. How do you feel? If you're anything like me, you probably imagine yourself getting wound up and feeling a bubbling sense of panic. See yourself saying something to the class. What is it? Perhaps you call out, 'If you won't be quiet, I'm going to keep you in at break!' Now consider whether you can be more effective if you say quietly, to a few sensible students at the front, 'Well done, you're listening beautifully, you obviously want to go to break on time.'

You may imagine that getting rewards right is fairly simple. A student does something good and you reward him. What's difficult about that? Unfortunately, you encounter all kinds of complicating factors when you're giving out rewards.

Using rewards is tricky because:

  ✔ You can end up giving a lot of rewards to your difficult students, in order to get and keep them 'on side', and you end up overlooking your 'good' students because they get on with the work without any apparent need or desire for rewards.

✔ Students can feel that they should do something just to earn a reward. From there, it's a small step to *demanding* rewards to do any work at all.

✔ You can easily slip over the line into bribing your students into doing something, instead of rewarding their efforts for what they've done.

✔ Your instinctive reaction isn't to reward, it's to punish. Overcoming this can be tough.

✔ In some schools a mismatch exists between the rewards you're asked to give and what the students really want.

✔ After a while students can get blasé about rewards – saying 'no thanks, sir' to a merit mark and thereby negating the value of the reward.

✔ You may find that some teachers in your school are good at giving rewards and others hardly bother. A few may scattergun rewards about like they're going out of fashion.

If you deal with these issues, you find that rewards are of great benefit in your classroom. You quickly see how they help you develop and maintain a good, positive and forward-thinking approach.

 Rewards often work best when they're unexpected – when you drop them in as a surprise, to show how genuinely pleased you are with a class. Take care with the alternative, where you say 'if you do *x*, you earn yourself *y*'. Doing this encourages your students to see work as something they do to earn a reward, rather than something they enjoy doing for its own sake. As a teacher, you walk a very fine line between rewarding and bribing your students.

Finding the right motivation

When you're considering how and why you use rewards, thinking about what motivates *you* is very helpful. Consider this question: what motivates you to turn up for work every day? Your initial reaction may be 'because they pay me a salary, and I've got a mortgage/flashy sports car/expensive holiday habit to maintain'. But this isn't the only reason. (And if it is, why not find an easier job that pays you more money?) As well as teaching being about earning a salary, it's also about a sense of vocation, a sense of achievement and enjoyment, a love of working with children, the need to make a difference in other people's lives.

Similarly, the situation for your students is very complex. Within a single class of students, you'll come across a whole host of different motivations. Some work hard because that's how their parents brought them up, or because they want to please you or do well in a future career. Others enjoy the sense of achievement when they're doing something well. Some need external signs of your approval or their success (such as stickers or certificates) more than others.

Intrinsic and extrinsic motivation

You come across some students who 'just do it'. No matter what task you set, they sit down and get on with it, without any apparent need for rewards. These students have 'intrinsic motivation'. They're self-motivating; they understand the worth of short-term pain (a boring lesson) for long-term gain (good career prospects). Some of them simply enjoy learning for its own sake, others have been brought up in homes where learning's viewed as a good thing.

Other students find motivating themselves very hard. These students need 'extrinsic motivation'.

They need you as their teacher to offer small motivators to keep them moving forwards with their learning. These are the students who most need an ongoing input of rewards.

Ideally, your students are sufficiently motivated by the 'joy of learning'. They're curious to learn, keen to work hard and take pleasure in finding out new things. But the reality is that many of your students need you to apply external motivators to keep them on track.

To make the most out of the rewards you use, you need to:

✔ Offer rewards that your students really *want,* which isn't necessarily the same as your school's written policy. If your students love verbal praise more than merits, then focus on giving plenty of specific positive comments in addition to using the school system.

✔ Remember that rewards don't have to be material goods. Many of your students really want to please their teacher. A smile or a quick word of praise from you can be more than enough. Physical rewards, such as stickers and prizes, often simply 'stand for' your approval.

✔ Use the 'praise one, encourage all' technique. When you face a problem, look around to see who's doing what you want and lavish praise on that person.

✔ Don't always pre-plan your rewards. Research shows that saying 'if you do this, you can earn this' isn't the best way to motivate students. Rather, drop in an unexpected reward for students to surprise them.

✔ Use the power of the peer group – get the whole class working together to earn a reward, such as 'marbles in a jar' (see the later section, 'Choosing and applying rewards').

You need to adapt your reward system over the course of time, and for different age groups. Talk with your students, too, about what kinds of motivator work best for them.

Choosing and applying rewards

Your skill as a teacher lies in choosing the right kind of rewards to suit your class, and then applying those rewards in the best way. For instance, some students respond really well to public approval, but others prefer not to be praised in front of the whole class.

You can use many different types of rewards, some for individuals, others requiring the whole class to work together to earn them. Here are a few examples, on a rising scale of how much effort they require to administer:

- A smile
- Verbal praise
- Stickers
- House points
- Merit marks
- Table points
- Positive note in planner or diary
- Visit to the head teacher to show work
- Certificates
- Star chart
- Star of the day/week
- Golden time (free choosing time, usually an hour at the end of the week)
- Filling a jar up with marbles for positive student effort, then rewarding the whole class when it gets full
- Positive postcards home
- Raffle tickets, with a draw to see who wins prizes
- A 'good' phone call home

Of course, you can use many other rewards. The only limit's your imagination!

Have some fun with the way you use rewards and the type of rewards you apply. Ask your students for their ideas as well – sometimes they surprise you with what they actually want. Here are other bits of advice to help you get rewards right:

✔ **Adapt your systems.** The kind of rewards you use depends on the type of students you teach. Young students enjoy smiley face stampers or stickers (many older students love stickers as well, even if they don't admit it). Older students respond well to rewards based on things they love, for instance the chance to listen to music during an activity.

✔ **Keep it fresh.** Don't stick to the same reward for weeks or months on end. Adapt and change the rewards you use to maintain student interest.

✔ **Make them tough to earn.** Make your students work hard to earn the rewards you give. This helps you maintain their value and minimises the amount of effort you have to put into giving rewards out.

✔ **Create a hierarchy of rewards.** Use simple, direct rewards for day-to-day positive achievements and more complicated or valuable ones for the most impressive work over a longer period of time.

✔ **Be creative.** Some of the best rewards are those that teachers invent themselves. Get creative with your reward systems – this helps you keep your students interested and engaged. You could create your own 'Student of the Week' award, with a specially designed certificate.

Remember, sometimes rewards need to be private. In a tricky class, the peer group leader doesn't want to look as if he's gaining your approval. In these situations, you're better off giving him a quiet word of praise in the corridor after the lesson.

Ideas for unusual rewards

Over the years other teachers have given me some wonderful ideas for unusual rewards. They may help you make a real impression in your classroom. Here are a few you can try:

✔ **The 'get out of homework free' card:** The teacher offers a card (one per lesson or per week) which entitles the owner to get out of doing homework.

✔ **'Deputy diners':** The students win the reward of dinner with the deputy head. Lay the table with proper linen and tableware, real glasses and flowers.

✔ **The weather chart:** The teacher (or class) creates a chart, showing a typical outdoor scene and with various weather-related pieces with Velcro attached. When the teacher's pleased with the students, he moves the sun up in the sky; if he's unhappy, the rain starts. And if the class is being absolutely brilliant, a rainbow appears.

Suiting rewards to the individual student

As with most approaches in teaching, rewards work best when they suit the individual. Of course, this scenario isn't always practicable or possible. But if a student's causing you real difficulties, aim to find out what really motivates him to do well. Then use this information to your advantage.

Your student may really want his dad to be proud of him and a positive phone call home can work wonders. Your student may love break dancing and be motivated by the chance to perform to the class. If you find the key to motivating a particular individual, you stand a great chance of success in your quest for a positive classroom.

Setting the Scene for Sanctions

Even when you're aiming for the most positive classroom atmosphere you can achieve, you still need to use sanctions from time to time (and perhaps much more often than that). Your students must understand that, if they push at the boundaries, you clamp down on them and make them serve a punishment.

No one likes punishment – just think of your reaction if you get a speeding ticket or a parking fine. You probably don't think, 'Fair enough, I deserved that'; you're more likely to think, 'Drat, they caught me!' Sanctions can damage the relationship between you and your students. The secret to limiting the damage is to get them exactly right, first time around. And the better you apply sanctions, the less often you have to do it, because your students soon discover that misbehaving doesn't get them anywhere.

Understanding how punishment works

You set the standards for your classroom – the 'I want' expectations Chapter 8 describes. This is all well and good, but you must also ensure that your students stick to those expectations. Often, you can use rewards to encourage them to do this. But you also have to know what you're going to do if a student refuses to comply with the rules you've set. You need to figure out what kind of punishment to use and how best to go about applying it.

Using detention time wisely

The classic sanction is detention – its message is, 'If you waste my time, I waste yours.' But what makes a *good* use of detention time? What kind of things can you get a student to do in a detention that serve some kind of purpose? The approaches you use tend to fall into four categories:

✔ **Something boring:** The student writes out lines, colours in squares on graph paper or similar. The purpose is to punish through tedium – the ultimate 'waste of time'. These sanctions don't really teach a student much about changing his behaviour, although some teachers feel the boredom inflicted is a lesson in itself.

✔ **Something reflective:** The student considers why his behaviour was wrong, and perhaps writes something about it. He might pen a letter of apology to the teacher or to the class, saying sorry for his actions.

✔ **Something useful:** The student finishes off work that he should have done in class, or picks up litter as part of a community sanction.

✔ **Have a chat:** Often, the most constructive thing you can do is to have a chat with the student about why you're detaining him. Explore the underlying issues in an effort to stop the problem occurring again.

The type of punishment you choose depends on the type of offence the student has committed. Clearly, if he didn't finish his work in the lesson, he should do it in the detention. If the student's one you don't normally have to sanction, you're wise to sit down and talk about why he got himself into trouble.

To use sanctions effectively, the punishment must be unwanted and it must fit the crime. The sanction must be fair and must not demean or ridicule the student. When you have to give sanctions, make sure they're ones your students don't want to earn. In some schools where the playground is a scary place, the students *want* to stay in at break. In these instances, a break-time detention is a reward and not a sanction. Students have a sense of natural justice. Whatever their 'crime', the punishment should have a connection to it. So a student who throws paper in a lesson can pick up litter; a student who vandalises a desk can scrub all the desks clean.

In deciding what sanctions to use, you must be realistic about what you can and are willing to deliver. You must follow through on your threats. If you repeatedly threaten terrible things but never actually deliver them, your students quickly learn that your words have no meaning. Your threats are empty. Similarly, don't threaten what you can't follow through on. Your students know, for example, that you can't keep them in every lunchtime for the next week.

Take care with the threat of 'somebody else'. Sometimes, when you run out of patience, you end up saying, 'If you do that again I'm going to send you to Mr X' (i.e. to a more senior teacher). While this may be justified in extreme circumstances, most of the time aim to deal with your students by yourself. If you always pass the buck, you suggest to your students that you can't deal with the problem by yourself.

If you have a student who's misbehaving, try a distraction first. In some situations you can distract a student away from misbehaving, so you don't have to go down the route of punishing him. This works especially well with young children, who are more easily distracted. You may ask the student to hand out some resources or to write something up on the board. Often, he complies and forgets all about misbehaving.

The options for sanctions are more limited than those for rewards – you can do less to punish your students than to motivate them. This is all well and good because you look for positive, rather than negative, approaches.

The type of sanction you use depends on your school's policy and also the kind of setting you work in. In most situations, give a couple of warnings first, before moving on to give the sanction. You may find yourself doing the following:

- ✔ Giving a verbal warning

- ✔ Following that with a written warning

- ✔ Giving a detention

- ✔ Moving a student to another seat

- ✔ Getting a student to pick up litter at break

- ✔ Drawing sad faces on the board

- ✔ Writing names on the board

- ✔ Taking golden time away from an individual or a whole class

- ✔ Sending a student to a separate in-school behaviour or referral unit

- ✔ Writing a letter home to parents

- ✔ Phoning parents to discuss the student's behaviour

Sometimes, you want or have to give a detention to a whole class, for instance if many students are talking and you need to get the class silent quickly. This is tricky, because not *every* student in the class misbehaves at once. At least a few of your students sit in silence while the others play up. My advice is to use whole-class sanctions in only a limited way, and to ensure that you let any well-behaved students finish their sanction first.

Applying sanctions

When you get to the point where a student repeatedly refuses to comply, the time has come to give sanctions. The way you do this affects the way the student reacts. You come across a range of student responses: from sheepish acceptance to downright aggression. Follow these guidelines and advice tips to get the best possible outcomes when you're applying sanctions.

General guidelines

To minimise the likelihood of getting into confrontations when you have to sanction a student, use the following approaches:

- ✔ **Explain *why* the behaviour is a problem.** Let the student know why his behaviour merits a sanction – what impact does it have on the class?

- ✔ **Blame the behaviour rather than the person.** Phrase what you say so you make clear that the behaviour's the issue, and not the person being punished. You can say something like 'Talking over me means no one can hear what I'm saying' rather than 'Jake, why are you always talking?'

- ✔ **Give the student time to consider.** Give the student a choice, allow him a few moments to consider what he's going to do, rather than jumping straight in with a sanction. See the next section for instructions on how to use this technique.

- ✔ **Keep the sanction private.** Don't shout across the room at a student – this ups the stakes and turns his entire peer group into an audience for your interaction. Move over to the student, crouch down beside him and speak quietly so that only he can hear.

- ✔ **Use a polite, calm and unemotional approach.** Limit the likelihood of confrontation by keeping your style very low key and calm. Remove all emotion from your voice. Be polite no matter what the provocation. Remember – you're the adult.

- ✔ **Aim for a note of regret, rather than revenge.** Try to sound as though you regret having to punish the student, rather than being delighted at the chance to get back at him.

- ✔ **Use repetition.** Don't assume that the student hears and understands the first time you outline the sanction. Repeat yourself a couple of times, using his name to ensure you have his attention.

- ✔ **Don't get sidetracked.** Students are clever at distracting their teachers from their main purpose (for example, to give a sanction). If a student starts blaming others, or claims mistreatment, simply pretend that you haven't heard. Stay on track with what you originally intended to do.

You may feel that this is a lot to remember, particularly in the heated moments after a student misbehaves. But with practice you're able to do all these things easily. In addition to these strategies, use 'the choice' as described in the next section.

Using 'the choice'

'The choice' is a great technique for limiting the damage that sanctions can do to your positive classroom atmosphere. It forces the responsibility for misbehaviour on to the student, and asks him to acknowledge that his behaviour is his choice. Your role is merely to outline the options according to the rules of your classroom, and to apply the relevant sanctions if the student fails to behave appropriately.

The idea behind 'the choice' is very simple:

- ✔ The student has a choice about his behaviour.
- ✔ The teacher can't force him to behave.
- ✔ The teacher's role is to make behaving well seem like the best option.
- ✔ The teacher lets the student know what happens if the student doesn't comply.
- ✔ If the student refuses to make the right choice, the teacher gives him a sanction.

The best way to understand how 'the choice' works is to see it in action. Here's an example:

> Sanjit refuses to do his work, so you move over to him and crouch down beside him. You say quietly, 'Sanjit, you have a choice. I want you to do the work now. If you choose not to do it during the lesson, I'm going to have to keep you in at break to complete it.' You then move away, giving Sanjit a few moments to consider his decision.
>
> If Sanjit complies, great. You can offer him a few words of praise for making the right choice. If he still refuses to work, you go back over to him and explain how the sanction is going to be applied.

Your students quickly get used to this approach. It takes all the stress and pressure off you. It encourages the students to take responsibility for their own behaviour and to accept the consequences of making the wrong choice.

Blame the policy

I was given a great piece of advice in my first year as a teacher and that was to 'blame the policy'. Your main role is *not* managing behaviour, it's teaching. Behaviour management is only ever a way of ensuring that you can get on and teach. Use 'blame the policy' to take all the personal challenge out of applying a sanction.

When you talk to a student about his problem behaviour (i.e. not wearing a tie), make it clear that you're simply applying the school policy, rather than being against him. Show him a copy of the school rules and say something like, 'Do you see how the school policy says, "Students must wear correct uniform at all times"? I want you to comply with the policy right now, please.' Simple!

Sanctions in your setting

The way you use and apply sanctions varies, depending on the type of educational setting you work in. Ideally, you should use the sanctions outlined in your school policy, although if you find that these don't work at all, you may like to develop some sanctions of your own. You also need to consider how students respond to being sanctioned – in some schools, the confrontational nature of the students means that sanctions are almost more trouble than they are worth.

The secret to effective sanctions is to find something that actually *changes* a student's behaviour in the long term. This, however, is very tricky to do. The way you use sanctions, and their ultimate success rate, depend on the following:

- The overall ethos of your school or setting
- The effectiveness of your school behaviour policy
- The way the students react to sanctions
- How well the staff use sanctions
- How consistently sanctions are applied throughout the setting
- Whether senior managers do their bit in supporting you when you need to follow sanctions through at a higher level
- Whether sanctions have any long-term impact on changing behaviour

As an individual teacher, you can't do much to affect many of the above issues. What you have to do is work out how best to use sanctions in *your* classroom with *your* students, so that you can all get on with learning in the most positive atmosphere possible. To help you make the right decisions, ask yourself:

- What impact are the sanctions I use having on actually changing student behaviour?
- How much stress does it cause me to apply and follow through on these sanctions?
- If I'm really tough with sanctions for the first part of the year, will this help me use them less later on?
- Would it cause me less stress to focus instead on delivering engaging lessons and building positive relationships?
- What kind of support and back-up do I get when I give sanctions and the students fail to serve them?

Ask around amongst the other staff at your school to see what they feel is the best approach, then tailor your preferred method to the classes you teach.

Chapter 10

Handling Challenging Situations

. . . .

In This Chapter

▶ Exploring the reasons why students become confrontational

▶ Understanding ways to avoid confrontations, and to deal with them when they happen

▶ Discovering how to 'win back' a challenging class

▶ Examining the best ways of minimising the stress you feel

. . . .

The vast majority of your work as a teacher involves the day-to-day delivery of lessons and the pastoral care of your students. You also have to deal with the typical classroom management issues that arise in every lesson, along with some low-level misbehaviour. And from time to time, in most schools or settings, you also have to handle situations where a student becomes confrontational, aggressive or abusive.

Although you're probably not faced with an angry or abusive student very often, when you are you feel awful. Your aim as a teacher is to do the best for all your children. When one of them turns around and hurls abuse in your face or becomes violent, you can feel as though you've somehow failed in your job. In addition, you can feel quite scared in some situations.

You need to know how to handle confrontations when they happen, in the sense of knowing both how to deal with the situation itself and how to cope with the emotional fall-out after the event. Put yourself in the best possible position to handle these challenging situations, and make sure that you keep your students, and yourself, safe from harm.

In most schools, confrontations are a rare and unusual occurrence. The vast majority of students are unlikely to fly off the handle and abuse or attack you or a classmate. Any students who do behave like this probably have a pretty awful life outside school. In the most challenging schools or settings, the senior staff should be well aware of the kind of support you need to deal with confrontations as an individual teacher. And if they're *not* doing what they should to help you, then consider whether you may be better off teaching somewhere else.

Dealing with Confrontation

The way you deal with a confrontational student affects the way the situation pans out. Handle it right, and you may even be able to calm the student down before she takes things too far. Handle it wrong, and you can unwittingly contribute to the problem, so that the student boils over or explodes in rage.

Put yourself in the best possible position to deal with confrontations by understanding what you can and can't do in these situations. Know your position in relation to the law. Often students say something like 'You can't touch me'. This statement isn't actually true. But unless you understand the situations in which you can restrain a student, you put yourself on the back foot. Read up on the relevant guidance, particularly on the use of 'reasonable force'. In the UK, Circular 10/98 makes for very useful reading.

Think long and hard about joining a union, if you don't belong to one already. The teaching unions do a great job of supporting, training, advising and backing up their members in some very challenging situations.

Understanding why confrontations happen

Before you can discover how to deal with confrontations, you need to gain an understanding of why they happen. Sometimes the flare-up comes without warning, but often you get plenty of warning signs about problems about to hit.

Students become confrontational for a whole host of different reasons. Often, not a single factor but a complex set of issues all come together at the same time. After you have an understanding of why confrontations may arise, that can help you avoid these situations in the first place. You're also able to handle these problems more effectively when they do occur.

Understanding why confrontations happen helps you to do the following:

- ✔ Stay rational when you're dealing with an aggressive student.
- ✔ Avoid taking the situation personally when a child's abusive towards you.
- ✔ Limit the likelihood of confrontations happening in the first place.
- ✔ Handle the 'fall-out' after the event.

Issues outside the class

Sometimes a confrontation boils up that's absolutely nothing to do with you or with the way you handle your students. It's about the psychological 'baggage' your students bring into the classroom. Some of your students have a lot to cope with outside of school.

They may be dealing with many difficult problems, such as:

- Issues within the family, like arguments, break-ups or divorce
- Illness or bereavement of close family members
- Parents or carers who have addiction problems
- Their own addiction or psychological and emotional issues
- Acting as a carer for family members who have a disability or illness
- Parents or carers who provide only aggressive, confrontational role models
- Verbal and even physical abuse

Often, you aren't given access to confidential information about a student's background. Look out for the warning signs of neglect, though, such as malnourishment or a dirty appearance. Keep an eye out too for indications that a child may be being emotionally or even physically abused. You may notice a student crying, appearing depressed or showing sexual behaviour inappropriate for her age.

As a teacher, you act as a key 'early warning' system for students who aren't being properly cared for at home, or who are being abused. If you suspect a student's being maltreated, your professional duty is to report your concerns to the Child Protection Officer (CPO) at your school or setting. *Don't* assume 'someone else' has done this – voice your concerns even if you think the problem's already been spotted.

As a classroom teacher, you don't always have access to the information you may want about a child's background. Sometimes, this happens because the information's confidential. Other times, no one thinks to tell you about the problems a student faces at home.

Get to know the Special Needs Co-ordinator (SENCO) at your setting. Talk to her in general terms about any students who cause you trouble. Ask her for advice on how best to handle these students. Should you know about any 'triggers' that may cause a child to explode? May you be able to avoid any issues with particular situations? Can she give you any tips on the kind of rewards that work best with a specific student?

Issues inside the class

While a background issue's usually involved when conflict arises, you may also contribute to confrontations by the way you handle your class. That's *not* to say you should blame yourself when confrontations arise. But you certainly do yourself a favour if you're aware of the mistakes you may make, and how you can avoid them. Discovering how to do this is a key part of developing your skills as a teacher.

You may create a situation where confrontations are more likely to arise by:

- ✔ Being in a foul, negative mood and nagging at your students.
- ✔ Using sarcasm to deal with misbehaviour, rather than more positive approaches.
- ✔ Treating your students unfairly (often without being aware you're actually doing that).
- ✔ Asking lots of rhetorical questions that contribute little to effective classroom management – things like 'Why aren't you working?', 'Why are you all being so noisy?' and so on. Try only to ask questions when you actually want an answer.
- ✔ Misunderstanding a student's behaviour or intentions because of the busy nature of the typical classroom – for instance, having a go at a child who's talking when she's actually just helping her neighbour by explaining the work.
- ✔ Taking on a student in front of the whole class, so that you pull her into playing up to an audience of her peers.
- ✔ Getting involved in an ongoing argument with a student, rather than dealing with the situation rationally.
- ✔ Being inconsistent in what you ask of your students – clamping down on minor infringements one day then ignoring them the next.
- ✔ Pre-judging a student or class – if you expect the worst, your expectations are more likely to be met.

Of course, you're a human being as well as a teacher. Some days you find being in a good, positive mood hard work. But making the effort's worthwhile if the alternative's dealing with a situation where a confrontation boils up.

You're more likely to contribute to confrontations in your classroom when you're feeling tired, stressed or run down. One of the best ways to avoid this is to keep a handle on the balance between your working life and your life outside school. Make sure you take your breaks while you're at work, and try to avoid devoting too much time to work beyond the school day. For plenty of advice on handling stress and balancing your workload, see 'Managing your Stress Levels' in this chapter and also take a look at Chapters 14 and 19.

Exploring what students get out of being confrontational

When a student becomes confrontational, you may feel that everyone suffers – you, your class and the aggressive student as well. Sometimes, though, your most confrontational students get something out of the situation, probably without even realising. If you understand that confrontations have some benefits for your students, you're better placed to minimise the chance of them happening and to cope with the stress they cause.

Your students may get:

- A feeling of catharsis – the opportunity to let out all those bottled-up emotions.

- A sense of 'getting one over' on the teacher, who represents the voice of authority.

- A way of letting off steam – often impossible in their home situation because of fear of the reaction they may get.

- The approval of their peer group, especially in a very challenging school where others 'look up' to aggressive students.

- A chance to 'model' the kind of behaviour they see in their own homes.

Remember that some students are subjected to consistently aggressive behaviour in their home situations. And for these students, the teacher becomes a kind of 'safety valve'. They can let off their aggression in front of you, because they trust you not to react aggressively in return. Bizarre as doing so may seem, it becomes almost like a compliment to you and your ability to remain calm. The student's saying: *I trust you not to react.*

Avoiding confrontation

You help yourself avoid confrontations by following the positive, effective approaches to teaching and classroom and behaviour management this book describes. If you use good practice for all or most of the time, you build up good relationships and bonds with your students. And once you've done this, they're less likely to react badly if you make the occasional mistake.

To avoid confrontation, you need to:

- **Use an assertive, confident and definite teaching style.** Your aim's to achieve the style that Chapter 2 of this book describes. This helps your students understand exactly what you expect of them, and feel safe and secure in your lessons.

- **Understand the need for flexibility.** At the same time, you need to balance an assertive teaching style with a willingness to be flexible. Understand when flexibility's appropriate, particularly when dealing with your most troubled students.

- **Stay calm and rational.** Do this for as much of the time as humanly possible. If you take a calm, unemotional approach, this puts you in the best possible place to deal with challenging situations. Even the most brilliant, self-controlled teacher finds difficulty in keeping her emotions in check at all times. So don't be too hard on yourself when you do get something wrong, but aim to get situations right as much of the time as you can.

When you're teaching, you want to go for maximum passion, interest and engagement. But when you're handling problematic behaviour, use what I call the 'robot response'. Remove all tone and emotion from your voice, to avoid exacerbating the situation. This helps you stay rational and also helps keep everyone calm.

✔ **Judge and respond to the mood of your students.** Develop the ability to 'read' the class or the individual and to handle the class or the student in the most appropriate way. If your students seem a bit wired, find ways to calm them down; if they seem tense, look for approaches that relax them.

✔ **Keep interactions private.** Don't give your students that audience of their peers, especially when you're dealing with misbehaviour. Remember that the stakes are higher for your students, because *their* peer group is watching, not yours.

✔ **Try not to let your students wind you up.** And yes, I do know this is much harder to do than to say. But always bear in mind that if your students realise they *can* wind you up, they probably take great pleasure in doing so!

✔ **Understand when you need to intervene.** Sometimes you're best intervening in a quarrel straight away, before things build up a head of steam. For instance, if two students are quarrelling over the ownership of an item, you can remove the item to deal with later and hopefully solve the issue at the same time.

✔ **Know when to ignore low-level misbehaviour.** On the other hand, sometimes simply ignoring silly, attention-seeking misbehaviour is far more effective. Knowing when you need to jump in, and when standing back is better, is a matter of experience and professional judgement.

✔ **Don't get into tit-for-tat arguments.** Always remember that you're the adult – be the one to walk away, rather than allowing yourself to get drawn into ongoing quarrels.

✔ **Judge the situation.** Understand that you don't have to deal instantly with every misdemeanour. Sometimes deferring your intervention until later, when everyone's calm (and that includes you!), is a better strategy. A good rule of thumb is that, if the misbehaviour isn't immediately interfering with your ability to teach, you can probably wait until an appropriate moment to deal with it. Let the student know you're going to be having a word, then get the class settled to a task before you continue dealing with her.

✔ **Be willing to apologise when you get something wrong.** You're human, you make mistakes. But be big enough and brave enough to say sorry when you're unfair to your class. You don't lower your status or image by doing this; rather, you show that you're willing to admit to your failings.

Different students respond very differently when the teacher has to intervene in the way they're behaving. Some students are able to take a strict and scary approach from their teachers; for others that's completely the wrong tack to adopt. Discover how to differentiate your behaviour management approaches, just as you differentiate your lessons. That's not to say that you should change the kind of standards you set, rather that you can change the way you apply those standards to suit the individual student.

Sometimes one of your students goes down a road that seems destined to lead to a confrontation. Let's say she ups the ante by calling you 'a fat cow'. How are you expected to respond to this? And isn't getting wound up by what she says perfectly natural? In these instances, the 'just agree' strategy is often a very effective approach. Here's how: you 'just agree' with everything the student says, sounding as genuine and straight up as you can manage. You respond to those comments that she means to be personal and abusive as though you genuinely appreciate the insight the student's giving you. So, in response to the 'fat cow' comment, you can say, 'Well, I know I'm a bit on the heavy side, but I've tried every diet I can find, and nothing seems to work, do you have any advice?'

Dealing with confrontation

When a confrontation begins to boil up, despite all your efforts to avoid it, your first reaction's likely to be one of nervousness or even fear. Perhaps two of your students get into a fight; maybe a child point blank refuses to do as you've asked. As a teacher, you feel very vulnerable when this happens. Know what you should do in the event of a confrontation arising, so that you feel confident about dealing with it in the most appropriate way.

As a teacher, in a position of responsibility, you need to be aware of the potential for complaints when you handle a challenging situation. When a confrontation sparks off, your very first step should be to *send a reliable student to get help*. This is important because it allows you to:

✔ Get the support and back-up you need to handle the situation.

✔ Ensure that you have a witness to what happens.

✔ Have a second 'body' available, for instance to deal with the rest of your class while you calm an individual down.

When a confrontation suddenly erupts, you can all too easily forget common sense and rationality and go with instinct instead. If two students start to fight, your instinct may well be to dive in and pull them apart. If you possibly can, take a moment to calm yourself down before you intervene. You're best placed to deal with the situation if you're in a rational frame of mind.

Remember that if you get the situation wrong, your career and your own health and safety are at risk. Don't get dragged into an instant response – take at least a few deep breaths before you begin to intervene.

Using behaviour management techniques

In order to deal with a confrontational student, you need to use behaviour management strategies:

- ✔ **'Remove' the problem.** Whether the problem's the student herself or an item that's causing an argument, if you can remove the problem from the equation you stand a far better chance of calming things down. This may mean asking the student to step outside the room; it can involve confiscating an object from a student until a later time, when you have the chance to deal with the problem in more detail. If two students are 'kicking off' with each other, you could remove the student who looks the least eager to be involved in the situation.

- ✔ **Take feelings and complaints seriously.** Sometimes, you can calm down an aggressive student simply by listening to what she wants to say and taking her concerns seriously. Try not to brush off what seem like minor matters – the student may be talking about something that's really important to her.

Using your body and voice

You can also use your voice and body to help you stop a fight, or to calm down a confrontational child:

- ✔ **Try shouting 'stop!'.** Sometimes this is enough to stop students in their tracks, particularly at the start of a fight or confrontation. Make your voice as loud and abrupt as you can manage, so they hear it over the general hubbub of noise.

- ✔ **Make repeated use of names.** Ensure that you have the student's attention by using her name repeatedly. A person's name is such an essential part of who she is: using the student's name can help you refocus her attention on what she's doing.

- ✔ **Remind the student of her options.** Hark back to the idea of choices – if you continue down this path, you have to face the consequences. Encourage your students to stop what they're doing and make a better, more considered choice.

- ✔ **Use a calming, hypnotic tone of voice.** Just as you can use your voice to liven up a flagging class, your tone of voice can also help you to calm down an over-heated situation. Aim for a flat, droning kind of sound – the sort of voice you hear when a hypnotist's putting someone under her spell.

✔ **Keep out of the student's personal space.** Everyone has a 'personal space' around them, and when someone intrudes on this space, they feel very uncomfortable. Keep at least a foot away from any aggressive student. Not only does this lessen the sense of tension, you also keep away from any flying elbows or fists.

✔ **Keep a barrier between you.** Keeping something physical, such as a table, between you and a threatening student can help. That way, she can't physically get to you so easily.

✔ **Get onto their level.** This is especially important if the confrontational student is sitting down. Crouch down beside her to talk one to one, rather than towering over her. This helps you minimise the perceived 'threat' you pose.

✔ **Remember: You don't have to make eye contact.** When you look a student in the eyes, this ups the stakes and tends to feel more threatening for her. If the student's sitting down, crouch beside her so your faces are in the same direction. She can still hear your voice, even if she can't see your eyes.

Other strategies to use

As well as using your voice and body to calm the situation, you can use plenty of other strategies. Remember to do everything you can to calm the situation, but put your own safety, and that of the rest of the class, first. Keep the following in mind:

✔ **You're not aiming for win or lose.** You can find yourself getting dragged into an argument with a student who refuses to back down and feeling as though you have to 'win' the quarrel. Always bear in mind that nobody wins in a confrontation – you really don't have to have the last word.

✔ **Stay polite and calm throughout.** No matter what the provocation, aim to maintain a calm exterior. This is incredibly hard to do, especially if a student's hurling abuse at you. But if you can manage to, remaining calm ensures that you stay in a rational frame of mind. You also deal with the situation intellectually, rather than emotionally.

✔ **Consider the rest of the class.** The rest of the students in the class remain your responsibility, even though your main focus is obviously on dealing with the aggressive student or students. If two students are fighting, get the rest of the class well away from the area. You can gather them in one corner of the room or ask them to leave the classroom and line up outside.

✔ **Never 'trap' a student.** However wound up or justified you feel, never ever try to stop a student from leaving your classroom. (I did this once, and had a chair thrown at me for my efforts.) Remember, you can follow up on the incident afterwards. Trapping your students in the room only adds to their feelings of aggression.

When a confrontation happens in your classroom, nobody ends up 'winning'. Your best hope is to handle the situation so that no one gets hurt, and the least possible damage is done. This isn't about saving face or maintaining your image, but about getting everyone through this unscathed and in one piece, both physically and emotionally.

Handling the aftermath

When you've been involved in a confrontation, you inevitably feel shaken and probably rather upset. Make sure that you handle the aftermath – that you take account of how you feel and what happened, and try to deal with your emotions rather than shrugging them off. To handle the aftermath effectively, you should:

- **Give yourself time to recover.** After you've faced an aggressive or abusive student, you need some time out to calm yourself down and settle your emotional state. If your senior managers don't offer you time to get over the incident, make sure that you ask. You need an hour or so in the staffroom, with a sympathetic friend and a hot, sweet cup of tea. What you don't need is to be asked to face your next class without even the chance to catch your breath.

- **Watch out for the adrenaline rush.** You may feel a bit 'high' after the event, but beware: this is because of the adrenaline rush you experienced during the confrontation. Take care not to carry on regardless and then suffer a sudden drop in your emotional state at the end of the school day.

- **Watch your confidence levels.** Your confidence levels almost inevitably take a knock when a student explodes in one of your lessons. Find ways to rebuild your confidence, particularly if you normally lack self-esteem. You may ask a more senior member of staff to come into your next session with this class, and again when the confrontational student returns to the lesson.

- **Reflect on what happened.** Take a few moments to reflect on your experience while it's still relatively fresh in your mind. Think through what happened and how you handled it. Aim to use this as a learning experience. Can you do something differently next time? Can you help calm the situation down before things get out of hand?

- **But don't blame yourself.** At the same time, though, make sure that you don't blame yourself for the confrontation. Any student who gets totally out of control obviously has some pretty serious problems. You are *not* responsible for other people's behaviour; you should *not* take the blame on your own shoulders.

✔ **Write a detailed report.** Make sure that you take some time to write a detailed account of what happened, again while the events are still relatively fresh in your mind. Include details about the time, date, who was involved, the names of any witnesses and all the steps you took to calm things down. Take a photocopy of this report to pass on to the relevant senior staff, keeping a copy of what you've written for yourself. This helps senior staff deal with the student in the appropriate way and also 'covers' you in the event of any follow-up.

Perhaps the hardest event of all is taking an abusive student back into your lesson after she's served her punishment. Aim not to bear grudges – try to put the events behind you so that you can both start afresh. Senior staff asking the student to apologise can help, either in person or in writing, before they allow her to re-enter your class. Remain in control, and look for solutions rather than problems.

Managing Challenging Individuals

When you encounter a student who's intent on causing you problems, being aware of the kind of strategies you can use is helpful. You can't find a 'one size fits all' solution to handling challenging individuals. You should always use your professional judgement to assess the best kind of approaches to take in your class, with your children.

Handling the refuser

A student who point blank refuses to listen or do as you've asked is incredibly irritating. She acts as though she can't hear you, or pretends that she can't see you and simply carries on with what she was doing. Young people are incredibly skilled at winding up their teachers by doing this. That 'speak to the hand, the face ain't listening' attitude is fully intended to get on your nerves.

You can handle the refuser by:

✔ Reminding yourself that she *can* hear what you're saying, even though she pretends she can't.

✔ Acting as though you believe she *is* listening, even though she's trying to get you to think she isn't.

✔ Setting out her choices – either do this or suffer the consequences.

✔ Following through on each level of your behaviour procedures, taking things right up to the top level if she refuses to comply.

The secret with a student who refuses to do as you've asked is to refuse to allow her behaviour to wind you up in return. Assume that she has heard, and is in a position to comply, then follow through on your procedures in a calm and polite manner.

Dealing with the aggressor

Some students display worrying amounts of aggression in the classroom. Most likely they've seen this behaviour modelled at home since they were very young. They can hardly help but pick up on the aggression, but that doesn't mean you have to put up with such behaviour.

To deal with an aggressive student, you should:

- ✔ Use a relaxed, calm and low-key approach.
- ✔ Keep your voice quiet and soft.
- ✔ Use language that offers the student a way out – 'Come on, I know you don't really want to do that' rather than 'Stop doing that immediately'.
- ✔ Avoid backing her into a corner – offer her a choice and then walk away while she thinks about it.
- ✔ Ask for help from more senior staff if a student's very aggressive.
- ✔ Check with your special needs staff to understand the root causes of the child's problems.

Never feel that you 'must' put up with a student who's really aggressive toward you. Insist that something's done, and if it isn't, voice your concerns to your union representative.

Coping with the verbally abusive student

Young people are very quick to pick up on the effect that rude, abusive language has on adults. They love its shock value and the way their peers admire them for talking in this way. To my mind, swearing and abusive language has various levels. The perceived seriousness of the language also changes over time. Words that may have been shocking just a decade ago seem barely worth worrying about today.

Differentiate between swearing that's aimed *at* someone and the occasional lapse into bad language that isn't directed at anyone in particular. If a student drops something on her foot and says 'Oh sh*t!', I don't feel the need to clamp down hard. On the other hand, if a student uses the 'F word' against someone, that's completely unacceptable.

To deal with verbally abusive students, follow these suggestions:

- ✔ Don't react by saying: 'What did you say?!' The student's likely to be only too happy to tell you.

- ✔ Calm yourself before reacting – aim to overcome your initial, emotional response.

- ✔ Make a clear statement about the language: 'That is unacceptable language and this is the sanction for it.'

- ✔ Remind the student that you don't use that sort of language, and neither do other staff or most of the students. Again, emphasise the need for mutual respect.

- ✔ Encourage your students to think carefully about the language they use and the effect it has on others, for instance by doing some activities around appropriate language in different situations.

A fact of modern life is that swearing's quite common on the streets and in the playground (and, indeed, on the television). What you need to do is remind your students that they must adapt their vocabulary to suit different situations. Find ways to encourage your students not to use abusive language. You might point out that such words lose their power to shock when they're used too much.

Winning Back the 'Lost' Class

You may well come across some times when you feel yourself losing your grip, not on an individual student but on a whole class. Perhaps the students are starting to push at the boundaries of good behaviour; maybe you're finding getting the class silent so that you can deliver the introduction to your lesson increasingly impossible.

To some, this might not seem like a particularly 'challenging' situation. But when you have to face a lost class day after day, it quickly begins to wear you down and cause you heaps of stress.

Losing a class is like a ball rolling down a slippery slope – it starts off slowly, but it soon gathers momentum. As soon as you feel yourself beginning to struggle, take action immediately. If you let things go on in a negative way for too long, the day comes when getting your students back to where they should be is impossible.

If you're new to teaching and you feel that you're losing one or more of your classes, ask for support and help sooner rather than later. No shame's attached to doing this – I can remember losing one class early on in my first year as a teacher. Without the help of my mentor in regaining control, that would have felt like an extremely long year!

Spotting the warning signs

You should have a sense of when a class is slipping away from you. You probably get a sickly, nervous feeling just before you face the students. Watch out for the warning signs and aim to spot them early. Stamp down on anyone who steps out of line, rather than letting things go on badly for too long.

You may see warning signs such as:

- ✔ Increased chatter in lessons and difficulty in getting the whole class to pay silent attention.
- ✔ More low-level misbehaviour, such as going off task, tipping on chairs and minor uniform infringements.
- ✔ More and more students arriving late to lessons, without any reasonable excuse.
- ✔ Your hard-working students beginning to complain that they can't concentrate or can't work because of low-level disruption.
- ✔ The start of more serious incidents happening during lessons.
- ✔ Less and less homework being handed in on time, or at all.

If you spot three or more of these warning signs, then you know the time's come to get your class back under control.

Getting a class back under control

Getting a class back under control is difficult but not impossible, even though you may feel that you've completely lost them and have no chance of getting them back. At the very least you should make a good, solid attempt. Because the alternative's far worse – having to deal with a challenging class who simply don't listen or behave for the rest of the year!

The very best time to regain control over a class that's slipping away is at the start of a term or just after a half-term break. At these times, everyone has the mentality of a 'fresh start' – not just you, but hopefully your students as well. Seize these moments as the best possible time to get your class back under control.

To regain control of a lost class, take these suggestions to heart:

✔ **Ask for support from senior staff.** Talk with a senior teacher about the problems you're experiencing, and exactly how she can support you. For instance, she can come into your lesson to help you settle the class. She may also offer to back you up when the students misbehave, talking with individuals or helping you instigate sanctions and ensuring they're employed.

✔ **Get senior staff into your lesson.** The key to re-establishing your expectations is to be able to talk with your class about what you expect. Unfortunately, with a class that refuses to listen, this is nigh on impossible. With a senior teacher standing next to you at the front of the room, you should at the very least be able to get your students silent and listening. That way, you can outline what you want and the students see that you're serious about getting it.

✔ **Reorganise your classroom.** As part of your plan to regain control of the class, a great idea's to re-jig your room to show who's boss. You may move the desks and chairs into rows rather than groups – always a slightly easier format for discipline. You can even turn the entire room round to face in another direction. The idea is to challenge your students' perceptions of what's going to happen in your lessons.

✔ **Reconsider your teaching approaches.** Sometimes, a change in the way you teach your lessons helps you resettle a class. Spending some time doing more individual rather than group work may help you limit the noise and disruption during lessons. Alternatively, you may need to be braver in your approaches and encourage the students to take more control of how and what they learn. Judge what works best in your situation and try some new approaches to see what helps.

✔ **Be realistic about your behaviour management approaches.** If you're setting a lot of detentions that students aren't attending, then you're effectively wasting your time. If your students get away without coming to detentions, then the threat of detentions to control behaviour is meaningless. Be honest with yourself about whether you're going to follow through on the sanctions you set. And if you're not, then use other approaches instead. For instance, you can focus on giving lots of rewards to those students who are working and behaving well, rather than wasting your energy on those who aren't.

You can't find an instant panacea for regaining control over a lost class. Losing control happens to many teachers in their first year in the job, often because you're unsure of how to set clear and firm expectations at the start of the year. But remember that this experience is all about getting to know what does and doesn't work for you, in your classroom. Next September, everything may be very different!

Coping with a lost class

Sometimes you may completely lose your class and feel that getting them back under control's practically impossible, no matter what you try. In these circumstances, you can still use some approaches to handle the situation and minimise disruption to your lessons and to those of other teachers working close by.

To cope day to day with a lost class:

- ✔ Minimise whole-class teaching, especially if you're really struggling to get the students to listen.

- ✔ Have an active, engaging starter on the desks for when the students arrive. Encourage them to get straight down to work, rather than trying to get them silent to take the register.

- ✔ Take down the names of any latecomers, to deal with later or to pass onto relevant senior staff.

- ✔ Focus on using rewards and motivating the good students, rather than getting hung up on punishing the difficult ones.

- ✔ Use approaches that limit the stress on you and put the onus on the students to do independent work.

- ✔ Set projects and longer tasks, so that those who do wish to work know what they need to do.

- ✔ Move around the room, sorting out any disruption one to one, but mainly focusing on helping those who are on task.

- ✔ In extreme circumstances, try to 'divide and rule'. Say to the class: 'If you want to learn something today, come to the front.' During the lesson focus on those students who come with you and choose to work. Take down the names of those who refused to learn, and pass them on to the appropriate senior member of staff.

The key to success is being willing to incorporate a bit of flexibility. Although as far as humanly possible you should avoid lowering your standards, you need to gauge which battles to fight and which ones aren't worth the effort.

Managing Your Stress Levels

Teaching is a stressful job. This stress comes from many quarters – from the workload, from the paperwork, from the pressures of 'getting it right'. And often, most of all, from dealing with abusive or aggressive students or very difficult classes (the 'class from hell', as I like to call them). Depending on the type of school you work in, the stress caused by your students may be either negligible or the biggest source of pressure you face.

Recognising signs of being over-stressed

A certain level of stress is both necessary and important – without the challenges that stress provides, your working life's very dull and boring. Remember that every time you deal with a difficult student, you find ways to improve your teaching skills. The secret is to understand when the stress is at manageable levels, and when it's getting too much for you and you need to deal with it.

Watch out for the signs that you're getting over-stressed. You may find yourself:

- Having trouble getting off to sleep, or waking up feeling unrested and unrefreshed.
- Finding difficulty in cutting off from worries about work, or having ongoing fears about particular classes or students.
- Getting into poor habits with what you eat and drink.
- Relying heavily on substances such as alcohol and nicotine to relax.
- Falling victim to colds and bugs.
- Becoming overly emotional, or feeling really down and depressed.

Strategies for dealing with stress

You need to differentiate between the inevitable pressures of the job and the feeling that everything's overwhelming you. But don't ignore the symptoms of stress in the hope that they go away of their own accord.

If stress is a real issue for you, you can:

- Make an appointment with your GP, or with a counsellor, to talk through your options.
- Talk to the senior staff at your school, to find ways for them to support you or help you minimise your workload.
- Look for ways to create a better home/work divide in your life. Don't be a perfectionist – allow some of the less important jobs to slide.

✔ Do something just for yourself each week, or preferably each day – a glass of wine, a bubble bath or a favourite film. Find ways to shrug off the stresses of the school day.

✔ Consider whether you're in the right school or setting for your needs. Maybe you should think about changing schools or even jobs to find something a bit less stressful.

Perhaps you feel that you're mostly able to cope with the stresses of the job. Even if this is the case, you can still use some practical techniques to minimise the impact of stress on your wellbeing. These approaches also help you avoid getting stressed and losing your temper in lessons.

The following suggestions are based on my own experiences of teaching in challenging situations:

✔ **React from the head, not from the heart.** Back to that 'rational over emotional' approach. When you face a problem, take a moment to calm yourself down first. Remind yourself to react intellectually and rationally, rather than emotionally. Most misbehaviour isn't personal – it's not about *you*. At the end of the day, remember that teaching is just a job.

✔ **Build a wall.** Create a metaphorical 'wall' between yourself and any abusive behaviour. An invisible barrier, like the deflector shields on the Starship *Enterprise*, which pops up every time a student's rude or aggressive towards you. That's not to say that you shouldn't *deal* with the rude behaviour after the event; just that you mustn't let it get through your defences.

✔ **Feel pity rather than anger.** Although you don't feel like this at the time, the most appropriate response to an abusive student is to feel pity rather than anger. Remind yourself that this child must have a pretty awful life outside school to behave like this in your classroom.

✔ **Forgive yourself.** You make mistakes as a teacher – everyone does. I've certainly dropped some clangers in my time. But you've got to discover how to forgive yourself – put your mistakes in the past and move on. Don't let mistakes hold you back from a brighter future.

✔ **Don't bear grudges.** When a child's really abusive, you may be hugely tempted to bear a grudge against her – to remember what happened in the past at every future time when you encounter that student. But this is no way to proceed. Some of the most challenging students never get a chance to prove that they can change, because their teachers have a fixed, negative perception about them. Remind yourself that you're a professional and aim for a fresh start every time, no matter how difficult the child.

✔ **Use your support systems.** Plenty of people are willing to support and help you. Your fellow teachers are one of the best sources of support you can find – especially in a challenging school where you feel that you're 'all in it together'. Other sources of support include the teaching unions, your mentor, senior staff, friends and family and the students themselves. Look around and ask for support when you need it, and give your support in return to others.

✔ **Create a home/school divide.** Find every way you can to divide your days into time spent working at school, and time spent relaxing at home. If your circumstances allow, staying on at school until you've finished working for the day is a great idea. This creates that mental divide that's so vital for cutting off from work – you literally leave your work at work. Consider taking up a physical or creative activity after work to help you shrug off the worries of the day.

✔ **Maintain a sense of perspective.** Sometimes you can feel like your classroom's your entire world: all that matters goes on within those four walls. But a sense of perspective is both helpful and necessary. Even if your class messes you around, this really isn't the end of the world. Bear this maxim in mind when you're feeling stressed: 'Even in your worst lesson, nobody died.'

✔ **Give yourself a pat on the back.** Teachers are generally great at giving praise to others, but not so hot on giving it to themselves. Make sure that you take a look at all the great things you're doing in your class-room – focus on your successes, rather than getting hooked up on your failures.

Remember that in most schools, the challenging situations this chapter describes are relatively rare. And when you do encounter a student who pushes you to the limits, you can use that as an opportunity to develop as a practitioner.

Part IV
Dealing with Different Kinds of People

'OK, that's settled then -- I read you a story, you show me how to operate the video.'

In this part . . .

You came into teaching because you love to work with kids. Well, I hope you did. Because one thing you can't escape as a teacher is the kids. You need to know how to build relationships with your students, and also with the other staff at your school and the parents and carers as well. By building up these quality relationships, you make your teaching much more effective. In this part of the book, I explore how to deal with all different kinds of people in the best way you possibly can.

Chapter 11

Getting to Know Your Students

In This Chapter

▶ Exploring a range of ways to build bonds with your students

▶ Handling different kinds of students in the best possible way

▶ Finding ways to develop the pastoral side of your role to its fullest extent

*O*ne of the greatest joys of teaching is the chance to build bonds with your students. You meet and work with a whole host of different young people. And as their teacher, you have the chance to be a major influence on their lives and on the kind of choices they make in the future.

If you know your students well and they feel a positive bond with you, you almost inevitably get better work and behaviour from them. They want to please you by working hard for you, just as you want to work hard to help them succeed. Building up these relationships with your students takes time and effort, but the effort's more than worthwhile.

A truth rarely spoken in teaching is that you like some of your students much more than others. You must put aside your personal feelings and build bonds with each and every child you teach. Always remember, those students who challenge you the most are probably most in need of the strong, positive role model you can offer.

Discovering How to Build Relationships

You have many different types of relationships in your life. Outside school you have bonds with your family and friends. Perhaps you're married or living with a partner and this relationship's probably central to your daily life. If you've got children of your own, you understand the importance of creating bonds with them as well. You also develop relationships at work – perhaps some of the staff at your school become close friends.

The relationships you build with your students are *not* the same as those you may have with friends, family and loved ones. While you do want to build strong relationships, you also need to keep a certain professional distance so that you can maintain good discipline. Sometimes you need to 'crack the whip' with your class and this isn't easy if the students see you as their friend. This is a tricky balance to achieve, because you almost inevitably get emotionally attached to 'your' children and 'your' classes.

Why good relationships are vital

You may think the concept that good relationships are vital within your classroom is fairly obvious, but spending some time exploring this statement in more detail is worthwhile. Consider exactly *why* these relationships are so crucial. Also think about how good relationships can contribute to your students' development and also to the effectiveness of your teaching.

While forming positive relationships is the human thing to want to do – it's a good, solid moral foundation for the day-to-day challenges of life – specific reasons exist in teaching why teacher–student relationships are important:

✔ You can use these relationships to encourage your students to behave themselves. If a student wants to please you, then he's more likely to behave well for you.

✔ Exactly the same applies for his work – if he feels a connection with you, he's going to want to make you happy by pushing himself to achieve his best.

✔ Some of your students have few, if any, positive relationships outside school. Even relationships with their friends, which they may view as positive, can be more about negative influences and peer group pressures. By creating a bond with them, you demonstrate the possibility of building up good, strong relationships with adults, ones they may decide to emulate with their peers.

✔ You can use the relationships you build to boost your students' self-esteem. By creating a connection with them, you show them that they are likeable and worth getting to know.

✔ If you feel a bond with your students, this helps get you through the tough times. If your aim's to do the absolute best for each and every child, then you're less likely to 'give up' on a class when they really test you.

✔ When you feel good about relating with your students and they with you, everyone feels positive, relaxed and in a good frame of mind to work.

✔ Relationships are one of the joys of being a teacher – teaching's all about communicating with your class, and passing ideas, facts and information on to them. Positive relationships make this both possible and enjoyable for you and for your students.

You also need to build up good relationships with the other staff at your school, and also with the parents and carers of your students. You can find tips for doing this in Chapters 12 and 13.

Building bonds with your students

You build bonds with your students by finding ways to 'click' with them and make connections. If you're a primary teacher with just one class to teach, this is slightly easier than if you're teaching in a secondary school. At primary level, you spend all day every day with your children, so you can get to know them quickly. Of course, this does have its disadvantages, not the least of which is the fact that you spend every day with them. And if you have trouble getting on, you have no escape!

If you're a secondary teacher, you need to be realistic about the depth of the bonds you can build with your students, and about how long you take to get to know everyone properly. You aren't able to discover all the ins and outs of every child in a single year. But if you stay at a school for several years, before long you find that you do get to know lots of students well.

To build bonds with your students, you need to:

✔ **Talk to them.** Clearly you're going to talk with your students during your lessons. But don't just talk to them about things related to their work; make sure you talk to them about *them* as well. What do they like? What hobbies do they have? What are their favourite foods? What music do they listen to? Make sure you relate your discussions to what makes your students tick and this helps you build up bonds with them.

✔ **Set 'getting to know you' type activities.** At the start of your time with a class, a great idea is to use lots of exercises aimed at getting to know your students. You may ask them to write down their five favourite things, or to do a one-minute presentation on 'All the things that are special about me'. The more you can get to know about your students – their likes and dislikes, their lives outside school – the better you're able to click with them.

✔ **Use your face and your eyes.** When you make eye contact with a student, this begins to form a connection between the two of you. As the saying goes, 'The eyes are the window to the soul.' Although you don't need to get quite that deep and meaningful with your children, do make sure that you use plenty of eye contact with every member of your class. Use your face, too, in a way that shows you are open, friendly and keen to build bonds. Smile when someone gives a good answer; raise your eyebrows to show that you're interested, and maintain a relaxed and open facial expression. Make sure your expression is genuine though – students can spot if you're faking.

✔ **'Visit' everyone in the course of a lesson.** Make sure you don't stick at the front of the room. Get yourself moving around the space, so that you physically 'visit' every member of your class. Crouch down close to students to help them with their work. When you set group tasks, make sure you drop in on every group within the class. Aim to touch all four walls of your classroom during the course of each lesson – that way you know you visited everyone.

✔ **Get involved beyond the classroom.** You can find lots of tips later in this chapter about this. Look, too, at Chapter 15, which deals with the extra-curricular side of school life in more depth. Perhaps your other commitments mean that you can't take part in lots of activities beyond the school day. Even so, you can still make the time to chat with students in the corridor or playground.

And don't forget that the most important aspect of all in building bonds is time. Getting to know the new people we meet, and working out what makes them tick, takes time. Don't expect instant results, but keep at the task and you succeed.

Using questions to 'click' with your class

You're aware that using questions is an effective approach for teaching in your classroom. But have you ever considered how well questions can help you 'click' with and connect with your class? When you ask someone a question you invite a response, whether it's an answer, an opinion, a description and so on. Make questions your friend – use them to develop your students' knowledge and also to develop bonds with them.

The more you use questions with your students, the more you develop an interactive approach with the class. And this helps you involve the students in their work and in the lesson.

Don't smile until Christmas – cliché or truth?

I'm sure you've heard the saying, usually aimed at trainee or new teachers, that you *shouldn't smile until Christmas*. In fact you have to be rather hard-hearted or humourless to manage this. But in any case, don't take this cliché too literally.

What I think this saying means is that you should aim to start off quite hard with your classes, or even very hard, if you think that works in your setting. That way you can get everyone toeing the line and make sure you outline your expectations clearly.

Even once everyone's working as you wish, don't relax your standards and boundaries too early in the first term. You can certainly crack a smile or two along the way, though, just to show that you do want to build relationships with your students.

Ask a lot of questions

Whenever you need to talk to your class about a topic, intersperse this time with many questions. Consider ways of incorporating questions into your lesson delivery. The more often you get individuals responding and contributing to the work, the better connections you make with them.

Focus on open rather than closed questions

Most questions fall into two types – *open* and *closed*. You use closed questions where a single-word, right or wrong answer usually applies. For example, you can correctly answer the closed question 'What's the capital of France?' only by saying 'Paris'. Open questions, on the other hand, invite opinions, feelings and ideas. With open questions, there's no one correct answer to give. So, if you asked 'Which places would you like to visit on our trip to Paris?', you may receive a whole host of different answers.

Limit the number of closed questions you use. Closed questions don't give you much chance of getting to know your students better, because all they ask is for that one 'right' answer. Although they're useful for assessing your students' knowledge, they don't invite any kind of personal or extended response.

By using open questions whenever you can, you draw your students out. Open questions help you encourage more open-ended and personal responses from your students. Because open questions don't have one 'right' answer, they invite feedback from your students about their opinions, emotions, perspectives and so on. You relate what you ask to the individual and his experiences, thoughts and feelings.

Move toward a student as he answers a question

When you've asked the class a question and picked out someone to answer, move toward the student as he responds. Use your face and body to show that you want to hear his answer. This stance helps you demonstrate an interest in the student's opinions or ideas, and again strengthens his perception of a connection between the two of you.

Take care how you respond to answers

Use praise when a student gives a good answer. Highlight what was good about the answer, whether it was 'interesting', 'a good idea' or 'imaginative'. If you're looking for ideas from your students, then aim to build on the suggestion the student gives, developing an idea laterally or showing your class how it may connect to another area.

When a student's answer is weak, respond with care. You may have difficulty knowing what to do when a student gives an answer that's obviously silly, wrong or a bit odd. Aim not to dismiss these answers in an off-hand way, especially if the student's one who doesn't normally volunteer to answer.

You can say something safe like: 'That's an interesting thought.' You may also respond by saying: 'Good idea, can anyone develop on that further?'

When your students put up a hand to answer a question, they're doing so in front of their entire peer group. Talking to the class may not feel like a pressurised situation for you, but for any shy students or those who lack confidence or self-esteem, speaking out in front of their peers can seem like a pretty big deal. Listen to each and every student with the same show of enthusiasm and interest so that everyone feels valued and involved. Stamp down on any instances where students laugh at each other's answers in a critical way.

Buddy or boss – getting the balance right

The temptation when you first start out as a teacher is to want to be your students' friend as well as their teacher. 'But you've just said I need to build bonds, connections and relationships!' you may cry. Well yes, that's true, but think about the big difference between forming a good relationship and being someone's buddy.

Q&A sessions: Getting everyone involved

Holding question and answer sessions isn't that straightforward. One of the issues you face is that some of your students are keener than others to give you their answers. The temptation is always to ask someone who has a hand up to answer the question. But if you do this, some of your quieter or less-willing students sit back and let everyone else do the work. And that doesn't help you build bonds with everyone in your class.

You can try other approaches, such as:

✔ **Anyone answers.** Once you've asked the question, give the students a little bit of thinking time or time to talk over their answer with a partner. Then pick out any student to answer.

✔ **Everyone answers.** Ask your question and then get your students to go round their groups, each person giving an answer to the group in turn.

✔ **Pick a card.** Use a pack of playing cards to show who answers a question. Before the lesson begins, place a card on each chair. When you ask a question, designate the owner of a particular card to answer, for example 'the Queen of Hearts'.

Take care not to put your more nervous students on the spot. Use an 'anyone answers' approach for straightforward questions or for ones that invite an entirely personal response. If you work with any really shy children, consider giving them the option to 'pass', and work on boosting their confidence.

You need to achieve a balance between getting on well with your students and keeping the necessary distance so that they still see you as their teacher. Yes, you do like some, most or even all of them, but relationships aren't about your personal likes and dislikes. Yes, some of them like you, but again, I'm not talking about their personal feelings towards you. What you're after is a feeling of mutual respect that allows effective teaching and learning to take place. This is a tricky balance to achieve, although it does become easier with experience.

You may find striking a balance with older students particularly hard, because they seem mature enough to be the kind of friends you have in your life outside school. You probably find this especially tricky if these older students are close to you in age. Perhaps you went straight to university from school, and then straight into the profession once you qualified. If that's the case, you're only a few years older than any sixth-form students you teach. Take care to maintain some distance between you and them.

To get the balance right, you need to remember:

✔ **You're a professional, in a professional role.** The relationships you form are designed to make your teaching better, not to build up your network of friends. Although you enjoy building relationships, make sure that you don't push things too far in the 'friendship' direction.

✔ **Keeping a distance helps you maintain consistency.** You almost certainly feel warmly towards at least some of your children, but you need to maintain a certain distance between you and your class. You may have heard some students complaining that a teacher has 'favourites'. What this probably means is that he allows his personal feelings about the children to become apparent in the way he treats them. You damage the relationships you're trying so hard to build if your students sense that you like some of them more than others.

✔ **Some children push to be treated as a friend.** Some of your students may have difficulty judging the kind of relationship they need to establish with their teachers. These students may lack effective adult role models outside school and find sticking within the appropriate boundaries tricky. While you don't want to shove these students away, you do need to work hard at creating a sense of distance between you and them.

✔ **Sometimes you need to crack down.** If you get too friendly with your students, when you do need to tell them off doing so is much harder. Your students more easily take a sanction from someone they perceive as a teacher figure, rather than someone they see as a friend.

✔ **You need to maintain your boundaries.** If your students see you as their friend, this can encourage them to push at the boundaries. They may start to use language that's inappropriate in the classroom setting and appear to believe that you should allow them to get away with doing this. You may sense that they're stretching at the limits of good behaviour because they're getting too relaxed in your lessons. You've got to strike a balance between good, positive relationships and the need to be firm about the kind of behaviour you expect.

Finding the right balance is tricky, and many new teachers let the line slip too far in the 'friendly' direction. Doing this in your first year of teaching isn't the end of the world. But remember that you make your life much easier, and your teaching much more effective, if you keep the limits firmly in place. For more on this subject take a look at Chapter 8.

Treating them as people as well as students

While your main focus is on teaching your students and getting them to succeed academically, you should never forget that these students are people as well as pupils. By treating your students as individuals, each special and unique in their own way, you get the most out of the time you spend with them. You also help yourself build up the kind of positive relationships I talk about in the previous section. You can show that you see your students as people, as well as seeing them as pupils, by:

✔ **Welcoming them to lessons.** At the start of the day or lesson, stand at your door and welcome your students into the room in a personal, and personable, way. The time taken while they're filtering into your room is a great opportunity for getting to know them better. By positioning yourself at the door, you also show very clearly that this is your 'territory', and that you set the rules and standards while they're in your room.

✔ **Remembering and using names.** A person's name is part of what makes him unique. Get to know your students' names quickly (see 'Names, names, names – knowing and using them', later in this chapter, for some advice on how to do this). And once you know their names use them as often as you can, particularly in conjunction with personalised and specific praise.

✔ **Noticing the little things.** Show your students that you care by noticing those little things that you can easily overlook. If a child's been absent for a few days, enquire after his health. When one of your students gets a new haircut, make a point of saying how great it looks. Spot those little things that show you really care about and take an interest in them as individuals.

✔ **Connecting outside the classroom.** Stop for a quick chat or give a brief positive comment as you pass by your students in the corridor outside lessons. When you're on duty in the playground, use this as an opportunity to have a relaxed chat with some of your students. Demonstrate that your interest in building and sustaining a relationship extends beyond the classroom walls.

✔ **Incorporating the personal.** Remember some of the minor personal details your students tell you and incorporate these into your conversations. For instance, if a child tells you about a forthcoming holiday somewhere exciting, make sure to ask afterwards how it went. If all your students are excited about the latest film, then you can use this as a way of delivering part of one of your lessons.

✔ **Incorporating their interests.** Find ways to incorporate a few of your students' interests into your lessons. For example, you can pick up on the latest playground craze and use it as a way into a topic or subject. Don't be afraid to bring objects and ideas into the classroom that are close to your students' hearts. Not only does this help you build bonds with them, it also increases their engagement in your lessons.

✔ **Staying up to speed on the latest trends.** Of course, you don't actually have to listen to the latest music at every opportunity or build a big collection of the latest trendy toys. But if you can at least show an interest in the things your students are 'into', you show them that you care about what makes them tick.

✔ **Getting involved in extra-curricular activities.** When you work with students outside lesson time, you can afford to take a slightly more informal approach with them. This allows you to build bonds and develop relationships in a way that isn't possible in a busy classroom situation. You can find advice about this aspect of your role in Chapter 15.

Remember, you're not pandering to your students and their every wish. Rather, you're finding effective ways to get them working to the maximum. You can't make every single lesson 'interesting' to each of your students on a personal level. And some days you just don't have the time or energy to work on building those personal connections. But do your best, build up bonds and your students are more forgiving at those times when you need a bit of a break.

Names, names, names – knowing and using them

You need to use your students' names for many different reasons: to get their attention, when you praise them, when you sanction them and also as a key part of the process of building up relationships. Of course, this means that a vital teaching skill is being able to get to know and remember names quickly. And that's not easy if you teach a large number of different students.

Using names is vital because:

- ✔ It shows that you care about your students as individuals.
- ✔ It allows you to personalise praise and to make that praise really count.
- ✔ It helps you gain the attention of a specific individual.
- ✔ It helps you 'click' with the students in your classes.
- ✔ It allows students new to a class or a school to get to know the names of their peers.
- ✔ It's polite!

Get to know your students' names as quickly as you can at the start of each school year, and after you know them, use them at every opportunity. If you're teaching a primary class where you see the same children day after day, getting to know names is a relatively straightforward process. You do it naturally because you're spending so much time with the children.

But if you're a secondary school teacher, and especially if you're working in a non-core subject (Modern Foreign Languages, say, or Music or PE), you teach huge numbers of different students. Can you really remember all those names? And how on earth do you do it?

You develop your own favourite ways of remembering names, and the process does get easier the more experience you have as a teacher. The following approaches offer a good starting point for your first few lessons.

You can get away without knowing every single name for quite a while, especially if the students only see you once a week. But don't get too relaxed about this. The day comes when you have to write reports about the students or attend a parents' evening to talk about them. And if you can't match the name to the student at this stage, you're going to feel very embarrassed and look rather unprofessional.

Use name games

Play name games with your class, particularly in the first few lessons together. You don't have to be a Drama teacher to do this – a name game works well as a quick starter activity in any lesson. You can:

- ✔ Ask the students to 'throw' their names around the room, one to another: Josie to Anya, Anya to Ranjit, Ranjit to Jasmine and so on.
- ✔ Get them to add in an adjective that describes themselves to spice things up a bit: Jolly Josie to Amazing Anya, Amazing Anya to Radical Ranjit and so on.

Use visual back-ups

Seeing a name actually on a student is a great way to help the name stick in your mind. Use visual back-ups to do this. For instance, for the first few lessons you can give your students badges or stickers on which to put their names. Or you may get them to make little cardboard name plates to sit on their desks. Collect these at the end of each lesson – you particularly don't want your students wandering out into the streets with their names emblazoned on their tops! Re-use the badges or name plates for each of the first few lessons with the class.

Use a seating plan

Using a seating plan is a great way to get your students to behave themselves, but it's also a helpful method for getting a handle on names. One of the simplest approaches for seating a new class is to put the students in register order. As you call the register, you can look up to see who answers. As you do this, start to fit the face to the name and fix it in your memory.

Perhaps you prefer not to put your children in register order or not to have a seating plan at all. Even so, you can still create a visual plan of where they're sitting by drawing desk shapes on a sheet of paper and then writing in the name beside each seat. You can refer to this when an individual puts a hand up to answer a question, so that you're able to use his name. With older students you don't even have to create this visual plan yourself – ask one of your trustworthy students to do it for you.

Use the names whenever you can

The more you use your students' names, the better they stick. So every time you address a student, whether you're answering a question or simply saying hello, make sure you use his name.

As time goes on, you start to get to grips with most of the names. You can then move on to use higher-level strategies to remember the rest.

Some teachers find remembering names really tricky – if that includes you then incorporate all the strategies you can find, particularly the memory tricks and techniques described below.

Use memory techniques

Memory techniques and systems can be really useful, because they offer a simple yet effective way to remember your students' names. You can also use these techniques to help you remember things other than names – shopping lists, birthdays, anything you need to memorise.

Me and my name

Here's a lovely activity to help you get to know your students' names. It's based around the idea that your name is a key part of what makes you the person you are.

Ask your students to write a short piece called 'Me and My Name'. The idea is to focus on their own personal feelings about, and responses to, their names. By getting them to give you this personal insight into their names, you can find the hooks and links you need to remember them.

You can ask them questions like:

✔ Where does your name come from? Is it a family name? Is it a name from this country or from somewhere else?

✔ How do you feel about your name? Does it suit you? Or maybe you don't like it and prefer to be called something else?

✔ What does your name say about you? Does it fit with the way you see yourself?

✔ Do you have any pet names or nicknames that your family or friends call you? Where do these pet names come from?

As an extension of this activity, you can bring in one of those 'baby names' books and get your children to look up the origins of their names and what they mean.

Most techniques for improving your memory are based on creating links and forming mental images. The more outrageous or bizarre these links and images are, the more likely you are to remember them. You may find using these systems a bit odd at first, but with time and practice they can become part of the subconscious range of techniques you use to remember your students' names.

You can get lots of great books on memory systems and investing in one of these really is worthwhile, especially if this is a weak area for you. I find Tony Buzan's books particularly helpful and accessible. You may want to try *Use Your Memory*, published by BBC Books.

Here are my top tips for developing your memory. I've related these tips specifically to the need to remember your students' names, but of course memory systems have many more uses than that. Some of the strategies you can use include:

✔ **Picking out the most striking features.** Look to see whether a student has a strong physical feature, perhaps really dark eyebrows, a large nose or red cheeks. Now try to find some way of linking that feature with the student's name. For instance, if you teach a student called Rose who tends to blush easily, you can use the rosy colour of her cheeks as a reminder of her name.

✔ **Looking for rhymes and rhythms.** If the connection you make in your mind rhymes or has a particular rhythm to it, it's easier to remember. So if you have a student called Billy and he's rather silly, that helps you remember his name.

✔ **What first comes to mind.** When you're aiming to create associations, the first thing that pops into your mind is the easiest to recall. Say you teach a boy called Alfie, and when you hear his name the song 'What's it all about, Alfie?' always comes into your brain. Aim to associate the song sounding in your head with the face of the child who has that name.

✔ **Stress what you never remember.** Similarly, when you find something hard to remember, stressing it can help you retain it in your memory. Imagine you have two students called John – the John you always forget is the one you should focus on, rather than the one you find easier to remember.

✔ **Weird or vivid images.** Creating a really bizarre or a very strong image helps you 'stick' something in your brain. For instance, if you teach a student called Luke who's always rather pale, you can conjure up the image that 'Luke is about to puke'. Not only is this memorable in its own right, it also uses the rhymes mentioned earlier in this list. Now create a mental picture for yourself of Luke being sick. Make the picture really vivid in your mind. Make sure you see that puke coming out of his mouth.

✔ **Sensory perceptions.** Making sensory links with an image can help your brain to drag it back up when you need it. If you can bear to keep going with the Luke image for a moment, see what sensory perceptions you can associate with him being sick. The bright colour of the sick, the hideous smell, the slushy texture of his vomit. Really fix the sensory parts of the image in your mind.

✔ **Size.** Large mental images tend to stick more than small ones. So take an image and make it huge in your mind. Imagine that Luke isn't being just a little bit sick, he's being sick like the magic porridge pot – more and more of the vomit keeps bursting out of his mouth. (At this point you're probably thinking I'm mad. Perhaps I am, but I promise you won't forget this image of Luke in a hurry!)

✔ **Action.** If you can get some action and movement into your mental image, so much the better. So, before you finally take poor Luke to the sick bay, get some action into the mental image you've created. If you don't mind, I'd like you to finish by imagining hundreds of teachers rushing in to clear up the giant pile of sick.

Of course, you definitely don't want to *share* this kind of mental image with your students, or for that matter with their parents either. But such an image really is a great way of getting those tricky names to wedge themselves in your memory. Just beware that you don't let your inner thoughts slip at the wrong moment!

More tricks for hard-to-remember names

Some names stubbornly refuse to stick in your memory. Often you remember the names of the most difficult students, and also those who always put their hands up or always work hard. The names of the quiet, shy, silent students are trickiest to learn, simply because you tend to have less interaction with them. You may also encounter difficulties with more complicated names or if you have several students with the same name.

For those names that just don't stick, or if you find learning names really difficult, you can:

✔ **Annotate your register or class list.** Write a few subtle annotations on your register or class list to help you identify the students. Be careful that you don't write anything rude, though, just in case someone happens to look at the register! You can put something like 'glasses' or 'blonde hair', but don't put anything too personal like 'sticky-out teeth' or 'dodgy haircut'. If you feel you must, use a code like SOT instead.

✔ **Do some verbal presentations.** You tend to remember names more when you hear a student speak up. But what can you do about those students who sit silently in lessons hardly ever saying a word? To help you learn their names, set an activity that involves a verbal presentation to the class. Do this in groups if your students are very young or very shy. Before the students start their presentation, ask them to state their names. And as they do that, make a mental note of the names that don't 'stick' for you. During the course of their presentation, make a point of trying to firm up those difficult names in your mind.

✔ **Check on their books.** All the students in your class have written their names on the front of their exercise books. As you move around the room and talk to an individual, have a quick look at the front of his book to check for his name. After you have the name, use it in your discussion of his work.

✔ **Leave by name.** At report time, if you're really panicking this is a simple and useful technique. At the end of the lesson, get all your students standing behind their chairs. Then explain that you're going to let them leave one at a time as you call their names. When the turn comes for those students whose names you don't know, look to see who moves. Make a quick written note for yourself about the kind of report you want to give this child.

✔ **Grasp some memory systems.** By getting to grips with a few simple memory techniques, you can make huge improvements to your ability to remember names. You may find that these techniques feel a bit 'odd' at first, and in fact you're right, because that's a key part of how they work. And they really *do* work.

The longer you teach, the more you're able to remember names. You develop your own techniques that work for you, with your students, in your classroom.

Dealing with Different Types of Student

You come across many different types of student during your career as a teacher. Each one of them's a unique individual, with his own skills, talents, positive attributes and negative ones too. As a professional, you have to know how to handle and work with each and every one of your students to help them achieve their very best.

Some children tend to fade into the background in a class; others you get to know very quickly, often the 'characters' in the class. I love the 'characters' – it's a dull old world without them. You probably have your 'class clown' who's always making the other students (and you) laugh. You may also have several more challenging characters who push you to your limits.

When you work with challenging students and their behaviour or attitude causes you problems in your lessons, you feel very frustrated. You want to get on and teach the class, but a minority of your students just don't let you do that. At the toughest times, remind yourself that these students push you to develop your teaching skills to the maximum. Your job as a teacher's rather bland if you only ever teach 'Stepford'-type students who are impeccably behaved at all times. Every time you face an issue or a challenge in your classroom, you're pushed to become an even better teacher. Go to Chapter 10 for information and advice on dealing with challenging situations and challenging students.

Differentiating your approaches

As a teacher, you must strike a balance between being consistent and using some flexibility. You need to know how to differentiate your approaches to suit the individual students you teach.

You can find advice about differentiating your lessons in Chapter 4. But as well as differentiating the way you format and deliver activities within a lesson, you also need to differentiate your approach according to the behaviour needs of your children. You don't change the standards you expect of your class; rather, you differentiate the way you ask for and apply those standards according to the individual student.

When you know and understand your students, you have a sense of which approaches are going to work best for them as individuals. If you've succeeded in building positive relationships, you've gained a feeling for the strategies you need to use with each child.

Even after you get to know your students as individuals, you still need to handle them in different ways according to the kind of mood they're in. If a student comes storming into the room and throws himself down in his seat, this is probably not the best time to come down hard on any minor infringements.

Take a look at an example of how this differentiation of behaviour approaches can work to help you understand what I mean. Imagine the behaviour issue you face is that some students are turning up to class without their ties on:

- ✔ With a student who's normally well behaved and amenable, you may simply say: 'I want you to put your tie on right now, thanks.' With this kind of student, you can do that at the start of the lesson while the class is entering the room, without the need to have a private word.

- ✔ If you're aware that the student has some personal issues at home that mean he may have trouble sorting out his uniform, you can have a quiet word with him: 'Did you have a problem finding your tie this morning? Shall I find one in the lost property box for you?'

- ✔ Perhaps you have a student who tends to become very confrontational with you and you've noticed a grim look on his face today. With him, the best approach may be to allow him some time to settle into the lesson first. After the rest of the students are on task, you can then have a private word with him to get him to sort out his uniform.

As you see from the examples above, you apply the same standard ('you must wear the correct uniform'), but take into account the differing needs of individuals.

Handling students with special needs

Over the course of your teaching career you work with students who have a whole range of special needs, from a child who has a serious physical impairment to a student who has a minor problem with socialising. Some students may have several different needs, all of which you must factor into your approach. Increasingly, schools are asked to take an inclusive approach, with more students given access to mainstream schooling.

Those students with the most serious special needs may have a 'Statement of Special Educational Needs'. This statement details the kind of support the student receives. All children with a Statement also have an Individual Education Plan (IEP) setting out short-term targets for that student.

Some types of special needs

Among many types of special needs, you may come across students who have:

- ✔ **Social, emotional and behavioural difficulties (SEBD).** This term is a 'catch-all' for those students whose needs are about behaviour rather than about learning. Some students struggle to socialise with their peers, while others are emotionally immature or have serious behaviour problems.

✔ **Dyslexia.** These students struggle with reading, writing and spelling, even though they may do well in other areas of the curriculum. Many children with this special need have a tendency to reverse letter sounds within words.

✔ **Dyscalculia.** These students have a problem in acquiring mathematical skills. They can struggle with basic concepts around numbers and other mathematical techniques.

✔ **Autistic spectrum disorder.** Students on the autistic spectrum find difficulty in communicating and understanding how to fit in with their peers. You may see them engaged in repetitive or obsessive behaviours. The conditions that fall under the autistic spectrum can range from mild to very severe. Children with severe autism are usually taught in a special school that's better placed to meet their needs than a mainstream school.

✔ **Hearing or visual impairment.** Students may have a slight loss of hearing or sight, or be profoundly deaf or blind. You need to adapt the approaches you use to take account of your students' physical impairments.

Your aim should be to meet the needs of all your children, and this includes finding out more about their special needs. Some students with more serious issues are allocated a specific learning support assistant to help them. Find the time to sit down with any support staff to talk through the best approaches to take.

Helping special needs students in your class

You can't take a 'one size fits all' approach to handling students with special needs. The advice below gets you thinking about the best strategies to use with students who have different kinds of needs. You also need to keep up to date on the latest research and thinking on the various different special needs.

To help your students, you need to:

✔ **Know more about your students' specific needs.** You can get advice from the special needs staff in your school. You can read some books on the subject or do some research on the Internet. For many of the special needs, specific charities and organisations can inform and assist both parents and schools.

✔ **Get support and help.** Your school or LEA should hopefully give you additional staff input if you're working with students with serious special needs. Unfortunately, this isn't always the case. Students with behavioural needs, in particular, can sometimes be left to 'sink or swim'.

✔ **Ask for additional training.** If you teach a student with a special need and you don't have any prior experience of this particular area, then ask whether you can get some additional training. For example, you may find benefit in attending a course about helping children who have dyslexia.

✔ **Differentiate your approaches.** Consider how your teaching approaches and your classroom set-up affect the likelihood of your students being successful. For instance, if you teach a child who has a visual impairment, he needs to sit close to the board.

✔ **Differentiate the activities you set.** Even when planning time is short, aim to differentiate for the bottom and top ends of the ability spectrum within your class. Bear in mind that not all special needs are about being academically weak – some students with special needs can be among the brightest in the class.

Those students who have serious behaviour problems, such as attention deficit hyperactivity disorder (ADHD), often benefit from time spent outside the classroom on developing key skills. Many schools now organise non-curriculum classes for their most challenging students, for instance in subjects such as anger management.

Don't assume that every student with special needs has had his needs noticed or identified. Some children with mild special needs get overlooked; others develop a special need during their time in education. Also, don't assume either that a child's special needs will always equate with low ability or poor behaviour. Remember that some students become adept at hiding any issues, either through embarrassment or even fear. If you have any concerns about a student, talk with the special needs staff at your school.

Managing the brightest learners

You may think that dealing with your brightest, most able students should be simple. Of course, much of the time working with really bright students is great fun. They push you to push yourself – you have to stay right on top of your subject to keep pace with them. But conversely, these can be some of the most difficult students to handle.

Your most able students should be on the school's gifted and talented register, and should be given the opportunity for accelerated learning. Ensure that your plans give plenty of opportunities for your most able students to progress so that their needs are met within regular lessons.

When you're working with the brightest learners, the kind of issues you can face include:

✔ The student who thinks he knows everything and behaves in an arrogant way towards you and perhaps also towards his peers.

✔ The student who finishes the work really quickly, then complains that he's bored because he has nothing to do.

✔ The student who challenges the approaches you use or your expertise in what you're teaching.

✔ The student who's clever about misbehaving, using subtle ways to undermine you while not doing anything that earns him a direct sanction.

✔ The parent who feels that you're not stretching the student sufficiently, or who perhaps has unrealistic ideas about how able the child really is.

✔ The parent who complains that you've placed his child in the 'wrong' class and you need to move him up a set.

You should also bear in mind that your brightest students tend to produce lots of work. And this can have a serious impact on the kind of time you have to spend marking.

To manage your brightest students, you need to:

✔ **Plan for plenty of extension tasks.** Think about how you can incorporate extension tasks into your lesson. Do you want to specify the extra activities these students should do, or are you going to give them an element of choice?

✔ **Be consistent about your standards.** Some bright students are very clever at getting you to vary your expectations of how they should behave. Stick to the clear standards you set right at the start of your time with a class, and make sure that you're consistent by demanding the same attitudes and approaches from every student.

✔ **Give them tasks that push them.** Look for activities that really push your very bright students. For example, you may ask a student to come to the front and write up some ideas on the board, or to deliver a presentation about the topic you're studying.

✔ **Look for opportunities for enrichment.** Find situations where your really bright students can go beyond the constraints of the traditional curriculum. For instance, you may suggest that they join a lunchtime chess club or get involved with the school council.

✔ **Set homework that students can take to the next level.** Outside the school day, your very able students have the time and opportunity to push their knowledge forwards. When you plan homework tasks, look for activities that give your brightest learners a chance to extend themselves. Extended projects offer a great way to do this.

✔ **Consider vertical banding.** You may gain from getting your brightest children working with some of the older students in a mixed-age class. Conversely, very able children often benefit from helping some younger or less able students with their work.

Some students who are very academically advanced find forming social relationships with their peers tricky. Success at school, and in life, isn't just about how able you are. Look around your class and aim to celebrate all different types of achievement – social and emotional skills as well as subject-related ones.

Boosting self-esteem and confidence

Some of your students may really lack self-esteem. Their confidence is at rock bottom; perhaps they have a negative image of themselves. They're too shy to speak out in class and they hate being put on the spot. These students often have difficulty forming social relationships with their peers. Some of them can be prone to becoming victims of bullying.

Conversely, some students with low self-esteem mask their inner fears, perhaps by misbehaving or seeming more confident than they really are. When you face a problem with misbehaviour, take care to consider whether this is actually rooted in issues with lack of confidence and low self-esteem.

You can use lots of different approaches to boost your students' self-esteem and to encourage them to have more confidence:

- **Praise, praise, praise again.** Use praise with those students who lack self-esteem. But take care not to praise them in front of the class, because these students can find peer group pressure a concern. Give a quiet word of praise when your shy students speak out. Write some complimentary words on a good piece of work.

- **Take things one step at a time.** Don't expect a very shy, unconfident student to turn overnight into your most outgoing or self-confident child. Confidence boosting's a slow, drip-feed process.

- **Give them an 'opt-out' clause.** Don't put your very shy students on the spot, particularly when speaking out in front of the class. Offer them the option to 'pass' during spoken activities.

- **Find their talents.** Your quietest students may just be hiding a secret talent. Perhaps that quiet boy's a regional chess champion, maybe that shy girl speaks four different languages. You can have difficulty finding out, because these students are unlikely to push themselves forward and tell you all about their talents. Take the time to ask about their interests outside of school and celebrate these as appropriate.

- **Give them volunteer tasks.** When you need someone to hand out some books or tidy a cupboard, don't always plump for the loud boy at the front who's waving his hand in the air. Make sure that you also choose quieter students for these volunteering jobs, perhaps offering the task to an individual rather than always doing 'hands up' for volunteers.

- **Use circle time activities.** These activities are very useful, particularly in a primary school class. The format of a circle takes some of the pressure off the students. Use circle time to focus on areas such as emotional intelligence and social skills. Get the student's peers to boost his confidence by talking about the things he does well.

Just as with building relationships, developing your students' confidence takes time and patience.

Dealing with those who opt out

As a teacher, you want to reach and teach all the students in your class. A child who 'opts out', either by refusing to do any work at all or by sitting back during group tasks and letting others do all the work, can be hugely frustrating. Sometimes the best approach is to ignore these students, especially if their opting out's designed to gain your attention.

You need to differentiate between those who opt out because they *can't* do the work and those who opt out because they *won't*. Adapt the approaches you use according to your understanding of the situation and the student's motives.

For the student who opts out because he can't do the work, you can:

- ✔ Differentiate the work so that the student can gain a sense of success – make sure the task's something he *can* do and he may well *want* to do it.

- ✔ Set small, achievable targets. If the task involves writing and this is a weak area for the student, draw a line a little way down the page and ask the child to write down to this point.

- ✔ Sit with the student for a while to help him get to grips with the task, particularly just after the class has settled to work.

- ✔ See if you can find a peer group partner who works well with the child and can help him gain a sense of success.

For the student who opts out because he *won't* do the work, you should give a straightforward statement about what you want: 'I need you to get on with this work now or unfortunately you'll have to do it at break.' Then walk away. Don't tower over the child waiting for an answer; this only puts him on the spot. A few minutes later, do a subtle check to see whether the student's started the work.

If he hasn't, move in close to give him a second warning and be very specific: 'John, I've explained that you must do this work now. You must complete all five questions properly by the time the bell goes. If you don't, you're staying in at break to finish.' If the student doesn't achieve what you've asked, then follow through on the sanction you've outlined.

During the detention, have a chat with the student about why he has to complete the work you set in class. Check as well that he doesn't have any specific problems understanding what he's meant to do.

Developing Your Pastoral Role

As well as being a classroom practitioner, you also have various pastoral responsibilities linked to your role. You must take care of the 'whole child' – not only focusing on the academic development of each of your students, but also keeping an eye on their personal, social, physical and emotional development as well.

If you teach in a primary school where you're with your class for most or all of each day, the pastoral aspects of your job intermingle with your day-to-day work. If a child's upset after break, you naturally have a quick chat to see what's wrong. If a student seems unusually quiet, you look into the situation to see what's causing the problem.

If you teach in a secondary school, these pastoral aspects of your work are traditionally part of your role as a form tutor. Although not all staff in a secondary school act as form tutors, this job falls to many class teachers. And it's a very rewarding job to do, because you get to know a group of students outside the pressures of the typical classroom situation.

Understanding what your pastoral role is about

In essence, your pastoral role's about caring for the 'whole child'. It's a separate issue to your teaching, although some cross-over may well exist between the two, especially if you're a primary school teacher. You want your students to settle well into school and to do their best during their time there. Your pastoral role's about making sure that this happens.

Getting fully involved in pastoral duties also helps you to grow as a teacher and as a person. It helps you take a real and honest interest in your students, and this is an essential part of being a fully rounded practitioner.

In recent years, various changes have happened to the type of tasks that fall under the teacher's remit. This means that you're no longer routinely expected to do jobs such as chasing up absence. While this means that your pastoral-related workload isn't quite as heavy as in the past, you still need to maintain an overview of any students who are experiencing problems.

You need many skills to do your pastoral role effectively. You have to be able to:

- ✔ Inspire your students to do their best.
- ✔ Boost their morale if they're feeling low.

✔ Listen to their worries and help them find strategies to cope.

✔ Celebrate their successes and share good news around.

✔ Counsel the students when they have fears or worries.

✔ Solve the day-to-day problems they face in school.

✔ Keep an eye on their progress – academic, social, behavioural.

✔ Help them develop social skills and build good relationships.

✔ Take an overview of any behaviour issues and understand how best to deal with them.

✔ Sort out low-level behaviour issues, encouraging proper uniform, punctuality and a good approach to learning.

✔ Deal with equipment issues, such as lost diaries and missing pencil cases.

✔ Support and nurture them to help them succeed, both in the classroom and in their lives beyond the school gates.

On a practical, day-to-day level, your pastoral role involves some or all of the following:

✔ Legal and administrative duties, such as registering your class and collecting in notes to pass on to the office.

✔ Helping your students settle into school and find their way around, especially if you're working with reception-age children or students just moving into secondary school.

✔ Dealing with those minor worries that all students face – things like making friends and getting homework done.

✔ Keeping a check on student diaries or reading logs, and writing in some comments or feedback for parents to see.

✔ Taking an overview of how a child's doing across the various curriculum subjects, or in different classes in a secondary school.

✔ Keeping an eye on those students who are earning lots of sanctions and finding out whether to flag up a specific problem with the special needs staff.

✔ Attending year-group or house meetings with other members of your staff team.

✔ Making sure that an educational welfare officer (EWO) is checking into any unusual patterns of absence.

In addition to all the tasks listed above, you may well be responsible for teaching personal, social and health education (PSHE), and possibly citizenship, to your class or form group. You probably also have to accompany your class or tutor group to assembly.

Sometimes a student comes to you to discuss an issue and asks you to promise that you 'won't tell anyone'. Never make this promise. Say that you're happy to listen, but that you can't promise confidentiality if the issue is serious. Your school handbook should give further advice on your position. If a child divulges an issue of abuse, or a situation around child protection, you're duty bound to pass on the information to the Child Protection Officer (CPO) at your school.

Developing your pastoral role

The day-to-day running of a class or tutor group is obviously your main focus, but you can also spice things up for your students by incorporating some other activities into your time together by developing your pastoral role in many different ways. The more effort you put in, the more you get out of your pastoral role.

As time passes, you'll build a strong bond with your students or tutees. In many secondary schools the form tutor follows his group throughout their time at the school, and this means you may spend several years taking care of your form class.

To develop your pastoral role you can:

- ✔ Arrange for your class or form group to do a presentation or performance in an assembly.

- ✔ Build up a pastoral-based rewards system, for instance giving certificates to the children for their achievements outside class time ('Friend of the Week', 'Most Helpful Student' and so on).

- ✔ Take the time to have informal chats with other members of staff about how your students are progressing.

- ✔ Set targets for each individual student, for both academic achievement and personal development. Some schools now offer staff time out from their normal timetables so that they can meet and have a chat with each of their students in turn.

- ✔ Have a class notice board where the students can post messages, photos and so on.

- ✔ Create some fun competitions for the class. For instance, get each student to bring in a picture of himself as a baby then play 'match the picture to the student'.

- ✔ Send little notes, cards or presents to your students to celebrate key moments in their lives. For example, send each student a birthday card or give them a small bag of sweets at the end of term.

✔ Take your group on a trip somewhere fun and educational.

✔ Create a class event, for instance a party at the end of term.

✔ Give your class some insights into your 'real' self; students love to hear little titbits of information about their teacher or tutor.

Think of lots of ways to bond with your students and to get them to bond with each other. The more imaginative your ideas are, the better. And don't forget to ask your students for their suggestions as well.

Chapter 12

Working as Part of a Team

One of the key skills you need to develop as a teacher is the ability to work as a member of a team. The team at your school or setting includes other teachers and teaching staff, and also support staff and those who perform administrative and premises-related roles. Every single member of staff works towards the successful running of your school, and you need to know how to value and support the job each of them does.

Being a teacher is a fairly solitary occupation. Although you have lots of students in your class, some of the time you may be the only adult in the room. Even if you work regularly with a teaching assistant or have the help of other support staff, you're still the one in overall control of what happens in your lessons. As such, you often become the leader of your own small classroom team. You plan and deliver your lessons, assess the students' work and do all the other jobs that make up your teaching role. But beyond that you may have little contact with the other staff in your school, particularly those who do non-teaching jobs.

The solitary nature of your teaching role can mean that you develop a bit of an independent mentality. But you should watch out for this insular approach; take the trouble to get to know as many members of the school 'team' as you can. Being an active part of the whole team enables you to contribute to the smooth running of your school.

Building a Positive School Ethos

The staff at your school are responsible for working together to build a strong and positive ethos: a 'feeling' within the school that everyone's valued and supported. Your school probably has a motto that reflects the kind of ethos the staff are being asked to help create. In a school where a clear and solid ethos exists, this has an ongoing impact on the success of all the students. But where the ethos is unclear or different staff members apply different approaches, this can damage the overall atmosphere and effectiveness of the school or setting.

As a teacher, you play a key part in developing a positive school ethos. You're in this together with all the people at your school, both staff and students, and indeed their parents as well. The 'ideal' is for everyone at your school to both feel and act like they're members of a bigger community. This sense of community is a key part of creating a highly successful school.

But a school's 'ethos' can be rather hard to pin down. It's not about one specific activity or approach you take – it's about everyone working together to make the place successful and effective.

Various approaches help you and the other staff at your school build up a positive ethos together. The lead clearly comes from your head teacher. But unless every member of staff 'buys into' the same ethos, it doesn't work to its fullest extent.

To build a strong school ethos, you have to do the following:

- ✔ Make sure that everyone understands the kind of expectations the school has – both of its students and of its staff.

- ✔ Achieve consistent responses to behaviour right across the staff.

- ✔ Make sure that you encourage good behaviour *outside* the classroom, as well as inside. In the corridors, in the playground, in the toilets – wherever they are, you must encourage students to behave in a good way.

- ✔ Celebrate all the positive things going on at your school. Of course you celebrate students who achieve good academic results. But you should also celebrate those who contribute to the arts and the sporting life of the school. And also those who contribute by way of their social and emotional skills, or in other non-academic areas.

- ✔ Have an ongoing process of evaluation and professional development, which supports the staff in whatever role they play.

A crucial part of building a positive school ethos is consistency – creating a sense of fairness and equity, and a feeling that the students are safe and secure within the school environment. For instance, in theory a student meeting *any* member of staff in a school should expect a similar kind of approach. If a student isn't wearing a tie, anyone she meets should respond in the same way, dealing with the issue rather than ignoring it. And if a child's in distress, anyone she meets should stop to see what's wrong rather than walking on past.

Fostering a Team Environment

Being part of a team makes you feel more confident that you're supported, and allows you to make the most of your teaching skills within your classroom and beyond. The various staff in your school have different levels of authority within the team, depending on the kind of role they have. Fairly obviously the head teacher's at the top of the tree. But an effective head's also able to make every member of staff feel that they contribute something important to the school.

When you're working as an effective team, the students perceive you as a 'united front'. They see you all sticking together and supporting each other in your day-to-day work. This is likely to encourage students to take on the same kind of attitudes and to be more respectful toward and co-operative with each other.

In my experience, the more challenging the behaviour or attitudes of the students (or managers) within a school, the better the staff typically support each other, as though the staff feel more inclined to stick together when school life is very stressful. You understand what other staff are going through and that means you're best placed to help them out. Watch out that you don't develop a 'them and us' attitude though, and remember to look for all the positive things that the majority of your students do.

Think about the way teachers, and other staff, at your school help each other out. Imagine yourself having a problem – who can you turn to within your school to help you solve this? Do you feel comfortable talking to other staff if you're having difficulties? Or are you more likely to lean on your friends or family outside work?

For effective team work to happen, you need to develop different skills. As well as helping you work as a team member with other staff, many of these skills also contribute to making your classroom practice more effective. If you're aiming to move into a managerial post during your teaching career, these are the kind of skills and talents you need to encourage from the staff under your control.

The first step in generating a sense of team work is to feel that everyone's acting in partnership together, in a co-operative way. Armed with this belief, you can take other steps, outlined in the following sections, to create an effective team atmosphere.

Supporting other team members

You should feel that you can turn to others in your time of need, and that equally they feel comfortable turning to you. For example, you may offer to take a difficult student into your own class for a couple of lessons if you notice a teaching colleague getting really stressed. In turn, she may take in one of your students for a while when you're feeling really under pressure. To support others within your team, you can:

- Offer a sympathetic shoulder for someone to cry on when you notice they seem down or stressed out.

- Make sure that you get to the staffroom at break times, so that you can have a chat with other staff or just switch off from the pressures of work for a while.

- If you're part of a secondary school department, make sure that you build bonds with teachers outside your department rather than sticking in a little clique of your own. You'll get a better sense of perspective above the whole school and you'll also get some great ideas for cross-curricular approaches.

- Share your ideas about effective teaching approaches with others. For instance, you can present a particularly effective lesson activity in a staff meeting.

- Offer to act as a mentor for other, less-experienced staff. For example, you may work with a new teacher as her induction tutor.

- Notice the efforts other people make, and offer a compliment or two when you see something good going on in your school.

- Offer your help with a really difficult student, perhaps giving advice about some strategies that you know work well.

As well as giving support to others, you're also offered support by the other staff at your school. Make sure that you:

- Never feel too proud to accept offers of help – no shame attaches to needing a bit of support. Being able to do something to help you makes others feel good. Accept that offer of support, even if you're not sure you really need it.

✔ Boost the skills of other staff by giving them responsibility. For instance, ask your teaching assistant to help you prepare some lesson activities for your students.

✔ Listen to the advice more experienced staff offer – they've been there and done that, and they have lots of useful tips.

✔ Say 'thank you' when someone helps you out.

Support's a two-way street. Not only do you have to support the other members of staff at your school, you should also welcome the support they can offer you. Again, the little things make the difference. When a feeling of mutual support exists within an organisation, everyone benefits. And the knock-on effect means a more positive feeling and ethos within the school community as a whole.

Taking a consistent approach

You need to know what standards your school expects you to set, and then go ahead and apply those standards as consistently as you possibly can. You (and others) let things slip a little sometimes – you're only human, after all. But most of the time you've got to keep those high expectations and standards in place. And every single member of staff at your school must apply this consistency of expectations. Because if they don't, and a few people let their standards slip, life's that much harder for everyone else.

Some teachers may not be willing to make the effort to chase up homework or insist students put their chewing gum in the bin. But if other teachers at your school don't set these standards, doing so is much harder for you. You look like the hard, nasty one and the other teacher looks like the nice one. As the saying goes, everyone must be 'singing from the same hymn sheet'.

Unless you're a member of senior staff, you can't do an awful lot about those staff who lack consistency. Grit your teeth and keep up your own standards. And remember that, in the long run, your approach will reap rewards in terms of better student work and behaviour.

Understanding different perspectives

If you can see things from other people's point of view, this helps you understand why they behave or react as they do. For example, you make a simple request for the premises staff to set out some chairs in the hall for a lesson in an hour's time. When you arrive at the hall, you find they've failed to do this for you. From your point of view, they 'haven't bothered' and they've mucked up your lesson. But from their point of view, an hour's notice is probably completely inadequate. They do have other tasks to perform, after all!

Valuing everyone's contribution

Being an effective team member means making sure that everyone respects and values each other – both students and staff. You show this through the way you behave towards others and through the attitudes you insist on. You 'big up' the role that supervisory and support staff play to your students. If you see a student being rude to a lunchtime supervisor, you stop and intervene rather than walking away. You present a positive role model to students, sending the message that every single person in your school is both valuable and to be valued.

Try not to assume that yours is the only important or difficult job. Yes, the classroom teachers do probably have one of the more stressful jobs in a school. But everyone else has work to complete too. Find ways to make this process easier for everyone and they're likely to reciprocate when you need support.

Some schools have different expectations about how students should behave toward different members of staff. If a student swears at the head teacher, she's immediately excluded. But when she swears at a classroom teacher or a member of the non-teaching staff, nothing's done. This kind of differentiation of attitudes towards staff is very damaging to a school and to the people who work within it. It sends a very negative message to the students about the value of various different members of the team. Make sure that you don't inadvertently do the same. Show your students that you believe everyone is entitled to exactly the same approach by clamping down on any disrespect.

Trying not to pass on your problems

When you're having a rough day, you can be tempted to pass your own problems on to somebody else – to overlook those little things you may do to make someone else's job a bit better. But doing these little helpful things does, in the long run, probably make your job that little bit easier as well. For instance, you should ensure that you leave your room tidy at the end of each day, with chairs put up on the desks. That way the cleaners can get on with cleaning it, rather than having to lug furniture around first. And as a bonus, you probably find that they do a better job of cleaning your room. If they feel that you're taking their needs into account, they help you out in turn.

Similarly, in a typical school 'fires' – issues and problems that *someone* has to solve – break out throughout the average day. Aim to 'swallow your own smoke'. Don't pass every minor incident of misbehaviour on to a more senior teacher; aim to deal with it yourself instead. This also ensures that your students see you as someone who *can* deal with these problems, and that you're someone who's willing to play your own part within the school team.

Getting the most out of meetings

As a teacher, you find yourself involved in some meetings. Sadly, some of the meetings held in schools are either a poor use of time or a total waste of time. In fact, the most effective meetings are often those where staff break up into groups for discussions, rather than the ones where the head teacher subjects them to 'death by PowerPoint'.

If you're fairly new to teaching and not working in a promoted post, you probably don't find yourself being asked actually to run meetings. But you certainly still find yourself being asked to attend them. Understand how to get the most out of meetings and also how they can help you play a more effective part in your team.

When you attend a meeting, make sure that you:

✔ **Consider what you want to find out.** Think about the kind of questions you want to be answered during the meeting. And if no one deals with these issues, then make a point of raising a hand and posing the questions. But don't overdo this. Don't spend hours quizzing the person holding the meeting about every minor detail. Although this may make you look keen, you lead to the meeting running on longer than strictly necessarily. And that doesn't leave you very popular with the other members of staff in attendance.

✔ **Contribute to policy development.** If your head teacher does ask the staff to give ideas about a new policy or the revamping of an old one, then make sure you put forward your ideas. No point moaning that the behaviour policy 'doesn't work' if you didn't offer your ideas when it was being written.

✔ **Come prepared.** Sometimes you may have to attend a whole-staff meeting in a large school, but you know that much of the time someone's droning on about stuff that isn't of interest or relevance to you. If that's the case, come prepared with some bits and pieces you can be doing while still giving the appearance of listening at the same time. A little bit of sneaky marking, perhaps, or reading through a new syllabus.

And if you do progress up the career ladder, when the time comes for you to host a meeting of your own, why not think about how you can take your own experiences of meetings into account? Make sure that the meetings *you* host are a good use of time. Encourage everyone to contribute in a positive way and to offer solutions rather than problems.

Sharing your ideas and resources

Many teachers waste their time by 'reinventing the wheel'. You may find yourself re-creating resources, or planning lessons, when someone else has already done something similar at a previous time. Be willing to share your stuff, perhaps within your department or across your key stage. By doing this you're playing your part within the team, spreading the 'good stuff' around so that everyone benefits. And by doing this, you should find that others are much more willing to share their own ideas and resources with you.

Rewarding and motivating others

Even if you're not a member of school management, you can still do your bit to help motivate other members of staff. Give a quick positive comment to another teacher when you see her achieving good results with a student. Express delight at the displays in someone else's classroom. Take the time to notice the little things that others do well, and this creates a strong sense of pride and achievement within your school.

Staff helping each other out leads to an atmosphere of team work and partnership. This attitude and approach pass on to the students, who follow the model you set and start to work better and more co-operatively with each other.

Understanding Who's Who in Your Team

The typical school has a whole host of different staff. The following sections identify teaching staff as well as support staff. These lists are by no means exhaustive, but they do cover most of the different kinds of staff working in the typical large secondary school.

In very small schools, some staff probably have to put on various different 'hats', doing many different jobs in addition to their main role. But very large schools have literally hundreds of different staff, all with different jobs and responsibilities. Several different staff may also perform the same role. For instance, you may have several assistant head teachers, each with responsibility for a different area of the school's development; you may have a number of learning mentors supporting students around the school, or a lot of teaching assistants giving support within different classes or departments.

The bigger your school, the harder getting to know all the different staff who work there is. You may find that you have almost no contact with many of the non-teaching support staff, apart from when you need to ask them for a favour. Bear in mind how you feel if someone you hardly know comes up and insists that you do something for them straight away!

In addition, the way staff work varies – some are full-time staff, employed by the local authority; others are on fixed-term contracts, working part time or coming into your school from an outside agency (for instance a supply teacher). Other staff may be working in a freelance capacity or as volunteers who come into your school. Some staff also visit your school from other settings to perform certain key roles, for instance an educational psychologist who works with particularly troubled individuals.

Regardless of whether the number of staff is large or small or somewhere in between, take the trouble to get to know all the staff at your school. Have a quick chat when you pop into the school office to ask for a letter to be typed. Spend a few minutes thanking the premises staff when they've helped you out setting up the hall for a school show. Get some little gifts for the cleaning team who've been working so hard all year to keep your classroom clean. These little moments of kindness all contribute to building up a better and more positive working environment for everyone at the school.

Teaching staff

Different kinds of teaching staff work with students. The following list is written roughly in order of that member of staff's position on the managerial ladder. Typically, the higher up the ladder you go, the fewer staff perform that job, with the head teacher on her own right at the top. You may find:

- ✔ A head teacher or principal
- ✔ Deputy head teachers
- ✔ Assistant head teachers
- ✔ Heads of year or house
- ✔ Deputy heads of year or house
- ✔ Heads of department or faculty
- ✔ Deputy heads of department or faculty
- ✔ Subject co-ordinators
- ✔ Key stage co-ordinators
- ✔ Advanced skills teachers
- ✔ Classroom teachers

Teaching support staff

As well as teaching staff, various support staff focus on helping students. These staff are responsible for supporting both the teachers and the children in their teaching and learning, making sure that everyone's needs are met. The student-based support staff at your school may include:

- ✔ A special needs co-ordinator (SENCo)
- ✔ Other special needs staff

- ✔ Staff working at an in-house student referral unit, a separate centre where students with more specialised needs can go to be supported
- ✔ An educational welfare officer (EWO)
- ✔ A child protection officer (CPO)
- ✔ Educational psychologists (EdPsyc)
- ✔ Librarians, or learning resource centre (LRC) managers
- ✔ Cover supervisors
- ✔ Subject technicians (usually in Science and ICT)
- ✔ Higher-level teaching assistants (HLTAs)
- ✔ Teaching assistants (TAs)
- ✔ Learning mentors
- ✔ Learning support assistants (LSAs)
- ✔ Parent helpers and other volunteers

Non-teaching support staff

Various non-teaching support staff don't have any regular contact with students. These are the people who assist in the smooth day-to-day running of the school. Your non-teaching support staff may include:

- ✔ A school manager
- ✔ Receptionists
- ✔ Office and administrative staff
- ✔ Photocopying technicians
- ✔ A bursar
- ✔ Finance department staff
- ✔ Premises staff, including a caretaker
- ✔ The head's secretary
- ✔ Examinations officers
- ✔ Lunchtime supervisors
- ✔ Cleaners

Unions

The teaching unions have done a great deal over the years to fight for teachers and school staff and to improve your pay and working conditions. Although you don't *have* to join a union, doing so really is a very good idea. A union can help you in many ways: answering queries about pay, offering you low-cost or free training courses, supporting you if things go wrong at school and so on.

A number of different unions exist, and the one you join depends on the kind of teaching post you have and your personal preferences. Getting to know the union representative for each union at your school or college is a good idea. The four main teaching unions are:

✔ **Association of Teachers and Lecturers (ATL):** www.atl.org.uk. The ATL represents 160,000 members, including college lecturers.

✔ **National Association of Schoolmasters Union of Women Teachers (NASUWT):** www.nasuwt.org.uk. The NASUWT is the largest UK-wide teaching union representing teachers and head teachers.

✔ **National Union of Teachers (NUT):** www.teachers.org.uk. Membership of the NUT is open only to fully qualified teachers.

✔ **Professional Association of Teachers (PAT now Voice):** www.voicetheunion.org.uk. Voice represents different kinds of education professionals.

You'll also find unions devoted to particular staff groups (support staff, head teachers and so on), such as the National Association of Head Teachers (NAHT).

Finding other sources of support

As well as the staff within your school offering each other support, you also encounter various agencies outside school who can offer some support. As a hard-pressed teacher you're wise to grab every offer of support with both hands.

You can gain additional support from:

✔ **A teaching union.** Your union can offer you advice on all aspects of your work – from assistance if a student makes a complaint about you to help with the financial or contractual side of your job. Get to know your union representative – she's someone to back you up if ever you need support.

✔ **Your local education authority (LEA).** Some LEAs are better than others at supporting their school staff. Your LEA may organise training sessions for new teachers or give you discounts on local services and in local shops. Take advantage of whatever's on offer.

✔ **Advisory staff.** Many local authorities now employ staff who specialise in various different areas. For instance, these staff may come in to give schools advice on improving behaviour and attendance across schools in the authority, or on the best ways of teaching the Literacy Strategy.

✔ **CPD trainers and training organisations.** These days, continuing professional development for teachers is much talked about. When someone comes into your school to deliver an INSET (in-service training) or to work with your department, grasp the opportunity to ask for advice on the specific issues you face.

✔ **Charities and voluntary bodies.** The Internet offers you a great way to find out about the various charities and other voluntary organisations that offer support and resources to teachers and schools. Whatever your query or problem (teacher stress, materials for teaching a subject, advice on dealing with bullying), lots of people are happy to help.

And because a school's such a key player within the local community, you may also want to ask around some of the local businesses to see what advice, support or materials you can cadge.

Working with Teaching Support Staff

In recent years, teachers have been asked to work more and more with other members of staff in their classrooms. This coalition has both advantages and disadvantages. Of course, having an 'extra pair of hands' is always useful. But the role of the teacher has changed quite a bit. Teachers have gone from being the 'masters of their own domains' to having to share their space with other adults. Adapting your role can cause you various issues and you need to work out how you're going to overcome them.

✔ **Deciding what approaches to use.** If you're used to working alone, then knowing how best to work with support staff can be tricky. Consider what kind of jobs you want your assistant to do and how you can get her using the kind of approaches you prefer with your students. Ask for her input on the kind of things she wants to do, rather than fobbing off all those jobs on her that you don't really fancy doing yourself!

✔ **Overcoming the feeling you're being 'watched'.** Having another adult (or adults) in the room can make you feel rather self-conscious. Although your support staff are probably less qualified than you, you may still feel as though they're passing judgement on what you do. Every teacher makes mistakes in the classroom; some days you feel like you're getting everything wrong. And if you lose your temper with your students or one of your activities is a complete wash-out, you can feel as though your support staff are thinking 'she doesn't know what she's doing'. Keep faith in your professional judgement and don't be too harsh on yourself when you make mistakes. Most support staff understand the pressure you're under. If you feel really awkward, have a quick chat after the lesson to clear the air.

✔ **Finding difficulty getting on together.** Sometimes you have to work with another adult who you don't really like, or who you don't feel has the students' best interests at heart. Remember, you're a professional. Do what you can to build positive relationships, but sometimes you may need to lay down the law with your support staff and insist that they work according to your rules.

To overcome these issues, find ways to get to know your support staff, using the suggestions given in the following section. Build a sense that you're working as a team and this benefits both you and your students.

Getting to know your support staff

The better you know your support staff, the better able you are to make use of their assistance. Of course, finding time to do this within the demands of the typical school day can be hard. But see this as one of your priorities, especially if you're going to be working regularly together.

When you have support staff, find the space early on in your time working together to sit down and have a chat. Aim to make this more of an informal discussion rather than a formalised meeting. Spend a bit of time getting to know each other and this helps you work out how best to utilise the support. During this chat or at other opportunities to talk, find out the following:

✔ **The kind of input they want to make.** Quiz them about the kind of roles they want to take on. While you may not be able to match what you need exactly to their wishes, you certainly benefit from understanding what they prefer to do.

✔ **Their insights about the school or the students.** Often, a teaching assistant or support teacher knows some of the difficult students better than you. She may have been working at the school for several years, while you may be brand new to the place. Ask for her advice on any students or classes where she has some 'insider knowledge'.

As the school year progresses, make sure that you have regular meetings to update everyone on how things are going and ensure that you build a solid team. Encourage your support staff to give you feedback and to feel comfortable about making suggestions or raising any issues.

Making the most of your support staff

Having additional staff within your classroom is great and you want to get the most out of any support you have. Look for ways to develop a sense of partnership between you and your assistants, so that your students see you as a 'team'. Remember, establishing this sense of a strong partnership between you and your support staff takes time.

The way you use any support staff depends on the particular type of role they are there to perform. Some support staff work with individual students who have particular learning or behavioural needs, for instance moving around to different lessons with a student who has autism. Others are there to offer general support under the direction of the teacher. Make sure that you find out what your support staff *expect* you to ask them to do, and what kind of jobs or tasks are included in their job description.

You should apply some general principles no matter what role your support staff are performing:

- ✔ **Offer her strategies and techniques.** As the class teacher, you've been trained in how to use specific techniques to help your students learn and behave. You need to share these with your assistants, particularly if they're new to the post or where they're not trained to a higher level. You may be showing her the best ways to develop a child's writing skills, or giving her advice about how to control the behaviour of a small group.

- ✔ **Ask her for strategies and techniques in return.** While offering advice, be aware too of the need to receive it. For instance, if you're not experienced in dealing with a student who has autism, then the support staff who work regularly with that child are able to give you lots of great tips on how best to meet her needs.

- ✔ **Build up a sense that you're a team.** You need your students to perceive you and your support staff as a partnership. You can find lots of different ways to do this. You need to use language that suggests you're working together – inclusive words such as 'we' and 'us'. You may also want to explain your assistant's role to the class, and be very clear that they should treat her in the same way as they treat you.

- ✔ **Have the same standards for everyone.** You absolutely *must* insist on the same standards for any support staff as you do for yourself, and indeed for the way your students treat each other. Make clear to your students that you expect certain behaviour and attitudes from them, and that these apply just as much to your assistants as they do to you. If a student's rude to a member of support staff, crack down hard and apply exactly the same sanctions as if they're rude to you.

As well as setting these key standards, you can find lots of other ways to make the most of the support you have:

✔ **Plan together.** Try to find time to sit down and work your way through your lessons together. For support staff to know what the objective of the lesson is, and how you're going to achieve it, is very important. Ask your assistant to come up with ideas about how a particular activity may run. If she's going to be working with a low-ability group, she can work out ways to differentiate the main task to better suit their needs and perhaps prepare a separate worksheet for the group. If her main focus is on working with an individual student, she can advise you how well a particular activity suits that child or whether you need to change or adapt it to fit her needs.

✔ **Assess together.** Your assistant needs to know the level of work she should expect from the students. Look at some examples of the children's work together and get your assistant to help you assess these. Show her the targets you're working towards – give her a copy of any official paperwork. Show her samples of student work that match the various strands within the different subjects.

✔ **Give her plenty of responsibility and creative activities to do.** Just as with your students, if you give your assistant lots of responsibility, this helps her to feel valued and also to develop her own skills. Having said that, don't just dump lots of jobs on her – make sure that she wants and welcomes any responsibilities you give her. A teaching assistant, for example, may be the perfect person to take responsibility for putting up the displays in your classroom. Make sure that you incorporate some of these more creative types of job into her role. You probably find that she seizes the opportunity with both hands, and that she does a far better job than you ever can!

✔ **Use her as a 'sounding board'.** Voice your thoughts out loud, using your assistant as a kind of sounding board. You may say something like: 'Aren't they working well together today?' or 'Who do you think deserves a special reward today?' By vocalising what goes on in your head to your assistant, you can help your students see her as a key part of your classroom team.

As time goes on, you develop your own ways of working together. And before long, you wonder how you ever managed without lots of support staff in your classroom.

Exploring useful roles for support staff

In the average modern classroom, particularly at primary level, you may have a couple of different teaching assistants working with you at various times during the week. You may also have the help of some parent volunteers. Knowing how best to make use of all this help can be difficult. You may feel tempted always to get your assistants working with the more challenging or least able students, feeling that this is the best use of their time. While doing this can be very valuable, support staff can support student activities within your classroom in plenty of other ways.

You can ask your support staff or helpers to:

- ✔ Work with the most able students in your class.
- ✔ Sit with an individual who finds staying on task hard, setting targets to keep her on track.
- ✔ Take on some creative tasks within the classroom, for instance acting as 'creative director' for your displays.
- ✔ Contribute some of their skills or talents to a lesson; for example if your teaching assistant speaks French, she can teach some phrases to the class.
- ✔ Take small groups into the playground to hunt for natural materials or to the library to choose some books.
- ✔ Deliver part of a lesson under your supervision, particularly if you're working with a higher-level teaching assistant.

Don't always give your assistant the least able or most disruptive children to work with. Offer a good balance of activities and students, based on what you know she enjoys and on what works best for the lesson.

Getting to Know the Right People

You may be part of a small primary school team of only five or so staff; you may equally be part of a huge secondary school team that has literally hundreds of different members. In either case, some people can smooth your path through your daily work, help you get better results with your students and generally make your life much happier. And others can make life incredibly difficult for you, throwing obstacles in your way at every turn.

The sections below are based on the idea that you should 'know your enemy'. Consider which kinds of people within your school you want to get to know, but be aware too of who you're best to avoid.

Good acquaintances to make

You're wise to get to know certain people at your school. Regardless of your personal feelings about these people, they can do a lot to smooth your path or make your job as a teacher much easier. Of course, you don't want to be fake or phoney about this. Aim to develop the kind of genuine relationships that you also want to build with your students.

You may want to focus your efforts on getting to know:

- **Office staff.** When you need a quick letter typed or the phone number of a parent, a good working relationship with the office staff in your setting is very useful. The role they play in the smooth running of your school is easily overlooked, but they perform a vital 'front-line' service. Be polite and friendly with them, and be respectful about the job they do.

- **Technicians.** Many schools now have a whole team of technicians on the staff – some in Science, others involved with ICT, maybe some in the arts/theatre department. The technicians at your school can be a great help to you, especially when your computer or DVD machine is playing up.

- **The head's secretary.** Grabbing a quick word with the head is that much easier if you've got to know her secretary. In some larger schools, the head's secretary becomes a kind of barrier between the head and all but the most important staff, or the most urgent issues. Get to know her, and she may lower that barrier and let you in when you most need to speak with the head.

- **The premises staff.** Just as with the office staff, the job that the premises staff do within a school is often overlooked. You may assume that the heating always works, that light bulbs always get changed, that seats always get put out and away for assemblies. But behind the scenes, someone (or a group of people) works very hard to ensure that this happens. Make sure you've got a smile and a quick word of praise for your premises staff – say 'thank you' when they do a job for you. And you should find that they reciprocate by smoothing your path when you need something moved/done/repaired.

- **The SENCo.** The special needs staff within your school have access to very valuable information about your students. They can't necessarily share every detail of this with you – some of it's highly confidential. But they can give you some insights into that tricky child or give you a few top tips for handling that aggressive student. Get to know your SENCo and any other special needs staff. Let them know that you appreciate the stresses and strains of their work and that you value their insights.

If you're working in a secondary school and you have a tutor group or teach a lot of classes from that year, building up bonds with the head of year of that year group is very useful. She knows all the ins and outs of the difficult students in that group. She may have a quick word with a challenging child, which makes all the difference to how that student works in your lessons.

Staff you're best to avoid

Within a few weeks of starting work at a school, you're probably able to identify certain characters who don't play their part in the team. These are the people who make everyone's life more difficult. Perhaps they undermine you in subtle ways; maybe they spread a negative atmosphere around the school.

These people aren't necessarily working in particular roles at your school – they may not all be teachers, for instance. Rather, they are particular character 'types' who can make your job more difficult to do. For that reason, I've dealt with some of the types of people you can encounter, ones you should definitely try to avoid, rather than with those who do specific jobs within your school.

Please note that I've tried to make these descriptions humorous rather than totally realistic. Because they're generalisations, they err on the side of being rather stereotyped portrayals. But you're probably able to spot aspects of at least one or two of the staff at your school in the descriptions.

You may come across:

- ✔ **The cynic.** A cynic, or a few cynics, exists at many schools, particularly the larger ones. Often she's someone who's been at the school for a long time and who's become a bit lazy or disillusioned with the job. The cynic takes great pleasure in voicing her negative feelings about the place and the students to anyone who listens. She shrugs off every new initiative or idea, believing instead that she knows everything already and has nothing left to learn. Just a word of warning, though: take care that you don't mix up the *rebels* at your school with the cynics. The rebels have an important role to play. Sometimes a bit of rebellion (particularly when aimed at inefficient senior managers) is entirely justified and a jolly good thing.

- ✔ **The dictator.** The dictator often has a slightly elevated role on the school ladder, perhaps working as a head's secretary or a head of year. But unfortunately, the power's gone to her head. She wants other staff to 'bow down' to her and if they don't, she puts all sorts of barriers in their way. One of the best ways to handle encounters with a dictator is to pretend to kowtow to her, but then just to go on and do things in your own sweet way.

- ✔ **The war monger.** The war mongers in a school have an urge to 'do battle' with others, particularly with students. They take every opportunity to create conflict and confrontation. They believe that only their way is right and that everyone else should fall into line. You may hear the war monger talking about the 'good old days' when students respected their teachers merely because they were in a position of authority. They bitterly resent the fact that they're no longer allowed to use corporal punishment on the students.

✔ **The slob.** The slobs are, as you may expect, the lazy staff in your school. They get others to do all the work and then sit back and try to take the credit. The slob often has an incredibly messy work area. She regularly asks you to help her find those really important papers she lost a week ago. And while you're busy trying to find them, she heads off to make herself a cup of tea.

✔ **The gossip.** These are the people who spread rumours around the school. Often the gossip talks to students about things that really should be kept private or between adults. She may 'let slip' to the children some information you've been trying to keep to yourself. Gossips also try to talk to you about other members of staff in a negative way. These people can poison the atmosphere at a school.

✔ **The snake.** The snake tries to undermine the other staff at every opportunity. She 'tells' on you if you make a mistake or makes your life more difficult in small but telling ways. If you book the computer room for a lesson, you may turn up to find the snake already in there and your booking crossed out on the bookings form. The snake often intends to slither her way quickly up the managerial ladder, without worrying who she squashes on her way. Watch out for this type of person within your senior management team!

As the saying goes, 'It takes all sorts to make a world.' The vast majority of the staff in your school are wonderful, hard-working people. Make the most of the ones who are and appreciate them to the full. And in return, they look out for you in your hour of need.

Chapter 13

Building Bonds with Parents

A great way to help your students get the very best out of their time at school is to build up positive relationships with their parents. You should think of parents as the third point on a triangle – a triangle that includes you, the students and their parents. Your aim is to work together as a team to help each and every child succeed.

Your students spend far more time at home than they do in your lessons. This is especially so in a secondary school, where you may see that student for only an hour or two each week. What happens in the home has a powerful impact on how well the student does while he's at school. By ensuring that you have support and back-up from home, you can boost every student's chances of success.

You've probably realised already that you can gain a good sense of what a student's home environment is like by the way the student behaves and works in school. In a home where reading and books have always been around and seen as something interesting and exciting, a young child turns up at school keen to discover how to read. In a home where aggressive behaviour's the norm, the student may well have learned to react to problems in a confrontational manner.

Remember not to make judgements about a student based on any knowledge you may have about his home background or his circumstances outside school. Many children from very disadvantaged backgrounds go on to great things. Indeed, school's part of the support network that can help this happen. Other students who have everything they want at home can cause you lots of grief in your classroom. They're so used to getting what they want at home that the school environment comes as a bit of a shock.

Have the highest standards and hopes for every child and give every student a 'clean slate' on which to prove what he can achieve. Pre-judging a child isn't fair. And if you have negative expectations of your students, they're likely to live up to these negative judgements.

For ease of reference, in this chapter I use the term 'parents' to describe whoever takes care of the child outside school. Be sensitive to the fact that some of your students may have other people taking care of them: grandparents, older siblings, foster carers and so on. Some may also be 'looked-after' children living in council care. When you're talking about parents with your class, for instance asking the students to bring something in from home, remember to refer to 'your parents or carers' rather than just to 'your parents'.

Understanding Parents

Just as with your students, if you can understand what makes their parents tick you stand a far better chance of getting on well with them. You're also able to gauge the kind of things they may be able to do to support their children outside school. Just like students, parents come in all different types. As a professional, you have to understand and work with every kind of parent, regardless of your personal feelings about them and the way they bring up their children.

Parents don't necessarily know what really goes on at school. In fact, they're often entirely oblivious to the realities of school life, usually for the following two reasons:

- ✔ **Their children don't tell them.** When a parent asks the typical child 'What did you do at school today?' the usual answer's 'Nothing'. Luckily most parents don't believe this, but they can have a tough job actually getting accurate information about what their child does during the school day.

- ✔ **It's a long time since most parents were at school themselves.** Things in education have changed a great deal over that time. Some parents may assume that your school's a bit like theirs was when they were children. Other parents believe every scare story they read in the media. Separating fact from fiction can be hard for them when trying to understand school.

Overcome these issues by finding every way you can to communicate the realities of modern-day schooling to parents. Let them know how your school day runs, how you approach the curriculum, how the school's supporting and helping their child and so on. Open up the lines of communication between the home and the school. Make sure that parents feel happy to ask if they have any questions or concerns, and that they have clearly defined ways in which to do this.

In the 'good old days' some schools maintained discipline through a climate of fear. Other schools 'wrote off' students at an early age, or failed to spot and deal with children who had special needs. Let your parents know how far education's advanced in the years since they were at school. Celebrate the advances that have been made in understanding how children learn and in meeting everyone's needs.

What parents really want from teachers

At this point I want to speak to you as a parent rather than as a teacher. When my son started at primary school, I wasn't sure how best to help support him and his teacher. And that's speaking as someone who spends a lot of time in schools and knows quite a bit about how they work. Now imagine how most parents feel – they're in a position where they have very little idea about the best approaches to take and how they can help the teachers do their very best for their children.

Crossed wires

Sometimes the lines of communication between home and school get crossed. When this happens, parents can misunderstand a situation or get the wrong end of the stick about something that's happened at school.

Sometimes a child may say something innocent about what happened in a lesson, but phrase it so that the parent thinks something awful's taken place. Students can also misunderstand something you've said to them and a passing comment gets blown out of all proportion.

Here's a true story of a time this happened, a classic example of the way in which wires can get crossed between home and school.

A primary school teacher was preparing for a lesson in which the children were going to hold a debate. This debate was going to use the format of a council meeting with local residents. The meeting was to decide whether or not the school field should be sold off to create a car park for a local supermarket.

First thing in the morning, the teacher handed out some very realistic-looking letters to the children about the school and the council's plans to sell off their school field. The lesson itself was going to take place after break. Unfortunately, one of the children in the class fell ill during break time and had to be sent home. And as you've probably guessed, the fake letter ended up going home with him.

I'm sure you can imagine what happened next. An irate parent phoned the school: 'What's all this about you selling off the sports field? It's outrageous!' and so on. For the head teacher to calm him down and explain what was really going on took quite a while.

Not all parents want exactly the same things. What they want depends on their own feelings about what a school should offer, and also on their knowledge of what may best suit their child. Some parents are more worried about their child's academic progress than others are. Those parents with a shy or nervous child obviously want to know that their child feels confident and happy at school. Some parents view school as a kind of babysitting service for older children. Other parents expect you to teach their child skills that they should really learn in the home – even simple things such as using the toilet or eating properly.

Bearing in mind that they have different perspectives, on the whole parents want:

✔ To know that their children are happy at school

✔ To believe that their children are safe at school

✔ To feel that their children can find their way around at school

✔ To believe that their children know who to go to if they're ever worried or in trouble

✔ To know that they can talk to someone if they have any concerns

✔ To feel that their child's going to be treated fairly at school

✔ To be sure that their child doesn't get bullied

✔ To be sure that their child's making progress

✔ To feel that behaviour at the school is good and that any misbehaviour doesn't interfere with their child's work

✔ To believe that the teachers and the school have their child's best interests at heart

And as a teacher, you want exactly the same kind of things as well. The secret is working out how to let the parents *know* that all these things are happening in your classroom and in your school. And to be sure that if they have any concerns, parents feel happy to approach you to talk these through.

Looking for the perfect parent

When you come across a 'perfect parent', you can breathe a huge sigh of relief. Here, at last, is a parent who knows how to support you and the child so that he can get on with his learning. Most parents, although not perfect, have at least some of the assets of the 'perfect parent'. Be proactive about communicating with your parents and you should be able to 'train them up' in some or all of the 'perfect parent' attributes listed below.

The 'perfect parent':

✔ **Has taught his child how to be independent.** With younger children, he's taught the child how to dress himself, how to behave at meal times, how to treat others with respect, how to take turns, how to use the toilet and so on. With older students, this parent has clear boundaries in place in the home and uses effective sanctions when the child steps out of line. He supports the student with his learning, but he doesn't actually *do* the work for the child.

✔ **Has set clear boundaries for behaviour from an early age.** Children need to know at a young age that certain behaviours are desirable or acceptable, and other behaviours aren't. They must also know that they may need to behave in different ways according to the setting. For example, while talking one way with their friends in the playground is okay, they may need to speak in a more formal manner in the classroom. A sad fact is that some children start school with very little idea about what constitutes 'good' behaviour. A lot of damage can be done in those first few years of life – teachers often have to spend a long time repairing this damage. The 'perfect parent' has set clear boundaries and used the same kind of techniques you employ in your classroom to help the child understand how he should behave.

✔ **Has encouraged his child to be creative and to take calculated risks.** Having talked about 'good' behaviour, you don't want little robots or 'Stepford children' in your class. That's boring! You want children who are willing to push themselves and use their imaginations. You want them to understand that being brave is good and that sometimes they need to stand up for what they believe in. Your 'perfect parent' has managed to instigate a sense of creativity and hopefully a little bit of subversion in his child. A few rebels in a class makes for a good mix!

✔ **Doesn't allow too many distractions in the home.** As you can imagine, this child doesn't have a television in his bedroom and he doesn't spend hours playing computer games every evening. The 'perfect parent' creates a good balance of things to do at home – from a walk in the park, to a wet Sunday afternoon spent cooking, to time spent sitting and playing with some toys together. He understands that children need to know how to focus on one activity for a sustained period of time, rather than being sat in front of the 'electronic babysitter' (the television) for hours on end, day after day.

✔ **Isn't a 'helicopter' parent either.** At the same time, this parent doesn't force the student to spend hours involved in every out-of-school activity he can think of. He gives his child some time just to be himself, to sit and slob out when he's tired, rather than spending every spare hour doing hobbies and activities. The perfect parent understands that children need time to themselves and that too many formal activities can lead to stress.

✔ **Encourages a sense of respect at home.** The 'perfect parent' chats with his child regularly, using a wide and varied vocabulary. He interacts with his child in a way that demonstrates respect. He understands that he needs to present a model of appropriate behaviour for his child. He tries to find an opportunity to sit down for meals together with his family. He encourages the child to show respect for everyone and everything.

✔ **Understands how best to support his child at home.** The 'perfect parent' understands the importance of sitting down and reading regularly to the younger child, and with the older child as he learns to read by himself. With the older student, this parent understands the need to give his child space to work, as well as the importance of setting clear targets and sticking to deadlines.

✔ **Understands how best to support you at school.** This parent knows that sometimes he's best stepping in and having a word with the teacher, for instance if the child expresses concerns about an issue at school. But he also knows when he's better standing back and letting you get on with doing your job. He finds a good balance between the two.

✔ **Allows the child to make his own mistakes.** This parent understands that sometimes young people need to learn from their own mistakes. He doesn't try to avoid every difficult or risky situation for his child, wrapping him up in cotton wool. He knows that to get on well in life people have got to learn from their experiences, both the good and the bad ones.

Of course, these ideas are only my opinion of what makes a perfect parent. You may disagree with some of what I've said, especially if you're a parent yourself. And if I'm honest, the 'electronic babysitter' makes quite a regular appearance in my own home. You probably also have many more ideas of your own that you can add to the list.

Working with the difficult or indifferent parent

Some parents make life difficult for you, and for their children. They may not present a role model for the child about how adults should behave; they may push their child too hard to achieve and put him under a lot of stress outside school. Poor parenting tends to be a vicious cycle. The parent may not have had appropriate role models when he was a child, and subsequently he finds difficulty being a role model for his child in turn. Some parents also lack the kind of support network that they need for effective parenting. In these days where people tend to move around the country for work, some of your parents may not have any family in the local area.

Some parents are 'difficult' not because they don't care, but because they care too much. These are the parents who question your every move as a teacher. The ones who complain that you're not stretching their child or who kick up a stink if he doesn't get the results they feel he should be achieving. These parents may insist that you should put the student up to a higher class when this isn't appropriate. They may also want you to set extra work or to spend additional time working with their child.

Aim to treat all parents equally, just as you do your students. Listen to their feelings and comments, but stick to the approaches you know are going to work best. Tread carefully when dealing with the difficult or indifferent parent, to protect yourself and the child as well.

You should:

- **Do your homework.** Before you make contact with a difficult parent, look into the situation more fully. This is especially important if you're going to say something negative about the child. Consult with your special needs staff or line manager to check whether a phone call home's appropriate or not. Make sure that you don't put the child at any risk by getting in touch with the home.

- **See things from their perspective.** Try to see things as this parent sees them, particularly concerning the world of education. Be conscious that this parent may have had a bad relationship with his teachers in his own school days. He may feel very negative about his whole experience of education; perhaps he left school early with few qualifications. He may not care about school or feel that working hard and behaving well for teachers is important. This colours the way he interacts with you and the kind of support he can offer you and his child.

- **Aim for a sense of empathy.** Some parents have very low expectations of what their child can achieve. Perhaps the parent has a low sense of self-worth and very low self-esteem, which he passes on to his child. If you can learn to empathise with this kind of parent, this helps you understand the student and why he behaves as he does.

- **Watch how you phrase things.** Sometimes you may need to explain to a difficult parent that the student has behaved in a completely inappropriate or unacceptable way. The parent can perceive this as an attack on him. He sees the child's behaviour as a reflection of his own skill (or lack of skill) as a parent. Take care how you approach negative subjects with a difficult parent. Think carefully about how much impact your criticisms are actually going to have before you let rip. Make sure that taking up an issue with these parents is worthwhile. Look for ways to say something positive alongside any negative comments.

When the time comes for formal communication, for instance reports or parents' evenings, you're probably keen to meet the parents of your most difficult students. Sadly, often the parents you most need to 'get to' don't bother to read the report you've written or actually turn up to a parents' meeting. And if they do turn up to the meeting, they may become confrontational or aggressive. See 'Handling the parents' meeting', later in this chapter, for more information about how to deal with this.

Imagine how a parent feels when receiving bad news about something his child's done at school. Really picture yourself, perhaps receiving a phone call from a teacher complaining about your child, or getting a letter from the deputy head outlining details of a serious incident. How does this make you feel? How do you react? What kind of things do you say in response? Bear in mind that your most challenging students probably get many home–school contacts that are all about negative things.

Now see yourself getting a 'good' phone call from your child's teacher. He's telling you about something great that happened that day at school, so great that he made the effort to call you. I'm sure you can feel yourself bursting with pride. Make sure that you focus on sending good news home as well as bad.

Getting to Know Parents

As well as getting to know your students, you should aim to build bonds with their parents too. This helps you to support your children, in terms of both their work and their personal development. Parents are the ones who know most about their own children – what their strengths and weaknesses are, what they love most, what makes them tick. Parents also spend a lot of time with their children outside school. Get to know them, so that you can get them involved in their children's work.

You need to be realistic about the kind of relationships you can build with parents. If you're teaching a primary class, you should be able get to know all the parents fairly quickly and you probably spend quite a bit of time communicating with them. But if you're teaching many different secondary school classes, or if you're working with older students at sixth-form level or beyond, getting to know every single parent in detail is hard.

You benefit by getting to know parents better. Doing this means that you can:

✔ Gain a sense of where each student comes from and the factors that go together to make up each individual child.

✔ Show your students that their parents *do* find out about what goes on at school. Often children assume they can get away with stuff at school that home may frown on because their parents don't ever find out about it.

✔ Tell them the best ways to support their children at home, whether by reading with their child each night or helping to get students to set and meet targets for doing homework or coursework.

✔ Find out more about the kinds of interests and hobbies your students have and think of ways to incorporate these into your lessons.

✔ Build a sense of community within your school. Develop the sense that a successful school gets everyone working together and sharing the same ethos.

By understanding more about parents, you discover more about what makes your children work and behave the way they do. And these insights help you use the best possible approaches in dealing with your children.

Many schools now build home–school communication through the use of reading or homework diaries. Schools ask parents to read and sign these diaries, perhaps daily in the primary school and weekly in the secondary school, which give parents a bit more insight into what's going on at school.

Building lines of communication

If you're going to do the best for your students and get to know their parents a bit better, you need to open up the lines of communication. You can build those vital lines of communication with parents in many ways. Some of the lines of communication you build are as an individual class teacher; others are methods that your school puts in place.

You may be far more tempted to make the effort to contact a student's home when that student's done something really awful in one of your lessons. Perhaps you throw out the threat of a phone call home if the student doesn't behave, and once you've done that you know that you must go through with what you've threatened. Unfortunately this sets up the very kind of negative relationship that you're working so hard to avoid. Make sure that the majority of your school/home contacts are for positive reasons. Phone home to say something *good* about your students as well as when you have to report something bad. Build up a good relationship with parents, and they're better placed to withstand the times you do have to complain about their child.

Use different ways to make contacts with your students' homes. You can:

✔ **Have an informal chat.** You're more likely to do this if you're working at the lower end of the primary school. You probably encounter many of the parents when they drop their children off at school or pick them up at the end of the day. This means that grabbing a parent for a quick word's fairly straightforward. In secondary schools these informal chats only tend to happen at school events, for instance at a fair or after a drama production.

✔ **Write a letter home.** Most schools now have a variety of standard letters that you can send to your students' homes. Get hold of some copies of these letters and make use of them when you need to contact parents. Watch out, though! Most of these letters are designed to deal with the more negative aspects of a child's behaviour or work. The fact that they are standard letters can also make them feel rather impersonal – they appear to come from the school, rather than from the individual teacher.

✔ **Send a postcard home.** Rather than an impersonal letter, you may find that sending some postcards home to your students' parents works far better. You can write a quick positive postcard about a student during a lesson, offering this as part of your system of rewards. Many schools are now using this approach and some have even got the students to design their own cards, as a way of increasing their sense of ownership. See 'Getting parents involved', later in this chapter, for an additional idea to make this approach work even better.

✔ **Make a phone call to the home.** This is a particularly useful style of communication because it's very direct, immediate and personal. Remember to offer 'good' phone calls home to your students, especially where you know that the parents really appreciate this. While you're on the phone, you can chat with the parent about some targets for future improvements or some ways in which he can support his child at home.

✔ **Send samples of work home.** Parents love to see examples of what their children are doing in school. And most students love to show off what they've done in class. Pick out some great bits of work to send home, perhaps adding a little comment about the work and why you feel it's so good.

✔ **Send rewards home.** Pop a little badge or sticker on a student's jumper to reward him. The parents should then hopefully ask the child about how he earned the reward. Bigger rewards, such as fridge magnets, could go home for longer-term improvements.

✔ **Use student diaries or reading logs.** You can use diaries to write little notes home, for instance highlighting a lesson where a student did something really great or talking about the kind of rewards a student's earned. Reading logs or diaries offer a great way to build up a 'conversation' with a parent. Make your comments quite informal and relaxed, rather than sounding too like a teacher.

✔ **Create a weekly, monthly or half-term newsletter.** Most schools now have a regular newsletter that goes home to parents from the office or the head teacher. But this tends to focus on the administrative details of running the school or advises parents about forthcoming events. In addition to your school newsletter, you may also like to create your own little newsletter, telling parents about all the exciting things that have been going on in your lessons.

Getting parents involved

The more involved your parents feel in what's going on at school, the better. Of course, some parents are happy to volunteer to come and help out in your classroom. You can find some more thoughts about how this can work in this section.

Try this great idea, which I nicked from a teacher I met (if you have a great idea, make sure you pass it around to the other teachers at your school). The fantastic thing about this approach is that it ensures you remember to touch base in a positive way with the parent of every single student in your class. By using this approach, you avoid a situation where you 'overlook' some of the quieter students – the ones who just get on with their work anyway and who can tend to miss out on the best rewards. Here's how it works:

1. **When you first meet your class, hand out a set of postcards, one for each child, and ask the students to write their parents' names and address on one side of the postcard.**

2. **Collect the cards back in and keep them safely somewhere (in your drawer, in a cupboard).**

   Make sure that the students see you putting them away, so that they know where they are and they can remind you about them.

3. **Explain to the class that your aim is to send a postcard home with a positive message about each and every student in the class.**

   Set some kind of time limit for this, for instance over the course of a half or full term, or even across the entire school year.

4. **During your lessons, work your way through the postcards in your drawer, writing home about all the wonderful things your students are doing in their lessons.**

   You may like to set yourself a target of three postcards per lesson, or you can use them as and when the class is behaving and working well.

One of the great things about using postcards is that parents are likely to stick them up on a notice board, or on the fridge with a magnet. The postcard then acts as a constant reminder of something positive about the student, about the school, and about you! Letters, on the other hand, probably make their way fairly quickly into the recycling pile.

Here are some other ways to get your parents involved:

✔ **Ask for support from home.** Of course you want to think that parents are willing to help their children at home. But parents do really appreciate you being *specific* about the kind of things they can do at home to support their children's work. In a primary school you can do this via book bags and reading diaries, encouraging parents to read regularly with their children. You may send home some sticky notes, so that parents can send in little examples of things a child's said or done at home. You can add these sticky notes to a student's profile as examples of the kind of skills he's developed over the course of the year.

✔ **Set tasks that involve the home as well as the school.** You can find lots of opportunities to get your students doing an activity that needs input from the home. For instance, the students may ask their families for the relevant details they need to create a family tree. Or they can interview their parents about their own time at school.

✔ **Get your students to bring in something from home.** Students love to bring things into school from home – this helps personalise the whole classroom experience for them. You can ask your students to bring in ideas, resources, objects, information and so on. For example, they can bring in some old toys for a project, or a photo of their house for some work on 'where people live'. Again, this encourages parents to become more involved in their children's education.

As well as things you can do as an individual teacher, your school or setting can create stronger links with parents in plenty of ways. If your school may benefit from developing better bonds with parents, why not suggest some of these ideas at your next staff meeting? Your school can:

✔ Set up a breakfast club, and invite the parents to come along to eat with their children and socialise with the other parents.

✔ Create an after-school homework club and ask parents to come along. This may be especially helpful in encouraging parents to support their children, and in showing them how to do this effectively. Homework clubs are also very useful for children who may not have access to resources such as computers or coloured pens (or even just a quiet space) at home.

✔ Make a home/school contract about the kind of behaviour you expect while the child's at school. Ask that parents, students and teachers read this and sign up to it. Refer back to this contract if problems do arise with a student.

✔ Hold informal events at school during the year and invite parents to attend these. You can get your class to do a little show at the end of a half term, or have a little party for your class at the end of the year.

✔ Host more formal events that parents can attend, such as school shows, music recitals, information evenings and award assemblies or ceremonies. Find lots of ways to celebrate the achievements of your students.

✔ Have plenty of seasonal celebrations during the year, when the parents can come in and celebrate with their children. The events you host may include a harvest festival, a Christmas party or a summer fair.

✔ Get parent volunteers into school to help in class or to work with individual readers. (See 'Using parent volunteers', later in this chapter, for more thoughts about the best approaches for doing this.)

✔ Ask parents with specific expertise to come in and share their talents with the class. For instance, a parent who speaks Arabic can do some lunchtime sessions with the children; a parent who works as a vet can come in and talk to the students about what this career involves and the kind of qualifications they need to get.

✔ Encourage parents to get involved with a friends' association or a parent–teacher group (PTA). This group can organise events such as barn dances, bingo nights, barbecues and so on.

Get your parents fully involved with the school, so they have a sense of your school being a vital part of your local community.

Using parent volunteers

Trying to get some parents to come into your school is a great idea, to help out with individuals or even to do some work with the whole class. You may find this especially useful with the lower primary age range, where the subject knowledge or skills required to work with the children are fairly low level. At primary level you also see the parents more regularly and this means that organising volunteers is often easier.

At secondary school level, your parent volunteers can come in to do a presentation to the class about a particular career path, or to share their skills or interests with the students. Encourage your students to ask at home about whether their parents are willing to come in and help out. Think of different jobs parents can do or roles they can take on to help you.

They can:

✔ Come in to help individual children with their reading.

✔ Take small groups of children to the library to help them choose books.

✔ Get involved with putting up some displays.

✔ Help out with some jobs that need doing outside the classroom, for instance painting a mural in the school changing rooms.

✔ Come along on a trip to help you out and to boost the adult-to-child ratio.

✔ Join in with 'crowd control' at a school event.

✔ Give a presentation to the class, for instance a parent who's a dentist can talk about tooth care.

✔ Sew some costumes for your school play.

Not only do you get the benefit of additional adults helping you with the children, you can also use the opportunity to build up bonds with parents.

Any volunteers you use in school need to have a police check, just as all staff do who are working in close contact with the children. Your school office should be able to organise this for you.

If you're getting parents in to work with your children, make sure that you:

✔ Take them through the best strategies to use. For instance, if the parent's helping readers, advise him to run a finger under the words in a book and explain how to help the children to sound out words.

✔ Give a few general tips about managing behaviour and about the kind of expectations you have in your classroom.

✔ Explain some of the best approaches for encouraging students and outline the kind of rewards they may offer.

✔ Give your support and back-up if they have any problems – set the same standards for volunteers as you expect for all school staff.

✔ Let parent volunteers know where the toilets and staffroom are and invite them along for a cup of coffee at break times.

Although they're rare, some parents prove to be more trouble than they're worth or don't really 'click' with the students. Be a little circumspect about the kind of parents you invite into your classroom – you don't want to end up giving yourself additional work and stress.

Reporting to Parents

As part of your role as a teacher, you need to make several formal contacts with the home over the course of the school year: you write reports and attend parents' meetings. These formal contacts are a key feature in your calendar. When you report to parents, you need to:

✔ Let them know how their child's progressing at school.

✔ Relate the student's progress to key statutory targets.

✔ Set targets for future improvement and progress.

✔ Let them know about any problems or issues that have arisen.

✔ Talk together about ways to solve these problems.

✔ Tell them about all the great things their child's been doing.

✔ Ensure that you answer any questions the parents may have.

If you're new to teaching, you may feel a bit nervous about these formal teacher/parent contacts. But don't worry, you quickly get the hang of them.

Handling the parents' meeting

Depending on the approach your school or setting takes, you may be asked to meet with parents in the evening after school, or you may be given time during the day when this happens. These daytime appointments make life easier for you as a teacher, but they do mean that some working parents find difficulty in attending.

Most of the time, parents' meetings run smoothly. You gain a sense of satisfaction from being able to communicate with the parents; they gain a better sense of how their children are doing at school and how they can support their work in the future. Occasionally, you do experience some problems at parents' meetings. The advice and strategies in this section help you avoid some of the main pitfalls and deal with any problematic situations that arise.

Successful parents' meetings

In a successful parents' meeting, you have a chance to get to know the parents a bit, to pass on any good or bad news about how their child's doing and also to check whether they have any questions or concerns. Often you don't have more than five or ten minutes to do all this, so think ahead about the approach you're going to take.

 If you teach a non-core subject at secondary level – Drama, Music, Religious Education and so on – you may be responsible for teaching hundreds of different students. Realistically, you're not going to get to talk with a hundred or more parents at one parents' meeting. When you make appointments with your students, encourage them only to book a time with you if they really want their parents to see you, or if their parents have any specific concerns.

Your school should have an appointments system, where you, the students or their parents book a specific time slot. Be conscious that some parents may be late, but try not to keep anyone waiting. If a parent wants a longer consultation, ask them to make an appointment for another time.

To ensure a successful parents' meeting, before the event make sure that you:

- ✔ **Present yourself smartly.** By the end of a school day you're probably feeling a bit jaded. Bring in a clean, smart suit or another fairly formal outfit so that you feel fresh and uncrumpled for the meeting. In some subjects you may normally be quite relaxed with your clothing (Art or PE, for instance). Dressing more formally for this event's a good idea.

- ✔ **Get yourself in the right frame of mind.** For evening meetings, make sure that you have a little bit of time to yourself before the event begins. Relax somewhere quiet; have a cup of tea and something to eat.

- ✔ **Stick to appointment times.** Try your hardest to stick to pre-agreed appointment times. Parents do tend to get irritated if they've booked a particular slot and the teacher's still chatting with another parent ten minutes later. You need to be fairly assertive about keeping to times.

- ✔ **Consider what you're going to say to parents.** Think about the kind of areas you want to cover. Comment on the student's behaviour and attitude as well as on their work.

Some teachers like to show a child's work to parents. This can work well at primary level, but is trickier to do in a secondary school. You don't want to end up sorting through piles of books to find the right one. Far better to talk naturally about your own impressions of the student.

Your first parents' meeting of the year may fall quite early in the first term. If you're teaching lots of different students, you may not have 'got' all the names yet or you may feel that you don't have much to say about each child. Plan ahead for this eventuality, checking on the names of any students you don't yet know. You don't do any harm by being honest with parents and admitting that you've only taught their child a handful of times.

Here's a suggested format for a typical conversation with parents:

- ✔ Stand up and shake hands as you introduce yourself and don't forget to smile.

- ✔ Identify whose parent this is. You find this easier if the child's turned up with his parents or if you have a small class.

- ✔ Give a brief summary of how the student's been doing in class. Cover his approach to work and also his behaviour and attitude to learning.

Aim to frame your comments in a positive way – this isn't the time to get revenge on that challenging student. For example, 'He does find keeping quiet a bit of a challenge' is much better than 'He's always chatting, he just won't shut up.'

✔ Aim to set some targets with the parents for ways for the student to improve his approach or work in the future.

✔ Ask the parents whether they have any questions or concerns.

✔ To bring the conversation to a close, stand up and shake hands again.

✔ Let the parents know that they should feel free to contact you if anything arises in the future.

Keep a close eye on your watch so you don't run over time. By doing this you keep the parents happy, and you also get to go home on time.

Difficult parents' meetings

Sometimes you come across a parent who starts to become difficult or aggressive at a parents' meeting. Perhaps he accuses you of 'picking on' his child; maybe he says that you're not doing your job properly. This isn't the time for an in-depth discussion, nor should you put up with being treated in an aggressive manner.

If your school hosts the parents' meetings in the hall or other large space, plenty of more senior teachers are around to deal with any difficult parents. Sometimes, though, your school asks you to host your parents' meetings in your own classroom. Maybe you feel nervous about how parents may behave, because of a prior experience with them or because you're new to teaching. If that's the case for you:

✔ Make sure that you keep your classroom door wedged open while the parents' meetings take place.

✔ Ask that a more senior member of staff drops in on you from time to time to see how you're getting on.

✔ Identify any parents who may cause trouble and let senior staff have a note of the times these parents are meant to be arriving.

If a parent does seem to be angling for trouble:

✔ Use the verbal and non-verbal skills you employ in your classroom to calm the situation down (see Chapters 3 and 10 for more on this).

✔ Don't feel that you have to deal with the problem right now, or on your own.

✔ Defer the parent to a more appropriate date or time, asking that he makes an appointment to meet with you and a senior teacher.

✔ If you're really worried, send quickly for help, or walk away.

For more information on dealing with challenging situations, see Chapter 10. Many of the techniques discussed in that chapter for handling difficult students also prove useful for dealing with confrontational parents.

Writing effective reports

Reports are one of the key formal methods you have for making contact with the home. If you get them right, you help the parents understand how their child's progressing at school. Reports also give you a chance to show what kind of teacher you are – professional, caring, thorough and so on.

Here are some general tips to help you get the best out of report writing. When you're writing reports, make sure that you:

- Start well ahead of time – report writing can take much longer than you may imagine.

- Make sure that you *finish* on time too – reports tend to be done to a fixed schedule. You have a date in the calendar when parents expect to receive them. Don't be the one holding up the process.

- Use a computer if you possibly can – this makes report writing much quicker, and also means that making corrections is easier. By using a computer you can create some 'standard' formats – comments for your weakest, average and most able students, which you can copy. Add in at least a couple of personalised comments for each child.

- Stick exactly to the format your school asks you to use, otherwise you only end up having to re-do reports.

  Ask for advice on the little details – for instance, what colour pen should you use to write or sign reports? Check as well whether you're okay to refer to students by their chosen rather than their given names. For example, can you refer to a student called 'Jonathan' by the abbreviated name 'Jon' in the body of the report, if that's what he likes to be called in class?

- Make sure that you know which skill or subject areas you're meant to cover. If you're a secondary school teacher, make sure that you refer to the various areas of your curriculum subject. At primary level, ensure that you cover Literacy, Maths and Science targets, as well as commenting on a student's achievement in the non-core subjects if you have space.

- Check your reports carefully before you pass them on up the line. Be the first line of defence against incorrect or poorly spelt reports getting sent home. Remember that those more senior staff who check your reports have lots and lots of reports to look at. Minor errors can easily slip through the net.

Some schools now have an internal system for writing reports over the school intranet. You may find this helpful, although it does mean that you have to complete your report writing at school rather than at home.

Writing the actual report

This section gives detailed advice on how to actually write your reports. You need to adapt this advice according to the age of the students you teach, and also according to how your school asks you to present and format your reports. You should:

- ✔ Start your reports with a general sentence about how the student's been progressing, then go into more detail about specific skill areas, subjects and so on.

- ✔ Give at least a couple of really personalised comments, especially if your school uses a bank of computerised comments to cover subject-related areas.

- ✔ Use a formal style, but avoid overly technical terminology. Watch out that you don't put in educational or subject-related terms that the parents may not understand.

- ✔ Bear in mind the audience for your reports – the parents, of course. Speak to that audience in a way that they understand, and in a way that helps them get a better sense of what you're like as a teacher.

   While I normally believe in straight talking, for reports you've got to practise the art of euphemism. Aim to phrase your comments in a positive way, to ensure that you don't put off those children you've struggled so hard to motivate.

- ✔ Make sure your comments sound as though you know who the student is, and that you have a positive relationship with him. This can be tricky at secondary level, when you may not actually know every child in great detail.

   If you're not sure who a student is, check in your last few lessons before writing reports. Perhaps the worst error of all is to get the wrong gender for one of your students. While this sounds highly improbable, I've seen it done with some unisex-sounding names.

- ✔ Take great care with spelling, grammar and so on. The report's a formal communication with the home; it looks very unprofessional if you make any mistakes. And make sure that you spell every student's name correctly and add in any accents on the students' names as well. Refer to your class lists or your register, and double check if you're not sure. If you're writing your reports on a computer, you may need to scroll through the bank of symbols to find the relevant letter/accent combination.

- ✔ Give comments on a whole range of areas of achievement. You obviously want to comment on the kind of skills and levels the student's achieved within the subjects. Make sure that you refer to the student's behaviour, general attitude, ability to work co-operatively and so on.

✔ Set some targets for future progress – talk about those areas you want the student to work on and be clear about how he can do this.

✔ Make sure that you don't let your emotions become apparent in the way you write the report. Put your 'professional' hat on, and avoid writing reports about students who irritate you when you're in a bad mood.

Leave yourself plenty of time for writing reports. Writing each report takes a while, and you also need to proof read them after they're done. You probably have to pass your sets of reports on to a more senior teacher for checking before they're sent home.

Delivering the reports

If possible, aim to talk through the reports with each student. Some schools give their teachers an opportunity to do this within the school day. If you can find the time to go through the report in more detail with each individual, this ensures that they actually contribute to a student's future achievement.

Make sure that the reports you write actually get to their intended targets – the parents. Many schools get the students to take their reports home. Unfortunately, if the student knows he's going to get a 'bad' report, he may choose to 'lose' that report somewhere along the way. For those students who may do this, you may be better posting the report home instead.

Do be aware of the potential for negative reactions from the home, particularly when you're reporting on a student who isn't doing well or whose behaviour's a concern. Make sure that you don't subconsciously see reports as a way to get your own back on those students who are always messing you around. Be conscious of the kind of response that your most challenging students may get when they take the report home.

Part V
Succeeding Beyond the Classroom

'Don't worry about the bill. I do special rates for teachers.'

In this part . . .

Your job as a teacher doesn't stop at the classroom door. You've got lots of other stuff to do as well, not least a mountain of paper to climb. The secret's to make sure that all this non-classroom stuff doesn't interfere with your ability to teach. Rather, you want it to add to, and build on, the work you do with your students.

Find out in this section how to cope with your workload, why getting involved in extra-curricular activities is such a good idea and how you can reflect on and improve your teaching skills.

Chapter 14

Climbing the Paper Mountain

. . . .

In This Chapter

▶ Learning how to handle your administrative load with the minimum of stress

▶ Understanding which paperwork is important and what to do with the bits that aren't

▶ Finding the most effective way of filing your paperwork

. . . .

*A*s a teacher, you have a mountain to climb. You may think the 'mountain' is the job of getting to know, teaching and managing your classes. But that's a small hill in comparison to the paper mountain you have to conquer. Teaching comes with a whole multitude of non-teaching demands. Recent changes to the admin you have to do mean your workload is somewhat smaller than it used to be. But don't underestimate how long jobs such as writing reports, filling out forms and so on actually take.

Dealing with Paperwork

I can remember being hugely excited the first time I got my 'own' pigeonhole. My name was on it, in lovely bold writing, and the empty box was just waiting to be filled. But before too long I realised that my initial excitement was misplaced. By the end of the day my pigeonhole was stuffed with miscellaneous bits and bobs of paper. And at that moment I realised that paperwork was going to be one of the more uninspiring aspects of my job. By the end of my first term as a teacher, I understood that many of the bits of paper I received were either pointless, unnecessary or a criminal waste of trees.

In addition to the useless notes, of course you also get some bits of paper that are important, vital and entirely justified. Class lists, for instance, or forms to assess a child's special needs. Similarly, reports to parents are a key part of a school's programme of annual assessment. The secret is to work out which bits of paper are vital, and which ones aren't.

Determining what's essential and what's not

Many different bits of paper pass through your hands over the course of a school year. Take a look at the following examples and put a tick beside any of them that you think are urgent, essential or important to keep for future reference:

❑ Lesson plans

❑ Schemes of work

❑ Agendas for meetings

❑ Information about staff training days

❑ Copies of school documents and policies

❑ Draft outlines of proposed new policies

❑ A copy of the school handbook

❑ A copy of the school prospectus

❑ A copy of your departmental handbook

❑ Details of courses and other continuing professional development (CPD) information

❑ Class lists

❑ Timetables

❑ Individual education plans (IEPs) for students who have special needs

❑ Other information about special educational needs

❑ Forms asking you to assess a student

❑ Forms asking you for feedback on a student

❑ 'On report' forms to fill out, for students who have behavioural issues

❑ Copies of reports you've written to check or amend

❑ Adverts and marketing for new books, resources, courses etc.

I stop there, but you can probably list at least ten more pieces of paper that you've received in the last month. To my mind, an experienced teacher can manage without quite a few of the items on my list. Newer teachers may appreciate their own copy of some, for instance the school handbook, for reference. But with many of these items, you'll find several copies kept else-where in your school that you could read.

To determine what's urgent, essential or important to keep, ask yourself these things:

- ✔ **Do I need this information to perform my daily activities?** Some things – like course descriptions or esoteric school policies – are important to scan but *not* important to have at your fingertips. These are non-essential and can safely go.

- ✔ **Is there a copy somewhere else I can use for reference?** Schools are full of documents that are replicated elsewhere. If your department has a centralised copy of that handbook, refer to that rather than hanging onto your own.

- ✔ **Could I read it quickly and then get rid of it?** When you receive an agenda for a meeting, have a quick scan through to see what it says, then pop it in the recycling bin. You're going to be *at* the meeting anyway so you can always make a few notes at that time if you really must.

- ✔ **Is it even aimed at me?** Many bits of paper in a school are really the preserve of more senior staff, but copies get circulated to all and sundry, 'just in case'. Dump anything that doesn't directly relate to you. Similarly, I'm sure your school prospectus is beautiful, but essentially it's a marketing exercise for the parents and not for the staff. Pass it back to Reception, so it can go to its intended audience.

Look at the preceding list again, this time asking yourself the same questions. What do you think now about what is and isn't essential?

Bin it, deal with it, pass it on: The three rules for managing paperwork

Early on in my career, I realised that the secret to dealing with paperwork is to make sure that you handle each piece of paperwork as few times as possible. Every time you look at a piece of paper and think 'I can deal with that later', you waste a little bit more of your time. Rather than putting it to one side for another time, you should try to make an instant decision about each piece of paper. My three rules for dealing with paperwork help you do just that.

Now, I must admit that I don't always stick to my rules, but they offer a great starting point for keeping on top of your admin load. You need to be firm with yourself about applying these rules, but if you can use them most of the time, they help you keep yourself organised.

To follow the three rules, take each piece of paper and decide immediately whether you should bin it, deal with it or pass it on. Any papers that you aren't able to bin, deal with or pass on fall into two categories: those for your 'to do' pile (go to the section 'Dealing with your "to do" pile', later in this chapter) and those that you must file away for later reference. You can find filing information in the section 'Learning the Art of Filing', later in this chapter. Here's a more detailed description of your three options.

Bin it

If the piece of paper is unimportant, or you know that someone has a copy of it in a centralised folder somewhere, put it straight in the recycling bin. This includes leaflets from external companies marketing their products, unless you're sure you want to buy something. And if you do, put that order in *right now* (see 'Deal with it').

Deal with it

If you need to deal with a piece of paper (such as a form that you must fill in), then, if at all feasible, do that the *first time* you handle that piece of paper. Take a couple of minutes to whiz through it. Far better to do that than to come across it in three months' time at the bottom of your 'to do' pile. If you simply don't have time to do it now, put it in your 'to do' pile but make sure you get around to doing it next time.

Pass it on

As soon as you've 'dealt with' a piece of paper, you can pass it on. Or you can pass on other bits of paper with a quick scribbled message or an 'action' note written on them. And as soon as you pass on a piece of paper, it becomes someone else's problem, part of someone else's 'to do' pile.

Dealing with your 'to do' pile

To start with, let me reassure you that I regularly have a large 'to do' pile on my desk. This pile tends to get 'done' when a holiday is rapidly approaching. Bizarrely, when time's really short I somehow find space in my schedule to finally get all those vital bits and pieces done. Chances are, you end up with a 'to do' pile, too. The trick to managing this pile is to keep it as small as possible by rigorously applying the three rules, explained in the preceding section, and by going through it regularly to take care of what's in it. And if you really don't have time, at least pile it up in one big heap. Psychologically, a neat pile will make you feel a lot better.

The bigger your 'to do' pile is, the more times you have to go through it and the more often you handle each bit of paper. That's just more time wasted. Plus you aren't doing any action items that remain in your pile. If you see a piece of paper every time you go through your pile but haven't yet managed to do anything with it, apply one of the three rules to it: bin it, deal with it or pass it on.

Sounds easy enough, but you obviously had some reason for hanging on to whatever now comprises your 'to do' pile and may have a particularly difficult time letting go. My advice?

- ✔ **Be ruthless.** Be as ruthless as you can. A good rule of thumb is: 'Does it make me cry to think of throwing this away?' If it doesn't, then chuck it in the bin. Even if you throw away a vital piece of paper, someone somewhere probably has another copy.

- ✔ **Don't procrastinate.** In teaching, you're not suddenly going to reach a moment when you have oodles of spare time. There's *always* something you need to do – paperwork, planning, report writing and so on and so on. Don't let paperwork take over your life – deal with it *now* rather than later.

- ✔ **Be picky.** Yes, you may go on one of the ten different training courses for which you receive marketing leaflets. But be honest, probably a couple look more interesting than the rest. Be very picky indeed about what you allow onto your 'to do' pile. Otherwise, you may not get around to booking any of the courses at all.

 Set aside a bit of time each week to go through your 'to do' pile. And each time you go through it, set yourself a target for getting X number of bits done. You may add this time to your personal timetable, for instance giving yourself ten minutes every Thursday evening, so that you keep on top of your paperwork.

Your 'To Do' List: A Lifesaver during Busy Times

At certain times of the school year, you suddenly get snowed under with essential tasks to complete. Often, this is toward the end of term. You want to get all those jobs done so you can head off on holiday in a relaxed mood. One way to keep track of all you have to do is to create a 'to do' list. Figure 14-1 shows an example 'to do' list.

If you're heavily involved with an extracurricular activity such as a school play (see Chapter 15), in the run-up to the show you suddenly need to do a long series of tasks urgently. The deadline of the show date means you can end up working long days and even nights. Make sure you stay on top of those essential tasks, and feel in control, by using a 'to do' list.

Figure 14-1:
A sample
teaching 'to
do' list.

To Do

Urgent – <u>TODAY!!</u>

Finish marking Year 11 coursework
Pass on coursework marks to John
Jamie– chase to serve detention
Send application for literacy course
Positive phone call home for Jayden (DON'T FORGET THIS TIME!)

Urgent – <u>TOMORROW!</u>

Book computer room for next week's lesson
Practice assembly with tutor group at lunchtime
Mark Year 9 homework
New student diary for Alex
Year group meeting 3:30pm (don't forget to take list of kids to get
certificates in assembly)

For <u>FRIDAY</u>

Mark Year 7 books
Write plan for lesson observation
List to Stacey with ideas for this year's show
Write Year 10 mock exam

Figure 14-1: A sample teaching 'to do' list.

At busy times, a 'to do' list is a very useful device because:

- ✔ You write down everything in one place, so you don't forget to do something crucial.
- ✔ You can prioritise the jobs, so you get the most urgent ones done first.
- ✔ You know how much you've got to get done, and the timescale in which you must do it.
- ✔ You may be able to delegate some of the tasks, perhaps to an assistant or a trustworthy student.
- ✔ You can ask for help if you don't think you've got time to get everything done.

✔ You can cross off the jobs as you do them, giving yourself a sense of satisfaction and progress.

✔ The list stops you worrying endlessly about whether you've forgotten to do something really vital.

✔ The list keeps you from fretting over school-related issues in the evenings, when you're meant to be relaxing.

To write an effective 'to do' list:

✔ Divide up the tasks you have to do into different types, each one with a separate heading or section. For instance, 'school show', 'reports', 'planning' and 'marking', or if your list is general but time-specific, 'today', 'tomorrow', 'this week' and 'soon'.

✔ If you have a long list, consider subdividing the tasks, so that under 'school show' you may have a section for 'publicity', another for 'front of house', another for 'rehearsals' and so on.

✔ Find a way of indicating which tasks are most urgent. This may be listing the most urgent tasks first, putting them in bold or with an asterisk beside them.

✔ If tasks have a specific date by which they must be done, write them in date order, with the most urgent first.

✔ Use a teaching diary or planner for your 'to do' list so that's it's stored in a safe and easily accessible place.

✔ If you have non-urgent tasks that can wait for another time, put these on a separate list, then file this away to deal with later.

As you go through your 'to do' list and cross off task after task, you feel a powerful sense of achievement. You also minimise the feeling of panic that can take hold as a deadline approaches.

Marking Papers and Writing Reports: Achieving the Impossible

The admin and paperwork side of your job can seem an impossible task. You spend the majority of your time working in the classroom and you don't have much time to spare outside of lessons. This feeling is particularly strong around getting on top of your marking, and also when report-writing time comes around.

As you tackle these two daunting tasks, keep this advice in mind:

✔ **Distinguish between essential and non-essential paperwork tasks.** As you gain in experience, you begin to see that some paperwork tasks are essential and you must do them within a tight time frame (report writing or assessing coursework, for instance). You also realise that some paperwork tasks are non-essential and you can put them off for when you come across that elusive spare time (or you can conveniently overlook them). You might ignore a non-essential request for feedback on a new policy if you're pressed for time.

✔ **Know the rules regarding teacher tasks.** Changes to teacher workload in recent years have made a difference to the kind of tasks you're expected to do. For example, the National Agreement means you don't have to undertake many routine or clerical tasks. Make sure that you read up on the relevant guidance, and that you stand firm if you're asked to do things that aren't within your remit.

✔ **Be realistic about what you can achieve and what you can put to one side.** Don't be a perfectionist, or you end up driving yourself mad with the administrative demands of the job. I once heard a great saying that applies perfectly to teachers: 'Good enough is good enough.' Better to get things *done* than to agonise endlessly about whether you're doing a good enough job.

Handling your marking load

Marking students' work is one of the biggest parts of your paperwork load. (You can find details of the various types of marking that I cover here in Chapter 6.) Consider the kind of marking methods you use, and how well they repay the time spent in added value when it comes to your students' learning. You can find lots of advice in this section to make sure that marking doesn't take over your life.

Marking methods

Marking your students' work is a great way to develop their learning. But remember this proviso: the marking you do must be worth doing – it must actually make a difference to how well your students learn. This isn't always the case, as you can see from the common types of marking listed here:

✔ **Tick and flick:** You put a tick or cross on each answer or page, and then flick over to the next one. The books *look* marked, but it doesn't contribute much to your students' overall level of understanding.

✔ **A mark with brief comments:** You give short comments in addition to your ticks and crosses. This style of marking helps students develop their work to a limited extent.

✔ **Marking for specific errors/strengths.** You set the students a target before they begin the work – perfect spelling, interesting ideas, detailed explanations. This approach is useful for learning, because it encourages students to concentrate on different aspects of their work.

✔ **Detailed marking.** You mark in great detail, correcting spelling errors and so on, and adding a lot of comments to show where the student has worked well and which areas still need development. This marking style is great for helping students develop their work but is hugely time consuming.

The approach you choose depends on how much time you have available and the type of work you're marking. Marking a set of 30 essays in detail can take you several hours but could be worthwhile for GCSE students. Marking a spelling test could be as simple as a quick 'tick and flick' exercise.

When you use a quick marking style, you may get some parents complaining that you 'haven't marked the work' or that you 'don't correct spellings'. Parents don't easily understand just how time consuming marking is. If a parent expresses serious concerns, have a chat to her about why correcting every mistake isn't always possible (or useful). Mostly, though, you're best to hold your tongue and take these comments on the chin.

Mark my words: Suggestions for marking effectively

Here are my top tips for handling your marking load, and for making sure that the marking you do has lasting value:

✔ **Balance the type of activities you set.** Use a good mix of longer exercises that require detailed marking, and some shorter ones that you can skim through.

✔ **Use plenty of verbal activities.** You can assess or mark these while the students are actually in the process of doing them. For instance, presentations, performances and debates.

✔ **Beware of the test!** Okay, so setting a test gives you a chance to sit back and relax in the lesson. But you may regret it afterwards, because you have a pile of papers to mark. Take a few moments to consider the marking load *before* you tell your class they're doing a test.

✔ **Balance your marking across groups unless special circumstances dictate otherwise.** If you teach several different classes, devote a fairly even amount of marking time to each one. However, if you're working with students in their examination year, you may want to spend a bit more time helping them develop their work.

✔ **Balance your marking across your timetable.** Take an overview of your timetable and think about which work you want to mark and when you can find time to do it.

✔ **Mark anywhere and everywhere.** Grab a spare few minutes (on the bus, while you're waiting for a class to turn up) to mark a few books. Chip away at the overall task and it doesn't seem too horrendous.

✔ **Encourage your students to *read* what you've written.** When you've made a great effort to mark work, students not reading your comments is an awful shame. Set aside some lesson time for students to read and respond to the marking you've done.

In addition to you marking your students' work, you can have your students assess their own work or that of their classmates. They can mark a spelling test, write an evaluation of a report, read each other's stories and write comments on them and so on. This self-assessment can take place during lessons and is useful for getting students to develop their own skills. If you're working on computers, try the 'doughnut' activity. Give the students a short time in which to do a piece of work on the computer, then ask each student to move one desk to her right. Now give the students some time to read that person's work and to type in some comments or suggestions.

You don't have to have all the students' books marked up to date all the time. Yes, if you're about to undergo an inspection or an observation that's a good idea. But you simply can't keep on top of everything at all times, unless you have a very small class.

Set yourself a realistic turnover time for marking – perhaps within three days for simple activities and a week for longer ones. Remember that if students feel their work is not getting marked, they may lose the motivation to complete it.

Dealing with report writing

Reports are one of the main, formalised ways in which schools report to parents, and they tell parents a lot about you as a teacher. But report writing is very time consuming. If you teach a large number of students, writing reports is going to be one of the most time-intensive aspects of your workload. Approach your report writing with care and attention, but use the following strategies to minimise the demands on your time:

✔ **Start early.** The time for report writing is written on your school's yearly timetable. Think ahead of time about how you're going to approach this job. Make a few quick assessments of your students in class, and perhaps a few notes about each individual.

✔ **Use a computer.** A computer can speed up your report writing. You can create an outline report and adapt this slightly for different types of students. Include at least one personalised comment on each report. Many schools now ask teachers to complete reports over the school intranet.

✔ **Be positive.** Phrase your reports so that the student feels positive about her achievements. Rather than saying 'Selina just cannot be quiet in class', say 'Selina finds it hard to focus and listen'. If you must write a negative comment, soften the blow with a positive straight after it.

✔ **Watch out for male/female.** You can't always tell just by a name if the student is male or female. Take the greatest care to get the gender right, especially if you don't yet know your students well. If you're unsure, check with another member of staff.

✔ **Remember the audience.** You may have to write hundreds of reports, but each parent only receives one for her child, so they must all be of top quality. Fit your writing style to the audience – don't use complicated terms or jargon. Be clear and straightforward in what you say.

✔ **Set some targets.** End each report by setting a few targets. That way your students have something to aim for in future lessons.

You can find a lot more ideas and information about report writing and reporting to parents in Chapter 13.

If you're a secondary school teacher working with hundreds of different students, one of the hardest tasks is figuring out who's who. If report time falls in the first term, you've probably only 'met' each class a handful of times. Realistically, you're not going to know the name of every individual. I advise that, in the weeks running up to report writing, you devise between three and five categories (perhaps weak/average/good or weak/below average/average/good/excellent). You can then make a note of the category for each student in lessons, to use when writing your reports.

Learning the Art of Filing

Filing is definitely an art – if you get it right, you should be able to put your hands on any piece of paper almost instantaneously. If you get it wrong, you regularly waste time scrabbling around to find resources or lesson plans. As a teacher, literally millions of pieces of paper pass through your hands over the course of your career. After you decide which of these you need to keep for the future, file them in the most effective and efficient way.

If your school likes you to keep materials, lesson plans and resources on a computer, this adds a layer of complication. Make sure that you divide your work up into different folders on your computer, and set aside some time each term for sorting through these and deleting anything that you no longer need.

Creating an effective filing system

You need to develop an effective system for filing the important papers you receive. In addition, you have to find somewhere to keep your files, and this can be a challenge in itself!

First, you need to decide what's worth filing. Only file those things that you're really going to use again. Stick mainly to filing lesson plans, resources, syllabus details and schemes of work – these are most likely to be useful to you in the future. Conversely, you don't need to file any paperwork for which a master copy exists somewhere else in the school (although do so if you like your own copy on hand). Master copies exist of paperwork such as school brochures and handbooks, school policies and so on.

Next, find a good way to divide up your paperwork for filing. Depending on the age group and subjects you teach, this may be by year group, topic, theme and so on. My own filing system for teaching English and Drama at secondary level divides into:

- ✔ Separate folders for Key Stage 3 Drama and GCSE schemes and lessons.
- ✔ Sections within those folders for each year group or topic, which I keep separate using cardboard dividers.
- ✔ Separate folders for photocopiable resources, each of which I keep in an individual plastic wallet so that they're easy to locate, remove and copy.
- ✔ Another folder for exam-related materials in each subject.

In addition to these subject-related folders, I tend to have just one large file for paperwork that isn't related to lesson planning, such as standard letters, lists of class rules and so on.

Finally, work out where you're going to put your files. Make sure you can refer to them easily. If you don't have space in an office, you may ask to have some shelves put up in your classroom. When you're thinking of a suitable filing place, keep these points in mind:

- ✔ Your students can take an interest in your files, so keep them out of reach. If you have to store them in your classroom, choose a high shelf (out of reach of younger students). If they're in a filing cabinet in your room, keep this locked for safety.
- ✔ Put resources that you use regularly in an accessible place in the classroom, encouraging the students to take them out and use them as appropriate.

> ✔ Consider filing on a computer – many lesson plans and the like are now done on a computer. Ask yourself whether you need to make a hard copy at all.
>
> ✔ Take care with any confidential papers – keep these in a separate file under lock and key.

After your filing system is up and running, set aside a regular time to file away new papers. Otherwise you end up with a 'to file' pile to rival your 'to do' pile!

Maintaining your filing system

Files can get out of hand pretty quickly. For that reason, I recommend you go through your files quickly, perhaps once a term, to get rid of anything you know you don't need or won't use again. Then once a year do a more detailed review, to get rid of old paperwork, such as a 10-year-old exam paper or an out-of-date syllabus. This process also reminds you of the fantastic resources or plans you've created but haven't used in a while.

Another good time for maintaining your filing system is when you move schools. This gives you the chance for a clean sweep of all those out-of-date materials. If you haven't used a plan or a resource in the past two or three years, you're probably safe to chuck it away.

Chapter 15

Getting Involved in Extra-Curricular Activities

. . . .

In This Chapter

▶ Understanding how extra-curricular activities can boost your teaching skills

▶ Exploring the type of activities you may like to get involved with

▶ Learning more about going on a school trip

. . . .

*A*s a teacher the bulk of your work is in the classroom. This is where you spend most of your time and where you build those vital relationships with your students. But being a teacher is much more than just standing in front of a class. You may also play the roles of counsellor, protector, friend, role model, mentor, supporter, coach and many more. The work you do outside the classroom gives you a huge amount of pleasure; it also offers a great way of developing and extending your teaching skills.

Inspiring Beyond the Classroom

Your main aim is to inspire your students inside the classroom. But never underestimate how much you can inspire them outside the classroom as well. The opportunity to see you in a different role (sports coach, theatrical director, ICT genius) means they see you as more than 'just' a teacher. You're an expert in many other areas as well!

Your students probably find some of the compulsory parts of school rather dull – they *have* to do lessons even when they don't want to. But when they choose to get involved with extra-curricular activities this is entirely voluntary. Consequently, they're more enthusiastic about taking part.

As well as inspiring your students, taking part in extra-curricular activities is inspirational for you. And you may be doing something that teaches you new skills, for instance rigging lights for a show.

Just how involved can you be?

Your degree of involvement with extra-curricular activities depends on:

- ✔ **The type of setting in which you teach:** In a private school, you probably made a commitment to extra-curricular activities before taking the job. In a state school, you normally have no obligation to do so, although these activities look good on your CV. In a small private nursery, you have limited chance to do so because of the children's ages. With older students, you have many more options and opportunities.

- ✔ **The subject or subjects you teach:** If you're a PE teacher, running sports clubs or coaching a football team is a vital aspect of your role. Similarly, if you're a Drama teacher, putting on a school production each year is part of the job. But even if you teach in an area with no extra-curricular demands, you can still offer your services or find other ways of getting involved.

- ✔ **Your willingness to get involved:** No statutory demand says you have to work beyond your contracted hours. But if you're keen to get involved beyond the classroom, you can always find something useful to do or someone willing to take advantage of your assistance.

- ✔ **The practicalities of your involvement:** If you have commitments outside school (for instance a young family), you may not be able to give up your spare time. Similarly, if you live a long distance from your workplace, it may be hard to stay on late after school. Don't discount involvement in lunchtime clubs, though, if you can spare the time.

If you're brand new to teaching, limit the amount of extra-curricular work you do until you're settled in your job. The first year as a teacher is very demanding – physically, emotionally, psychologically. Put your classroom practice first, rather than devoting a lot of your spare time to extra-curricular activities. Limit any commitment you make – you have plenty of time for more involvement in the future.

Why extra-curricular activities matter

Education isn't merely about teaching your students skills, information, facts and concepts. It's also about helping them develop into fully rounded human beings. This means taking their cultural, artistic, creative and emotional development into account, as well as teaching them how to read, write, add up and so on. The curriculum now touches on many of these wider areas. But you only have a limited time to develop the 'wider' person in your classroom.

A chance to shine

Some students get a reputation for being 'difficult' in lessons – a reputation that follows them around during their entire time at school (and one that may be fully justified). Teachers come to expect these students to be a problem in class. This turns into a vicious cycle: the students never get the chance to prove themselves 'good' again.

These 'difficult' students often find their chance to shine in extra-curricular activities. A lot of extra-curricular activities involve non-academic subjects such as sports, Drama, Art and so on. And these subjects are practical, hands on, creative and imaginative. Just what your 'difficult students' most need.

When you see a problem student performing like a star at sports day, or dancing like a pro in the school show, you feel wonderful. It can seem like a risk to get them involved (what if they misbehave?), but when it works the results are more than worth the gamble.

You face a limit to how much you can do as an individual teacher; parents or carers should be responsible for many of these aspects of a child's development. But not every child has the chance to go on trips, visit art galleries and theatres or learn a fun new skill like karate or Spanish. Extra-curricular activities can introduce your most disadvantaged students to aspects of life they may otherwise never encounter.

When you're teaching, you're under a lot of time pressure. A single lesson is only a limited length. And you don't always have time to deviate from the curriculum if your students want to explore a topic in more detail. But outside the school day you have more time to develop and extend skills – not only your students' skills, but also your own.

Different types of extra-curricular activities

You can find a multitude of extra-curricular activities on offer in the average school. This can range from a few lunchtime and after-school clubs in a small primary school, to a daily diet of exciting activities in a large secondary. Obviously, the more staff your school has, the more likely you are to have volunteers able or willing to run extra-curricular activities.

Some of the types of extra-curricular activities you may come across, and get involved with, include:

✔ **Sports:** Schools typically run regular training sessions for members of sports teams (football, hockey, netball, rugby and so on). They may also offer more unusual sports in a less competitive environment, for instance a karate club. Even if you're not a sports expert, consider helping out with or supporting school sports teams. Show your face at a football match on a Saturday morning and your students may be eternally grateful to you for giving up your time.

✔ **Drama:** Even if you teach in a tiny primary, your school may still have at least one drama production each year. In some larger secondary schools several productions take place over the course of the year – perhaps one 'serious' play, a musical or Christmas show and a sixth-form or other 'niche' production. Drama teachers welcome any offer of help – with making costumes, collecting props or running 'front of house' on the night. You may also have drama clubs, which are not about putting on a specific production, but simply about allowing students to enjoy drama activities and improvisations beyond lessons.

✔ **Music:** Many schools have an orchestra or smaller chamber groups where keen musicians can practise their skills and play as part of a unit. Similarly, you find school choirs or other singing groups in many schools. Sometimes the students set up their own extra-curricular music groups, for instance a band practising in the music room at lunchtimes. There may also be extra-curricular music and singing lessons taking place at your school, perhaps run by a peripatetic teacher.

✔ **Computer clubs:** Teachers who aren't ICT specialists may find that their students know more about computers than they do! Running a computer club is often more about giving students supervised access to school computer resources than about actually teaching them new skills. This access is especially important for students who don't have computers at home.

✔ **Language clubs:** Modern foreign languages have suffered a bit in recent years – secondary students seem less keen to study them, and taking them is now optional at a higher level. In contrast, a number of primary schools now offer extra-curricular language clubs, particularly in popular languages such as Spanish. You don't have to be an expert to get involved: as long as you know a little bit more than your students, you can learn the rest alongside them.

✔ **Gardening clubs:** Gardening at school is enjoying a real upsurge of interest, particularly as teachers see how much students can learn by getting involved with growing their own food. If your school site doesn't have space for a garden, ask around locally to see whether you may be able to use a senior citizen's home or an allotment.

✔ **School magazines:** You may enjoy getting a team of students together to develop and create a magazine for your school. This, of course, can have brilliant links to the subjects of lessons, and you can ask for magazine contributions from all the students at your school.

✔ **Cadets:** You find a cadet group in many private schools. These groups offer students the chance to try physical activities such as sailing, orienteering and so on.

✔ **Duke of Edinburgh's Award:** This award is designed to encourage personal development in a non-competitive environment. Students can take part in physical activities, community projects and so on.

Whether you get involved on a small scale by helping out or you set up and run an activity yourself, you boost your teaching skills and have a great time getting to know your students better.

The more extra-curricular activities available at a school, often the better the establishment. This guide is useful when you're looking for a new teaching job. If staff are willing to commit themselves outside the classroom and have the energy left over to do this after teaching, this is a good sign of the quality of the school.

The ups and downs of getting involved

As with everything in life, getting involved in extra-curricular activities has both positive and negative sides. Your job is to decide whether, for you personally, the upsides outweigh the downsides. You've got to figure out whether you can afford to spend the time on extra-curricular involvement, while still doing your best in your classroom.

Extra-curricular involvement means a bit of time out from the pressures of the normal school day. You can let off steam in a fun and friendly environment. As the following sections show, you can find many other good reasons for getting involved with your students beyond the classroom.

Getting to know your students better

When you spend time together outside the classroom you discover what your students are really like as people. And they find out the same about you.

Some of the benefits of getting to know your students better include:

✔ You get to see how your students respond to pressure. Seeing how your students behave and work when they're pushed is very instructive. Often, they surprise you with how strong and able they are. The demands of starring in a school show, or leading the school football team, are huge. Watch and enjoy as your students rise to the occasion.

✔ You develop an informal relationship with students. When you're working with students outside the structures and strictures of the classroom, you can afford to be a little bit more relaxed.

✔ You meet students you don't teach at the moment. And when you come across these students in the future, they already know what you're like to work with, and hopefully have a positive impression of you.

Because you're in a more relaxed situation outside of lesson times, you can find achieving the right kind of teaching style tricky. You must stay in charge and in control of the students and ensure that no behaviour issues crop up. You've also got to be aware of health and safety and other technical details, such as insurance, risk assessments and so on. If you're running a study club, use the same kind of rules that you would in your classroom, although you can probably afford to be just a little bit more relaxed.

Sometimes, students get overexcited, particularly in the run-up to a big event such as an important sports competition or the performance of the school show. If you're working with large groups make sure you balance a slightly more relaxed style with high expectations and tough standards. A good rule of thumb is to take a 'professional' approach with your students: demand the kind of standards they need if they're working as professionals. But don't forget to have a good laugh along the way as well. They're giving up their free time, just as you're giving up yours.

Creating bonds with new and different staff

If you offer to help out in an area where you don't normally teach, you get to meet and make friends with staff you don't yet know. These kinds of links can be hugely beneficial for your day-to-day teaching. You might team up with another staff member to team teach a few cross-curricular lessons together. You could ask another teacher to visit your class as an 'expert'. For instance, an Art specialist could show your students how to design a stage set in your Drama lessons.

Increasing your own set of skills (and adding to your CV)

Getting involved in extra-curricular activities is a great way for you to learn new skills. These skills may well be ones you don't otherwise learn in the classroom; they certainly boost your teaching and your current level of teaching skills. Similarly, extra-curricular activities enable you to develop skills that you already have. This may mean extending your knowledge of football coaching, building up your repertoire of plays or learning all the ins and outs of a software program.

By taking part in extra-curricular activities you gain great experiences that look good on your CV in the future.

A word about the downside of extra-curricular activities

There are, of course, downsides to extra-curricular involvement as well, although in my experience the positives far outweigh them. The downsides include:

✔ **The time commitment involved:** This time commitment can be heavy, particularly in the run-up to a big event. Be sure that you can spare the time from your regular teaching role. Similarly, before you offer to help, think about whether you're willing to give up your spare time. Sometimes you may have to work on weekends, for example.

✔ **The lack of recognition about what's involved:** Sometimes senior managers, or regular staff, don't quite realise how much effort and time you put in. This can be frustrating, so be aware that your commitment may not be recognised as fully as you like.

✔ **The paperwork:** If you're in charge of an extra-curricular activity, you may have to deal with letters to parents, risk assessments, insurance forms and all those other boring but necessary administrative tasks.

✔ **The after-effects and clear-up:** When an extra-curricular activity's over, you can find yourself tired and a bit 'down'. For instance, with a school show so much effort goes into preparation, you often feel a sense of anti-climax when the production finishes. Similarly, a lot of clearing up often needs to happen in the aftermath of an extra-curricular activity. Your students may be less willing to help clear up their mess than they were to make it in the first place. Recruit some student volunteers to help tidy up after the event, rather than doing it all by yourself.

Taking Time Out for a Trip

Your school or setting should offer students a range of trips over the course of the school year. Some of these may be part of a compulsory programme of study, for instance a geography field trip for GCSE students. Other trips are organised for a year group, or even for the whole of a smaller school, for example a visit to a local city farm. Although the school asks for voluntary parental contributions, school funds should cover the cost of any trips directly related to learning and lessons. Your school may also run some non-compulsory (and pricey) trips, such as skiing holidays or overseas excursions.

School trips are hugely beneficial, both for students and for their teachers. Among many other benefits, they:

✔ Boost student learning both for the classroom and in a wider context.

✔ Give students access to and enjoyment of the wider world around them, whether in cultural or physical activities or the environment.

✔ Encourage positive teacher/student relationships.

✔ Allow staff to get to know each other better outside the normal school environment.

✔ Give everyone a chance for a day out in a fun and more relaxed situation.

✔ Can offer significant personal challenges for students (for instance on an activities break).

✔ Can provide a real 'growing up' moment for students, making a long-term change in their attitude to learning and life.

When you take time out for a trip, both you and your students should return to the classroom refreshed and re-enthused.

If you're fairly new to teaching, you may be in the lucky position of being invited to come on a trip without having to take overall responsibility for its organisation. If this happens to you, seize the offer with both hands. A day out of school in a new environment is like nothing else in boosting your enthusiasm and giving you the energy to keep going through the daily routine. After the event, you find the students responding to you more favourably and wanting to talk about where you went and what you did. If you're in a more senior role, it may be that you're actually responsible for organising and leading the trip.

School trips only take place through the goodwill and hard work of teachers. These days, organising a trip is quite an undertaking, and you should look for the support of senior staff in dealing with paperwork and health and safety issues. But if you decide to take the plunge and organise a trip of your own, the benefits usually far outweigh all your hard work.

Deciding to take a trip

Although a trip's a great opportunity for the students, deciding to organise one means a big commitment for you. You have to convince your head teacher that a valid reason for your trip exists (see the preceding list for a whole host of possible benefits for your students).

Ask yourself the following questions:

✔ **What can the students learn from this trip?** A trip to a museum allows them to see and handle original historical artefacts.

✔ **How can this feed into their learning in the classroom?** Students bring back photos and notes from the museum trip to add into a class project and display.

✔ **Do any opportunities exist for wider student development on this trip?** At the museum, students interview an archaeologist for an article in the school magazine.

✔ **What are the potential hazards of going on this trip?** All those glass display cases mean good behaviour is essential. You'll need to keep students focused so they don't wander off and get lost.

✔ **What are the organisational issues in setting up this trip?** You may need to hire coaches to take you to the museum, recruit extra staff to accompany you and fill out risk assessment forms.

✔ **What can I get out of organising and leading this trip?** A deeper and more enriched approach to learning in History and an enjoyable day out of school with your students.

The technicalities of trips

The procedures for organising and running trips are continually changing. Talk to your head teacher about the current guidelines from your LEA or governing body and where possible get the advice and support of staff experienced in organising trips. You also need to gain parental consent for students going on the trip and to obtain emergency contact numbers, complete risk assessment forms and organise transport as required.

Make sure that you're up to speed with the current regulations, and refer to your union for advice as well if you're unsure about your LEA or school procedures. You can use the general advice outlined in the following sections as a helpful starting point. For in-depth and detailed advice about all the technicalities of organising and going on a trip, see the DCFS booklet *Health and Safety of Pupils on Educational Visits* which you can find online at `http://publications.teachernet.gov.uk/eOrderingDownload/ HSPV2.pdf`.

Who's in charge here? The up-front planning

Start your planning well ahead of time; depending on the type of trip, leave yourself at least a few weeks to get things organised. Your employer (the LEA or governing body) must have a written procedure and should maintain insurance cover for trips. Get hold of the paperwork and study it carefully. You will also need to gain the approval of your head teacher before you go any further.

Here are some other points that you need to consider:

✔ **Decide who's in charge:** You'll need to have a group leader for the trip. This person has a lot of responsibility and in most cases having a senior teacher in charge of the overall running of the trip is a wise move.

✔ **Determine your student/teacher ratio:** You must have the correct number of adults to students (staff and also parent volunteers as applicable). The numbers vary according to the age of the students (you can refer to the DCFS booklet *Health and Safety of Pupils on Educational Visits* at `http://publications.teachernet.gov.uk/eOrdering Download/HSPV2.pdf` for more details).

> ✓ **Find out who's responsible for managing budgets and collecting money:** Your head should have set up a separate area within the budget for educational trips. Check whether staff in your school office are happy to collect in monies. Where the trip takes place within school hours, parents can be asked for a voluntary contribution, but this isn't compulsory.

> ✓ **Take care with the timing:** Take an overall view of the yearly timetable and be wary of planning a trip at 'peak times' (for staff or students), for instance around exams or close to coursework deadlines.

Preparing for the risks involved

The DCFS booklet *Health and Safety of Pupils on Educational Visits* (available online at `http://publications.teachernet.gov.uk/eOrdering Download/HSPV2.pdf`) gives much information about preparing for and assessing risks. With the current climate of litigation, making yourself fully aware of your responsibilities is a vital step to take.

To prepare yourself for the risks involved in taking time out for a trip, remember to:

> ✓ Check for potential hazards and do risk assessments as appropriate.

> ✓ Think carefully about doing high-hazard activities. Do you have staff with the relevant training and expertise to supervise these? Have you done the correct risk assessments properly?

> ✓ Ensure that staff have read the relevant guidelines (local or national) and summarise the key points for helpers. Refer to your LEA or governing body guidelines and also read any guidance from the Department of Education covering your region.

> ✓ Make sure that everyone knows what their tasks and responsibilities are during the day.

> ✓ Talk to supervising adults about behaviour. How can they help you ensure that the students behave appropriately while they're out of school?

Getting the necessary info to parents

Keep parents well informed about the trip and why it's taking place. Ensure that you have their written consent as appropriate. Refer to your LEA, governing body and education department guidelines for more information. The DCFS *Health and Safety of Pupils on Educational Visits* booklet gives lots of detail on this, and also provides model forms for you to use when contacting parents.

Try not to be put off from planning a trip by the organisational workload involved. Trips are so hugely beneficial for your students that putting yourself out to run them is worthwhile. Make sure you read and follow the guidelines, and take all reasonable precautions. The DCFS booklet gives a useful summary of your position – you should 'exercise the same care a prudent parent would'.

Handling behaviour on school trips

Inevitably, your students get excited about going on a trip. This excitement and enthusiasm form one of the key reasons for going. As their teacher, your responsibility is to manage their behaviour and also to ensure that you minimise any risks to their safety. During a day trip, the students are normally too busy to think of messing around. Clearly, any trips that involve an overnight stay offer the potential for more pushing at boundaries.

To help you handle behaviour on your trip:

- ✔ Have a meeting with students before you leave to talk to them about the standards you expect from them.

- ✔ Focus on the positive: all the exciting things they may do and all the benefits that the trip may mean for them.

- ✔ Make clear that they're representing the school while they're on the trip.

- ✔ Give a clear warning about sanctions if anyone misbehaves. Think carefully about the punishments you can offer (and don't threaten to 'take everyone home immediately' unless you really mean it).

- ✔ Explain that you're not going to allow a tiny minority to spoil the trip for everyone. Have a plan for what to do if a few individuals play up.

- ✔ Try to ensure you have lots of staff and volunteers on hand so that if you do have to separate individuals, you can do this without interrupting the trip.

- ✔ Accept that they're excited young people, and allow a little bit of flexibility in your normal regulations (but not too much).

- ✔ Share your expectations with the rest of the team of adult helpers to make sure you're all on the same page.

- ✔ Relax and try to enjoy yourself.

Most young people 'rise to the occasion' when you take them on a school trip. They love the chance to get out of the daily routine, and respond by proving themselves trustworthy and mature.

Getting the most out of a trip

When you've put all that effort into organising a trip, you definitely want to get the most out of it while you're away. Do some effective preparation beforehand to benefit from the educational opportunities that happen on the trip. To exploit your trip to the full:

- ✔ Remember to take a camera so you can snap some photos of all the exciting things you do to share with your class. (If you want to feature some of these photos in a newsletter or school magazine, however, be sure to check first that the school has parental permission forms for every student in the photo.)

- ✔ Avoid the dreaded worksheet. Your students are out of school, so having to fill in the blanks on a worksheet only reminds them of what they want to escape.

- ✔ Think about timing: How much time do your students get to spend on each activity? Is doing a few activities in detail better than skimming over everything?

- ✔ Consider groupings: Do you want to pick the groups, or are you going to allow the students to do this? If you're taking a range of age groups, mixing up students of different ages can work well.

- ✔ Plan some follow-up activities for after the event, perhaps including a presentation to the rest of the school in assembly.

Put in the time with your students outside of lessons and you can have great fun together. And at the same time, you boost your teaching skills for when you get back in the classroom.

Chapter 16

Evaluating and Furthering Your Teaching Skills

In This Chapter

▶ Discovering where you are now with your teaching skills and how you can develop them

▶ Understanding how to get the best out of observations and inspections

▶ Exploring ways to further yourself as a teacher

▶ Finding some things you can do for your own personal development or enjoyment

As a teacher, you never come to a point at which you can say: 'I've finished discovering how to teach, I know exactly how to do this.' You're always able to find some way to improve your lesson delivery, refine your classroom management skills or develop your relationship with your students.

You may also come across new research that makes you think about how your classroom works: perhaps a new study about how students learn best, or an examination of how our brains work. Similarly, new resources and materials can always make your lessons more interesting and educationally effective.

At various points in your career you may want to take a course or do some studying to improve your teaching skills. And the more you know about yourself as a teacher, and indeed as a person, the better the teacher you are.

Taking Stock of Your Situation

Perhaps you're a newly qualified teacher, fresh to the profession; maybe you're an experienced teacher with many years under your belt. Whatever your personal situation, taking stock regularly is important, to think about where you are and what you're doing at the moment. That way, you can work out how to build on your current levels of skill and experience and keep on improving as a teacher.

Understanding your strengths and weaknesses

The first step in evaluating where you are now, and where you want to go next, is to understand your strengths and weaknesses as a classroom practitioner. This isn't about beating yourself up; it isn't about making yourself feel that you're hopeless at the job. Rather, the evaluation's an honest appraisal of what you can do to improve your teaching.

You can identify your own strengths and weaknesses as a teacher in many ways. You can:

- ✔ Sit down somewhere quiet after a lesson or a teaching day, and spend some time reflecting on what went well and what didn't.

- ✔ Take some more informal, 'instant' reflections on how well you're doing, during the course of a lesson.

- ✔ When an incident or problem happens in your classroom, write a detailed account afterwards – what led up to it, what happened during the incident, what the aftermath was. With more serious incidents, sending a photocopy of this account to the relevant member of senior staff is helpful.

- ✔ Ask any assistants or support staff who work with you to let you know what they think you do well and what you're not so good at.

- ✔ Get another teacher to come and observe one of your lessons informally, to identify areas where you may improve. (Be aware, though, that the presence of other staff in the room may alter the way your students behave.)

- ✔ Tape record a lesson so you can get a better idea of how you sound to your students. Listen out for the number of times you use a particular phrase, or how often you raise your voice.

- ✔ Ask your students for some feedback – they're often far more honest than a fellow member of staff.

With time, you're able to reflect *as the lesson happens* on whether the activities or strategies you're using are actually working. You can see your students' responses to what you're doing and incorporate them into the way your lesson runs. This process of continual self-reflection is one of the best ways of improving your teaching skills.

The kind of things you can reflect on include the following:

- ✔ How well the activities you set match the needs, abilities and interests of your students.

- ✔ How quickly your students progress.

✔ Whether misbehaviour ever gets in the way of their achievement.

✔ Whether you're good at planning interesting, engaging activities.

✔ How effectively you use your voice and body to communicate with the class.

✔ What your reactions are, whether you have a tendency to get angry when things go wrong – to lose your calm and shout at the class, for example.

✔ How effective you are at focusing on the positive more than on the negative.

✔ Whether you're good at keeping a sense of perspective on what really matters in your classroom and beyond.

✔ How effective you are at the non-teaching bits of the job – paperwork, writing reports and so on.

✔ How good you are at developing strong interpersonal relationships with your students.

Even if you've never sat and reflected on your teaching skills before, you probably have a sense of how well you're doing in each area. For instance, I'm well aware that staying calm is one of my biggest weaknesses, but that I'm good at thinking up really interesting lessons for my students.

One of your weaknesses can also be one of your strengths. For instance, I'm a bit disorganised when it comes to lesson planning. But sometimes this very lack of organisation works in my favour, because it brings an element of flexibility. On occasions I've grabbed a resource as I walk into my classroom and somehow conjured up a really meaningful lesson from it. Of course, the lesson doesn't always turn out to be fantastic, but I'm good at thinking on my feet when things don't go to plan in my classroom.

Considering where you go next

After you identify your strengths and weaknesses, you need to work out where to go next to improve your teaching skills. Use the advice in this section to increase your skills in the areas where you're weak. Just as you'd set targets to help a student improve her work, so you can set yourself goals that you work towards during the school year.

Improving weaknesses

To build on your weaknesses, take a look at the following suggestions:

✔ Set yourself a few targets for each week or half term – three at a time is about right. Make these targets reasonably easy to achieve, so that you don't over-burden yourself on top of your normal workload.

✔ Write yourself a little card with some key words on it. Have this easily accessible in lessons to remind yourself of your targets, perhaps taped to your desk. My key words are: *calm, positive* and *relaxed.*

✔ If appropriate, ask a friendly student to act as a kind of neutral observer and to give you a signal as a reminder if you do start going off track. For instance, if your aim is to stop raising your voice so much, your student observer can raise a hand in the air if you begin to talk too loudly.

✔ When you feel you've achieved these targets, remember to give yourself a pat on the back, a little treat of some kind.

✔ Take a course to help you build your skills. For instance, if you're not so great at using your voice properly, a voice training course may be ideal.

Building on strengths

To build on your strengths, you can simply play to them. If you're good at creating engaging lessons, then use this as a technique to motivate and reward your students. For example, you may ask them to learn key vocabulary for buying and selling in a languages lesson. When they've achieved this, they get to set up market stalls where they buy food and other goods in the target language. Your ability to plan and deliver these exciting sessions becomes a 'carrot' for pushing forwards with the work.

You can also find ways to share your knowledge and skills with others. Check these out:

✔ Offer to do a demonstration lesson on a staff training day, or apply to become an advanced skills teacher, who visits other schools to share good practice.

✔ Share the resources you make: Give copies to other staff teaching the same subject or age group; or upload your lesson plans and worksheets onto the Internet.

✔ Support other staff who are having troubles or who've less experience than you – for instance, you can offer to mentor a newly qualified teacher.

Obviously, you should also practise a little humility. Avoid mentioning to all and sundry how great you are, but don't be too embarrassed to pass your ideas on to others. That way everyone can benefit from your skills, not least the students.

Getting the Most Out of Observations

From time to time during your career, you're observed by another teacher or a member of management. This happens most frequently during your first year as a teacher – you should have at least three opportunities for formal observations, with feedback after each one. As you progress in your career, you're still observed from time to time, for instance during an inspection.

To get the most out of an observation, you need to feel calm and confident during the lesson. Clearly, this is tricky because you're aware that someone's watching you: you want to do your best, but you may be feeling rather nervous.

You may be strongly tempted to try to deliver a really whiz-bang, thrilling, exciting lesson when you're being observed. However, this can backfire, particularly if you don't normally teach in this way. Rather than coming up with an entirely new kind of lesson to try to impress your observer, you're far better to stick to tried-and-tested approaches and activities that you know work with your class.

Preparing for an observation

One of the keys to a successful observation is to prepare properly before the event. If you're well prepared and know exactly what you're going to be doing in the lesson, your students get a sense of security from you that allows them to relax. You also feel more in control and hopefully more confident about being observed.

To prepare in the most effective way, you need to think about the planning and delivery of your lesson:

- ✔ **Have a clear, detailed lesson plan to show your observer.** If you prefer to work from a set of scribbled notes, make an additional plan especially for the occasion, to show the detailed thinking behind what you're teaching.

  On this detailed plan, show all those little strategies that you normally incorporate, but perhaps in an informal way. For example, how you differentiate for any students with special needs.

- ✔ **Check with your observer whether she wants you to use a particular format.** If your school has a 'formal' lesson plan layout for inspections, you're probably best to use this for an observed lesson as well.

- ✔ **See if your observer wants to join in.** In an informal observation, getting your observer actively involved in the lesson can work really well. She may help you by working with a small group or could even do the activity itself, to see how it works.

✔ **Aim to demonstrate a wide range of approaches to teaching and learning** – a little bit of teacher talk, some group activities, some individual work and so on.

✔ **Consider how you may appeal to the different kinds of students in your class, and how you can get all of them 'hands on' with their learning.** Look closely at the ideas and suggestions in Chapters 4, 5 and 6 of this book to help you.

✔ **Gather your resources well in advance of the observation lesson.** Make sure you've done any photocopying well ahead of time.

If you're using any resources that may go 'wrong', for instance a DVD player or an electronic whiteboard, ensure that you test these shortly before the lesson begins.

✔ **Make sure that the students' books are marked up to date.**

You also need to think about and plan for the kind of classroom and behaviour management issues that may arise:

✔ Consider how to deal with any issues that arise in the lesson, such as misbehaviour, latecomers or missing homework.

✔ Reiterate your expectations with the class ahead of time – go over the kind of behaviour and work you expect to see from them.

✔ Don't deviate too far, if at all, from your normal routines, as this can 'throw' a class into being unnecessarily difficult.

✔ Consider whether you're best to tell the students that someone's going to be observing the lesson. With some classes this pre-empts the inevitable question of: 'What's she doing here?' With other classes, this is an invitation to mess around! If you're good at bluffing you could always tell the students that the observer is coming to watch them.

After you're fully prepared, make sure that you're at your classroom in plenty of time before the lesson begins. Give yourself a few minutes to think through the activities, to check on your resources, to calm yourself and relax.

Being observed is always a rather artificial situation. Your observer appreciates that you probably don't go to quite this much trouble in your day-to-day teaching – you just don't have the time. Strike a balance between showing yourself at your very best and being honest about what normally goes on in your classroom.

During the observation

When the time for your observation arrives, use it as an opportunity to show how good your teaching skills really are. Aim for a confident and relaxed manner, even if things start to go wrong. And if everything goes completely pear shaped, don't panic. At least if the class is really difficult you get to demonstrate your brilliant classroom management skills!

At the start of the lesson you should:

- ✔ Check with your observer what she wants to do during the lesson. Some observers like to participate in the lesson, for instance sitting and working with a group. Others prefer to sit at the back as surreptitiously as possible, to watch and make notes.

- ✔ Bring the class into the room in a calm and controlled manner. Remember to deal with any minor issues, such as incorrect uniform. Sometimes you can overlook these little things because of the stress of the situation.

- ✔ Remember to use lots of praise and positive comments – drop a few of these in at the start to show how positive your approach is and to get yourself and your students into the right frame of mind.

- ✔ Demonstrate how you go about getting your class's silent attention. Don't be tempted to talk over students in your desire to get on with teaching.

During the lesson you should:

- ✔ Take your time, particularly when giving instructions to the class. Don't allow nerves to make you rush and fluff your introduction to the lesson.

- ✔ Avoid dealing differently with your class – the students may well helpfully point out: 'You don't normally do things this way, miss.'

- ✔ Keep a close eye on your watch. You're far better to finish a little ahead of time, so that you can end the lesson in a relaxed and calm manner, than to rush to fit everything in.

- ✔ Ensure a tidy end to the lesson. Get the students to collect or hand in any work as appropriate. Make sure that they leave the room as they found it, with chairs tucked in under the desks, and in a calm and orderly manner.

And after your observation's over, take a few minutes to reflect on how well the lesson went. You get some more formal feedback from your observer in due course. But don't forget to think back over the lesson for yourself while it's still fresh in your mind. That way you can respond to any points she brings up.

Sometimes your observer doesn't stay in the room for the entire length of the lesson. If you're being observed by someone who's a member of the senior management team she may be called away, for instance to deal with a problem in someone else's classroom. This is very frustrating for you, particularly if you've just got to the best bit of your lesson. Sadly, you can't do much about it.

Getting feedback after an observation

An observation's only useful to you for improving your teaching skills if you get the feedback you need after the event. Sometimes this means chasing up a more senior member of staff to sit down and talk with you. Your observer may talk you through the lesson in detail, point by point, or she may simply give you an overview of what went on.

Your observer should set you some targets to work on for the future. View these targets as an opportunity to make improvements, rather than as a criticism of your teaching skills. Every teacher, no matter how experienced or brilliant, always has room for improvement.

Dealing with inspection and inspectors

From time to time in your teaching career, the school where you work is subject to a formal inspection. The format of these inspections has changed quite a bit over the years – these days they place more emphasis on a school evaluating its own strengths and areas for improvement, rather than on assessing individual members of staff or departments.

If an inspector does come to visit your lesson:

- ✔ Follow the guidance in the previous sections on dealing with observations. Be well prepared beforehand and try to stay relaxed during the lesson.

- ✔ Maintain confidence in what you do in your day-to-day classroom life; don't change things around too much in an attempt to 'please' the inspectors.

- ✔ Remember that an inspection's only ever a 'snapshot' of what normally goes on in a school. Those poor inspectors probably never get to see the most brilliant lessons.

- ✔ Remember, too, that as an individual teacher you don't have responsibility for the effectiveness (or not) of the entire school.

- ✔ Focus on your own classroom practice, rather than worrying about how your school's doing. This applies especially if you're teaching in a challenging situation.

Even the new 'short' inspections are a stressful experience for all concerned. Keep faith in the long-term work you do with your students, rather than seeing inspection as a definitive judgement of you and your teaching skills. Remember that the inspectors aren't looking for a chance to 'fail' you, but are there to be objective observers of what goes on in your school.

Furthering Your Personal Development

After your first few years as a teacher, you probably start to think about the future direction of your teaching career. Some teachers choose to stay in the classroom and never even consider going for promotion. These days, you can stay as a classroom teacher but still continue developing your skills in various ways. A post such as advanced skills teacher celebrates the vital work of classroom teachers, and allows you to share and extend your skills to the benefit of other staff and other schools.

If you're thinking about moving up the career ladder at your school, look at the kind of extra qualifications you may find useful. And even if you simply want to stay as a 'normal' classroom teacher, think about doing some training or development just for your personal satisfaction and enjoyment.

Taking additional qualifications

A great way to develop yourself, and your teaching skills, is to take an additional qualification. If you're thinking about going for promotion, taking an extended course is a good way to demonstrate that you're keen to further your career.

You may consider:

- ✔ Doing a postgraduate degree, such as an MA, perhaps via part-time or distance learning.

- ✔ Taking a short course leading to a diploma or similar, for instance in a specific area of your practice, such as working with students who have dyslexia.

- ✔ Studying for a qualification that lets you contribute in a wider way to school life – for example a first aid course or a licence to drive the school minibus.

- ✔ Taking a qualification for a more senior post, such as the National Professional Qualification for Headship (NPQH).

If you do decide to take some additional qualifications, find out if your school's willing to support you, for instance giving you help in financing a course.

Doing something just for yourself

Teaching has a habit of taking over your life – of course, teaching's more of a vocation than a job for many (perhaps most) teachers. But you aren't doing your students any favours if you don't take care of yourself. If you're relaxed and happy outside school, you're bound to be more positive about your work as a teacher.

Set yourself some personal goals over the course of each school year. Choose things that are going to make you feel more positive and relaxed when you're in school, rather than anything that simply adds to the feeling of being over-burdened.

You can:

- ✔ Take up a new hobby – choose something different to what you do each day in school.

- ✔ Consider taking up a creative activity – this is often a great way to let your mind settle and relax after a long day at school. Perhaps pottery or art classes tickle your fancy?

- ✔ Get involved in a sport. This is a great way to relax after a long day at school; doing something physically active is good for getting rid of the stresses and strains of the day.

- ✔ Set up a weekly social activity with some other staff from your school – a trip to the pub, the cinema or the theatre may be just what you need to relax.

- ✔ Make the most of those lovely long holidays by booking a trip some-where relaxing. This is especially useful in the February break, when the days are short and dark and the rest of the school year stretches ahead.

One of the great things about teaching is that it's a very 'mobile' job – you can teach pretty much anywhere in the world. If your personal situation allows, going to teach overseas for a few years is a fantastic way to broaden your experience and deepen your teaching skills. Some schools help you organise a sabbatical: going to work in another school for a year or so, with your job kept open for when you return.

Part VI
The Part of Tens

'It was the way he would have wanted it – He was a terrible English grammar teacher.'

In this part . . .

No time to sit and digest lots of information? That's no problem. Because this part's your one-stop shop for all those top tips, bits of advice and strategies that really make a difference in your classroom.

Chapter 17

Ten Great Ways to Engage with a Group

. . . .

In This Chapter

▶ Building strong relationships with classes and students

▶ Creating lessons that are exciting and relevant for your students

▶ Understanding how to reveal a little of your true self

▶ Discovering how to take classes into the great outdoors

▶ Using peer-group power to boost your success with a class

▶ Keeping your students on their toes

. . . .

*Y*ou can boost the impact of your teaching by finding a lot of ways to 'click' and bond with a class. And once the members of a group engage with you and with the lesson you're teaching, they focus that much better on their work. You'll probably find you engage naturally with some classes or students, but with others establishing a connection requires much more effort.

Students want you to understand them and their issues. Work out exactly what makes them tick: peer-group pressure, playground crazes, imaginative lessons. And once you've worked out which buttons to press to make that connection, get pressing like mad!

You can find lots more ideas about how to get and keep your class engaged in Chapter 5. In this chapter, you can discover ten ways to start making those vital connections.

Build a Relationship

When your students have a positive relationship with you, they *want* to behave well and work hard for you. The desire to please you is a strong incentive to do as you ask. You can build good relationships by:

✔ Treating your students as you want them to treat you

✔ Being in a good, positive mood as much of the time as you can

✔ Involving your students in decisions about how and what they learn

✔ Using inclusive language – saying 'us' rather than 'you' (discover more about this in 'Use Inclusive Language', later in this chapter)

✔ Incorporating some of their favourite things into the way you teach

✔ Viewing your students as *people* and not just as pupils

Good relationships take time to develop – no instant formula exists for engaging with a class. But stick at your relationship building, give it time and it does happen.

Creating strong relationships while retaining some distance between you and your students is tricky. This is particularly difficult if you work with very young students or with the oldest ones. Young children can view you as a 'stand-in' parent, especially if they're not getting much emotional input at home. If you're close in age to older students, they may prefer to see you as a friend rather than a teacher. No harm in getting close to your students, but maintain some distance too. Build a relationship based on mutual respect, but one in which you are still the adult in charge. Avoid the temptation to use slang or casual language to 'get down' with your students. That way, when you have to tell them off (which you do), doing so is that much easier.

Use Inclusive Language

The way you speak to your students and the kind of language you use have a powerful impact on the results you achieve. The modern classroom is one where everyone's included. Using inclusive language helps all your students feel involved in your lessons and connected to you as their teacher.

To help your students feel connected to you and the lesson, follow this advice:

✔ Talk *with* them rather than *at* them

✔ Use words such as 'we', 'our' and 'us'

✔ Involve your students in making decisions about their learning

✔ Move toward a student when he answers a question

✔ Use loads and loads of personalised verbal praise

The more inclusive your classroom feels, the more you get the sense of you and the students working together as a team. And the more you engage and 'click' with your class, the better results you achieve together.

Create Imaginative Scenarios

When your students come to a lesson they expect to do 'normal' things, like reading, writing, looking at textbooks and so on. What they *don't* expect is for you to present them with an imaginative scenario, ask them to take on a character and then invite them to dive into that scenario to see what they can discover. At nursery and in the first few years at school, children role-play in various different settings (a home corner, which becomes a shop, a doctor's surgery and so on). As they get older, they get less and less chance to experiment through imaginative play. This is a shame, as doing so is a great way to engage students and to help them learn.

Imaginative scenarios work so well because:

- ✔ They're unexpected and unusual
- ✔ They encourage a healthy sense of curiosity in your classroom
- ✔ They let students *live* the experience and get immersed in learning
- ✔ They require students to use a wide range of thinking skills
- ✔ They're relevant and connected to real life
- ✔ They're a lot of fun!

Choose an imaginative scenario to suit what you're teaching, and also to fit the age of the students with whom you work. Older students respond well to becoming detectives and investigating a 'crime scene'; younger children enjoy being explorers and going on a 'treasure hunt'. You can add writing and speaking tasks as an extension of your imaginative scenarios. For instance, a crime scene activity lends itself to a police report, a taped interview, a courtroom scene and so on.

To get the most out of imaginative scenarios, follow these tips:

- ✔ Incorporate plenty of props for the students to handle
- ✔ Use some costumes (for you or for the students)
- ✔ Add some authentic extras, such as police crime-scene tape
- ✔ Appeal to all five of your students' senses
- ✔ Ask the students to take on adult attitudes and approaches, just like the characters they're playing

You can use imaginative scenarios in a whole range of subject areas, not just in Drama. A crime-scene scenario works brilliantly in English lessons and also in Modern Foreign Languages (talking about what *happened*), Science (forensics), Law (legal technicalities), Maths (drawing an accurate plan) and so on.

Remember Their Names

Your name is a central part of what makes you the person you are. You've lived with your name since you were a baby. You've heard the word over and over again, often in close and emotional situations. Even if you don't particularly *like* your name, you still grow into it and learn to live with it. Knowing your students' names is essential because:

- ✓ You can get their attention easily and politely
- ✓ You personalise the relationship you have with them
- ✓ You show that you're interested in really getting to know them
- ✓ You can use names to boost the value of the rewards you give
- ✓ You can use names when you need to give a student a sanction
- ✓ You need to know names to write reports and talk with parents

Mastering names is tricky, especially if you teach a lot of different students. Make a start as soon as you meet your class, and use many activities and games to help you. You can find advice on this process in Chapter 11.

Give a Little of Yourself

You don't *have* to give of yourself to be a good teacher: some teachers keep a barrier between themselves and their students, which works well for them. They never get close to the students and the students don't feel close to them. But to my mind something's missing if you don't give your students access to you the person, as well as you the teacher. Your personality plays a central role in the type of teacher you are. Students love to get little insights into what you're really like – and you're helping them engage with you.

You can talk to them about the kind of music you like, the books you enjoy reading, the television programmes you watch. Of course, you may also let slip that you're a black belt in karate to keep them on their toes!

You don't need to use up loads of lesson time talking about these things with your students. These conversations crop up naturally while you're doing a playground duty, an extra-curricular activity or taking students on a trip.

Find Out What They Love

When you're young you get really 'into' things: the latest music, fashion trends, hot Internet sites or playground toy crazes. Whatever age your students are, they're into something. Find out what that is and see if you can incorporate it into some of your lessons in some way. To show you how this works, here are some examples from my own teaching:

- ✓ **Tamagotchi:** Remember this craze from a few years back? Little electronic pets that you had to nurture constantly. I had so much trouble with them in one class that I ended up devising a crèche, which the students ran, where they kept the Tamagotchis during lesson time.

- ✓ **Top trumps:** Perennially popular card games are a particular favourite with boys. I've used them to study characters from plays in English and Drama lessons.

- ✓ **Pop music:** I've used song lyrics to talk about 'tone' in poetry with older students. And with one tricky class, I set a 'pop group' project where the students had to devise, market and write songs for a new group.

So the next time a craze hits your school, don't see it as a pain, see it as an opportunity for some creative teaching.

 Think back to the kind of things you were into when you were at school. Perhaps you were a culture vulture, who loved the latest music, films, books and TV programmes? Maybe you were the sporty type, who loved to go to matches, buy the latest kit or kick a ball around with your friends? Remember how important these crazes and fashions were to you then (even if they're hugely embarrassing to you now). Then bear in mind what the equivalents mean to your students and think about how you can utilise them.

Use Imaginative Rewards

Does your school or setting stick to the traditional type of rewards: merits, commendations, golden time and so on? If so, consider spicing things up by using more imaginative rewards. When you offer interesting rewards, this encourages your students to work hard to earn them. Your classroom is also a more interesting and engaging place to be. Here are suggestions I've used myself and also some ideas other teachers have given me:

✔ **Deputy Diners:** The students get to dine with the deputy head, with proper linen and tableware and flowers on the table.

✔ **Ask Me What I Did:** The student is given a badge saying 'Ask Me What I Did'. This encourages other teachers (and students) to ask him, and by doing so to reaffirm how well the student has worked or behaved.

✔ **Get Out of Homework Free:** The teacher has a card that he can give to one student in the lesson. That student receives a 'pass' and gets out of doing the homework.

✔ **Treasure Box:** The teacher has a box full of interesting treasures, and the students get to pick their own prize.

You can find more advice and information about using rewards in Chapter 9. You can also find a downloadable list of rewards on my website: www.suecowley.co.uk. Click Downloads on the left side of the home page.

Take Them Outdoors

I'm sure you can remember the feeling of long, hot summer days trapped in the classroom, days spent peering out of the window at a clear blue sky, resenting the teacher who kept you inside. A class can discover so many things when you take it outside. And getting out in the fresh air is a great way to refresh your students and keep them engaged in their learning. The outdoors is also the perfect place for messier activities:

✔ Blast some rockets into the sky in a science lesson

✔ Tend a school garden or vegetable patch

✔ Mess around with water, sand, clay or paint

✔ Play some letter or number games chalked on the playground floor

✔ Explore forces by experimenting with different forms of transport (skateboards, rollerskates, bikes and so on)

✔ Inspire some creative writing by lying on your backs and looking up at the clouds

When you take a class outside, lay down the law on behaviour *before* you leave the classroom. Some of your students may take advantage once they get outside, so make the limits clear before you leave your room. Being allowed to work outdoors is the perfect incentive for excellent behaviour. Use this to your advantage. Insist on perfect behaviour if the students want to stay in the great outdoors. Otherwise, sadly, you'll have to take them back inside.

Use the Power of the Peer Group

Many of your students are more influenced by their peer group than by anyone else, including you. They feel the need to build or retain status within the group by making friends. They also feel a powerful urge to avoid embarrassing themselves or losing face with the group. These are very powerful incentives to keep in with their peer group.

Luckily, you can use the power of the peer group to help you engage with and motivate a class. You may do this by:

✔ Encouraging a peer-group leader to be an active participant during a lesson. He may write some notes up on the board or even deliver part of the work for you.

✔ Using whole-class motivators where everyone must work together to earn the reward.

✔ Talking about how well another class in the same year group (or the one below) can do a particular task, then challenging your class to do it as well or better.

Get the peer-group leaders on your side and the rest of the class normally falls in line.

Give 'em a Surprise

Although routine and security are useful, it pays to keep your students on their toes. Make sure they stay interested in and engaged by your lessons by giving them the occasional surprise. That way, they never know quite what's coming next.

Try these ideas:

✔ Rearrange the classroom furniture so the students are facing in a different direction.

✔ Turn up to the lesson dressed in an interesting costume connected to the topic you're teaching.

✔ Bring a new and really original resource into the classroom, for example a giant potted plant called Henry.

✔ Spring a special visitor on the class: the head teacher, a visually impaired person with a guide dog, a local celebrity.

Not only do these approaches keep your students on their toes, they also add fun and interest to lessons for you.

Chapter 18

Ten Key Strategies for Handling Difficult Behaviour

*M*any teachers cite difficult behaviour as one of their key issues in the classroom. The problem is, if you can't get your class to behave, then you can't get on with teaching them. And that's what you're there to do. You're not a behaviour manager or a social worker, you're a teacher. Sort behaviour out and you can get on with the bit of the job you enjoy.

In this chapter you find my top ten strategies for handling misbehaviour, whether an individual student is causing you problems, a group of students simply won't settle or an entire class refuses to do as you ask. Many of these approaches are about fighting your natural, instinctive responses to misbehaviour. None of these strategies provides a one-off, magic solution to behaviour problems. You need to try different approaches until you find a combination that works.

Stay Calm

Sounds so obvious, doesn't it? Stay calm, so you can maintain control of your classroom, keep your emotions in check, minimise your stress levels and deal with any problems in a rational way. The thing is, staying calm is possibly the hardest thing you have to do as a teacher. When a student misbehaves or is rude or defiant, losing your temper may come entirely naturally to you. But somehow, you have to stop yourself.

Your students can sense the moment you start to lose your cool. They seem to have some kind of radar that pings into action the second you begin to get irritated. And when you're a kid, seeing your teacher go red, start sweating and begin to shout is incomparable. What a sense of power those young people must feel. We did that! We made the adult furious!

The secret is to have an internal alarm bell that rings for you the minute your temper begins to rise. Like a circuit breaker you use with a lawnmower, find a way to stop yourself mid-flow: something, anything, that makes you say 'stop' to yourself *before* you lose the plot.

You can find much more information about why you should stay calm, and how you can do it, in Chapter 8.

Ignore Attention Seekers

Your attention-seeking student wants one thing: your attention. And she does anything to get it. When you react every time the student misbehaves, she quickly discovers that this is a great way to get your attention. And the more you respond to her misbehaviour, the more you reinforce misbehaving as a useful thing to do. The secret, of course, is to teach yourself to ignore her, and in turn to teach her that misbehaving *isn't* the way to get your attention.

Imagine yourself talking to the class at the start of a lesson. Suddenly, from the back of the room, you hear the sound of a pencil tapping on a desk (or whistling, humming or whatever noise your students know most upsets you). What do you do next? See yourself responding in your mind's eye. Do you do something that reinforces the attention-seeking behaviour? Can you do something else instead?

You can ignore a lot of low-level misbehaviour, so long as it isn't having an impact on the rest of the class. This approach is known as the *tactical ignore*. If the student sees that she can't get a rise out of you, her misbehaviour is pretty pointless.

Constantly remind yourself that you don't have to respond to attention-seeking misbehaviour. Instead, you can:

- ✔ Focus only on those students who are doing as you wish, ignoring anyone who isn't doing what you want.
- ✔ If you feel you have to intervene, make a small hand signal to show you've spotted the problem.
- ✔ Move nearer to the student while continuing to teach the class.
- ✔ Wait until all the other students are getting on with their work before going over to the student to deal with the problem.

Students who crave attention love to be given it for positive, as well as negative, behaviours. Use tasks such as handing out resources or writing up points on the board to give attention in a positive way. Sometimes, taking an unusual tack is the best way to handle the attention seekers in your class. In the example above of tapping a pen, you can stop what you're doing and say, 'Great idea! Let's all tap out the rhythm of this poem with our pens. Come on everyone!' This turns a potentially tricky situation into something much more positive and interesting.

Be Reasonable, But Don't Reason with Them

Young people have an innate sense of natural justice – 'it's not fair!' is one of their favourite phrases (often said when what you're doing is entirely fair). This quest for fairness can spill over into constant demands that you justify everything you ask them to do.

A great rule of thumb to apply is 'Be reasonable, but don't reason with them'. What this means is that as long as what you're asking them to do is fair, realistic and practical, they should just get on with it. Don't feel you must constantly explain yourself – doing so is far too time consuming. It's also a way for students to wrestle control of a situation from the teacher. Show that you're in charge by having belief in yourself and your demands.

Suppose you ask a student to get on with her work (a perfectly reasonable expectation). She complains that she doesn't have a pen (not your problem, as one of your rules is 'turn up with correct equipment'). You tell her to get hold of a pen quickly or you have no choice but to sanction her (a reasonable consequence). She whinges: 'That's not fair, miss, someone borrowed my pen last lesson and didn't give it back.'

At this point, you may be dragged into a lengthy discussion about how she's responsible for her own equipment, or asking her who borrowed the pen (trying to reason with her). Instead, simply reiterate your expectation that she gets on with her work. If she refuses to do so, or if she doesn't sort herself out by borrowing a pen, simply carry on and apply the sanction.

The same approach applies to many different behaviour issues. A student arrives wearing trainers and then tries to reason with you about why this is 'fair' for her ('I've got bad feet, miss' she whines). Expecting students to wear shoes is perfectly reasonable, unless they have a medical note that says otherwise. You *don't* have to explain yourself!

Give Troublemakers a Choice

Life is all about making choices and accepting the consequences when you take the wrong decision. If you speed and get caught, you must pay a fine. If you choose a job that you don't enjoy, you must stay and cope, or work out your notice. If you eat burgers and doughnuts for dinner every night, don't be surprised if you put on weight. This is a vital lesson for your students to learn. It's also a great way to help you manage their behaviour in a calm and rational way. Here's what you need to do:

1. **When a student misbehaves, state the behaviour you want and the consequences of not complying.**

   For example, 'I want you to get on with your work right now, otherwise you have to do it at break.'

2. **Give the student a chance to think this through and comply, by walking away for a few moments.**

3. **If you notice that she's not getting on with her work, give a second warning.**

   For example, 'You know the rule. Get on with your work right now, thanks, or I have to give you a break-time detention.'

4. **Again, give time for the student to comply. If she doesn't, apply the punishment.**

The great thing about the choice is that it takes all the emotion out of the situation. You simply outline the required behaviour and the consequences of not behaving as you ask. You *police* behaviour according to the agreed rules. Save your passionate side for your teaching. You can find out more about using this strategy in Chapters 8 and 9.

When you use the choice, you teach your students an important lesson about life. Outside of school and after they leave education, the choices they make potentially have a far more powerful impact on their lives. Help them to understand this now, so they're better prepared for life in the future.

Stick to Your Guns

Some of your students accept your rules and serve any sanctions they earn with good grace (probably the students who behave well for you most of the time). But other students try their hardest to avoid sticking to the rules or to get out of the punishments you give them. They plead innocence, injustice, illness, incapacity – anything to make you soften and let them off 'just this one time, miss'!

The problem is, 'just this one time' never is just once. The moment you relax your standards and allow things to slide, you let the genie out of the box and things are all downhill from then onwards. You can't get that genie back in once he's escaped. Keep a firm handle on problem behaviour, particularly those low-level disruptions that can waste so much teaching time. Focus on the little things and the more serious issues often don't arise.

Stick to your guns. When you promise to do something, do it. When you say behaviour '*x*' must happen, make sure it does. Except, that is, in rare and exceptional circumstances. You have to use your professional judgement to work out what 'rare' and 'exceptional' means in *your* classroom, and you can discover more in 'Know When to Be Flexible', later in this chapter.

Know When to Be Flexible

Teaching is a balancing act at times. You balance the need to get a class settled and silent with the equally pressing need to get on with some work. You also balance the need to handle behaviour issues with the need to avoid confrontations with your more unbalanced students. And finally, you must balance the need for consistency with the need sometimes to apply a bit of flexibility to a tricky situation.

You have to work out for yourself when to push hard and when to ease off, when to go in firm and when to use a gentler tack. Keep your ultimate goal in mind (good behaviour, get this work done, survive to the end of today) and do what it takes to achieve that.

Sometimes you have to allow for a bit of flexibility, agreeing to disagree with a student, or compromising a bit to calm a tricky situation. You might need to be flexible when:

- ✔ The class has had a disruption – a change of room or timetable or the absence of normal staff, for example.

- ✔ A student turns up to your lesson in a foul mood – something has obviously gone wrong earlier in the day.

- ✔ Environmental factors intervene – for example, wind, hailstorms, full moons, a swarm of bees in the corridors (and yes, that really did happen to me in one school!).

- ✔ The end of term is approaching.

The secret is to pick your battles. Before you set out your demands, think carefully about whether they're realistic and achievable.

Imagine this: you're on the last day of the Christmas term and snow's been falling for hours. The wind is howling (tricky customers, those windy days). Santa Claus has been touring the classrooms, giving out coloured sweets and fizzy drinks to all the students. You've been off sick, so your class has had three different supply teachers in the last three days. And the England team is playing in the World Cup Final tonight (yes, I *know*, but this is a fantasy!). When your class arrives at the lesson, they're *completely* psyched up and wired. They race in, bob about and generally look like they're about to burst. And you were planning to do an end-of-term test. Up to you. Do the test? Don't do the test? I know what *I'd* do in that situation.

Turn on a Penny

Most of the time you should be calm, confident and reasonable – a stable feature in your students' lives. But on occasion, maybe once or twice a term, when it's really justified, let them see that you do have a fierce side lurking beneath. And that your fierce side comes out to bite if they try to take things too far. When a student's really pushing at the limits or a class is really messing you around, try 'turning on a penny' to give them a shock.

You may have your own way of making that sudden change in personality, but you can do some or all of the following:

- ✔ Suddenly go very still and silent
- ✔ Emit a low, growling sound, like a dog about to pounce
- ✔ Give the deadliest of deadly stares
- ✔ Hiss a furious 'how dare you!' at the class
- ✔ Instantly return to being all sweetness and light

By doing this, the class sees that it can only push you so far before you snap. That even though you're normally very self-controlled, they can't push you beyond a certain limit without getting a reaction.

Turning on a penny only works if you're normally calm and self-contained, with vast reserves of self-control. If you're deadly and dangerous most of the time anyway, the approach doesn't have quite the same effect.

Apply Lateral Thinking

Sometimes you come across a behaviour problem that seems to have no solution. You try all the obvious strategies, but none of them has any impact at all. In these instances (and indeed in any other situation where you fancy doing something a bit different), try applying some lateral thinking. *Lateral thinking* means taking your thinking sideways, rather than using the more usual linear thought processes. Instead of doing the obvious, you do something unusual, something from 'left field'.

In life, and in your classroom, sometimes the most obvious solution isn't the best. And sometimes the most sensible solution isn't obvious at all. If your class isn't behaving on a Friday afternoon, you could slog on and hand out punishments (obvious, but high stress and not likely to be terribly effective). Alternatively, you could try something lateral instead:

✔ Take them for a lesson outdoors – this may inspire them to work.

✔ Offer them ten minutes of 'golden time' at the end of the lesson if they complete the work properly.

✔ Move them into a spare classroom, or into the assembly hall, to see if a fresh room freshens up their attitude.

✔ Take them to a computer room – often students focus much better when working on a computer.

✔ Bribe them with a treat, such as listening to the radio while they're working.

✔ Ask *them* to run the lesson for you!

Thinking laterally helps you come up with new, creative approaches for handling behaviour in your lessons.

React from Your Head, Not from Your Heart

Your first, instinctive response to misbehaviour comes from your heart. This is your emotional reaction: anger, upset or nervousness. You have to short-circuit that emotional response, because it does you no good whatsoever. When you're handling misbehaviour, you need to use the rational, 'head' response instead.

When a class is on the verge of a riot, your heart says: 'Oh my god, what am I going to do, they won't listen to me, what if the head teacher turns up now, what will she think?' On the other hand, your head says: 'Okay, they're about to riot. What can I do about it? What's going to work? I know, I can send someone for help/give them a blast of my whistle/write a punishment on the board.'

Your heart sees the negatives, downsides and problems in a situation. It makes you flap, feel panicked and do the wrong thing. Your head sees the positives, upsides and solutions to a situation. It helps you cope and find a good way out of a difficult scenario. Make sure your head wins out over your heart every time.

Put Yourself in Their Shoes

If you want to understand why your students are misbehaving, you need to put yourself in their shoes. When a lesson isn't working as it should, what might your students say was wrong with it? When your students begin to mess around only minutes into a class, think about things from their perspective – what's making them misbehave? That's not to say you should blame yourself for their misbehaviour, rather that by understanding *why* they're misbehaving you may be able to find some solutions to the problem.

Think back to when you were at school. I'm sure you can remember some days that seemed to drag on for ever. Or some topics that you just didn't 'get', no matter how the teacher tried to explain them. And when you were bored or mystified, I bet the option of misbehaving occurred to you.

Some topics *are* a bit boring or hard to grasp, so your planning has to be tip top. Some students misbehave just because they're young people and that's what you do when you're young. As the saying goes, 'Walk a mile in their shoes'. Think like them, ask them for feedback, be responsive to what they feel. Then you stand a chance of understanding where they're coming from, why they're behaving as they are and what the solution may be.

Chapter 19

Ten Tips for Dealing with Stress

*T*eaching is a stressful job, no doubt about it. This stress can come from many sources: student behaviour, a heavy workload, excessive demands on your time. Discovering how to cope and deal effectively with stress is a key part of a successful teaching career.

Think of all the things at work that make *you* feel stressed. Then look through this chapter to see which tips can help you to deal with those things more effectively. When you've finished reading, why not write down your three top tips and refer back to them whenever you feel yourself getting stressed.

Keep a Sense of Perspective

When you're stuck in a classroom with a difficult class, you can easily lose your sense of perspective – to feel that this moment is the be-all and end-all of life and that the problems you have are completely insurmountable. In a more rational moment you don't think like this, but caged in that difficult lesson you feel emotional and vulnerable.

Keep a sense of perspective about what really matters. I was once given a great quote: 'Even in your worst lesson, nobody died.' Yes, the students were throwing paper aeroplanes or you couldn't get the kids to shut up and listen. But really, that's not the end of the world. Shrug the problem off, dust yourself down and get back to the chalk face.

Don't Take Things Personally

A student being abusive toward you is absolutely horrible – when he swears at you or tells you that your lessons are rubbish (probably using a more direct and graphic term). A class that just won't settle to work or students refusing to be quiet while you're trying to teach, no matter what you try, is equally depressing.

The thing is, though, you can't and shouldn't take things personally. Because 99% of the time the problem isn't you, it's them. Any student who feels that swearing at you is okay probably has some pretty serious issues outside of school. The swearing is about his lack of self-esteem, not about the quality of your lesson.

And if a class is completely impossible to control, something's probably wrong in the overall school systems and approaches. Look for ways to make life better for yourself and your students, but don't take things going wrong personally.

Build a Support Network

Thankfully, you find many sources of support in your working life as a teacher. I've always found that the more difficult the school is, the more supportive the staff are of each other. Look around for support and ask for it if it's not freely given, especially if you're new to teaching. Potential sources of support include:

- Your line manager or head of department at secondary level
- Your mentor or tutor if you're a new teacher
- The other staff at your school (and not just the teachers)
- A teaching union
- The local education authority (sometimes)
- Friends and family

Sometimes you even find that your (nicer) students offer you unasked for support, that they understand and care when you're finding things tough. Look for support wherever you can and take any offers of help you receive. Don't feel you have to suffer alone. Every teacher has his high and low moments. Look around and you soon find a shoulder to cry on or someone to make you laugh off your worries.

Create a Home/Work Divide

The thing about teaching is that it's a job without an end. You can work all day, every day and still not get everything done. When you're new to teaching, you take piles of marking home and stay up burning the midnight oil every night to get it done. As you get more experienced, you learn that this isn't a sensible use of your time.

You have to rest when you're outside of work, because that way you're a better teacher when you're in the classroom. If school is on your mind 24/7, you're not a relaxed or fully rounded person in your home life. You must find that 'downtime' for yourself after the school day's over so you can recharge your batteries for the next day's challenges.

If you find cutting off from school really hard, you can:

✔ Take up some kind of physical activity after school, something like swimming or walking that's not too mentally taxing.

✔ Write a 'to do' list of all the things on your mind, then put it to one side for tomorrow.

✔ If your home circumstances allow, stay at school until your work is done for the day.

Achieving a home/work balance is essential for a long, happy career as a teacher, so put yourself first and don't feel guilty about doing it. Jeni Mumford's *Work/Life Balance For Dummies* can help you to achieve this.

Put Up a Wall

On the popular, long-running TV show *Star Trek*, the crew has a secret weapon to use when aliens shoot at them: they put up their deflector shields to repel the attack. Aim to create a similar shield for yourself to deflect any unwanted abuse. Build yourself a metaphorical wall that you put up if a student is rude or aggressive – basically a block that stops the abuse from getting through to you emotionally and hurting you.

To build your wall, remind yourself that abusive behaviour is *not* personal. Abusive behaviour is not about you but about him – about how he's been treated in his life outside of school. Aim to see even the most aggressive teenager as the innocent baby he once was. Somewhere along the way, something went awfully wrong, but this isn't *your* fault, and you mustn't take it as a reflection on yourself, because it simply isn't useful for either of you.

That's not to say that you don't deal with the abuse by taking things further at a later time. But at the moment when the alien attack strikes, put up your wall so it just doesn't get through to you. Feel the verbal missiles bounce off your wall and retain a sense of confidence and self-esteem. Maintain a feeling of inner calm and security. Then you can deal rationally and not emotionally with the situation.

Maintain a Sense of Humour

A sense of humour is an essential tool in your teaching kit bag. It helps you lighten the mood in your classroom and it stops you from taking things too seriously. Maintain a healthy sense of the ridiculous – so many things in teaching are a bit daft or even downright crazy. Figure out how to laugh at yourself and at some of the situations you find yourself in.

Never direct humour at individual students, unless you know they welcome and enjoy it (your 'class clown' probably doesn't mind). Some teachers use a sarcastic put-down directed at an individual to get a cheap laugh from the rest of the class. While this may make you feel better in the short term, it can do a lot of damage to the individual's self-esteem. Young people often take what you say far more seriously than you may have intended. If you do have to make cutting remarks, save them for the staffroom, when the students are safely out of earshot.

Feel Pity, not Anger

If you're faced with a difficult or abusive student, feeling cross and hard done-by is perfectly natural. Although this instinctive response may be justified, it's not the most helpful way of keeping yourself calm and in control. It also does nothing to minimise your stress levels. Far better to feel pity for the student than anger against him.

Take a mental step back from the situation: look at the student as though you're an outsider and you don't know him at all. What may be going on in his head that's causing him to behave in this way? What must his home life be like if he's this awful to an adult in a supposed position of authority? See the small child he once was, then put aside your feelings of irritation and feel sorry for him and the life he leads.

Learn to Forgive Yourself

You're likely to do some things as a teacher that you later come to regret. Often, this happens when you're tired or under pressure. You may shout at a class or say something sarcastic to an individual. You can do something petty such as tearing up a student's work. When you make a mistake you have two choices. You can either let the error prey on your mind and cause you heaps of worry or stress. Or you can learn to forgive yourself and put the mistake behind you once and for all.

Nobody's perfect. Everyone makes mistakes, especially when they're in high-pressure situations. The secret is to learn from your mistakes and try your very hardest not to repeat them in the future. Oh, and don't forget to say sorry if that's warranted!

A Fresh Start Every Time

When a student is really difficult in your lesson or does something horrible to you, you may be tempted to bear a grudge for days and days. Every time you meet the student after that, you always have the thought of his past indiscretions in your mind. Things can get to the point where you dread having a particular student in your class and you sigh with relief when he's absent.

You are the adult in this relationship, so you are the one who needs to mend the fences. Some students are in trouble so often, making a fresh start is really hard for them. Give your students a second chance. This doesn't mean you let them get away with bad behaviour. But once they've served the appropriate punishment, put the problems of the past behind you and start over again.

Give Yourself a Pat on the Back

Have you ever noticed how you're expected to continually motivate and reward your students, but no one ever remembers to motivate and reward you? I want to finish this chapter by asking you to give yourself a 'pat on the back'. I want you to identify and acknowledge all the great things you do as a teacher and say 'well done' to yourself.

Imagine yourself walking down the corridor at your school or at the setting where you work. Ahead of you is a small group of your students. They're chatting quietly among themselves and they don't notice you approaching. As you get closer, you realise that they're talking about you. But they're not saying anything bad about you – they're discussing how great you are instead. What three things are these students saying about you? What aspects of you and your teaching do they think are so great?

Perhaps they love the way you give your time when they need help. Maybe they think the lessons you teach are fantastic: entertaining, engaging, just all-round good fun. Or perhaps they feel they have a really strong relationship with you and that you're great at getting the best out of their class. Narrow your thoughts down to three words or phrases that define what's great about you as a teacher. And once you've thought of those three things, I want you to write them down. Now.

If you found this really hard to do, it may be that you're causing yourself extra stress by being overly self-critical. Learn to be positive and to look for the best in yourself. Acknowledge all those things you do well, rather than focusing on the negative aspects of you as a teacher.

In times of great stress or when the job's really getting you down, think back to those three great things that you do for your students. And never forget, in 10 or 20 years' time when your current students have moved onwards and upwards, you may be the person they remember as making a difference to their lives. As the saying goes, no one forgets a good teacher. Be a great, fantastic, passionate, caring teacher and they do a lot more than that. They remember you as someone who inspired them for ever.

Chapter 20

Ten Best Book and Website Resources for Teachers and Trainers

. . . .

In This Chapter

▶ Finding resources to inspire and engage your students

▶ Exploring different sources of support and help

. . . .

*R*esources for teachers come in all shapes and sizes: from objects you bring in to inspire your students to a range of organisations to help, support and advise you. I'm sure you've found that one of the best resources of all is your fellow members of staff. Other teachers and staff in a school know exactly what you're going through and are in the very best place to advise and support you. The students themselves are often a great help as well. The other chapters in this book go into quite a bit of detail on how to take advantage of those resources.

This chapter focuses on books and websites that you, as a professional educator, are likely to find informative and inspirational.

Hopefully you find this book a useful resource as well. If you want to talk through a specific issue with me or get advice on something teaching related, do contact me via my website, www.suecowley.co.uk, or email me on sue@suecowley.co.uk.

Books

When I first started writing teaching books, I did so because very few practical guides were on the market. These days, you can hardly move for practical teaching books. The following sections contain some of the most perennially popular titles.

Cracking the Hard Class

Written by Bill Rogers (Paul Chapman Publishing), *Cracking the Hard Class* is a classic guide to managing behaviour, particularly that of the most difficult classes. Rogers gives lots of practical and useful tips.

The Craft of the Classroom

This book, written by Michael Marland (Heinemann Education), is a guide to all aspects of classroom life. It has an old-fashioned style, reflecting when it was written, but gives common sense advice that still applies today.

Getting the Buggers to Behave

Written by yours truly (and published by Continuum), this book is a thoroughly practical guide to managing behaviour. It contains all the practical strategies and techniques that I've picked up over the years, teaching in a range of very different situations.

Surviving and Succeeding in Difficult Classrooms

This book, written by Paul Blum (Routledge) is a guide for teachers working in very challenging situations. Blum gives realistic advice about how to both survive and succeed in the toughest schools.

The Teacher's Toolkit

In this book, Paul Ginnis suggests lots of ways for teachers to make use of the most effective teaching strategies. He shows the best ways to get your students learning effectively.

Useful Web Sites

The Internet has brought a whole host of opportunities to find useful resources for your classroom and more generally for you as a professional. The Internet does have its downsides, though, because you can waste an awful lot of time looking for exactly the right sites to visit. To save you that time, I give a run down of some my favourite resource sites here.

Primary Resources

www.primaryresources.co.uk

This site is a free forum for sharing resources and ideas. Online for over ten years now, this site is full of useful lessons and downloads to support teaching in the primary classroom. The ideas are all contributed by teachers for teachers.

Teachernet

www.teachernet.gov.uk

Teachernet is a useful source of accurate information about educational issues and policy. This website also contains some useful teaching materials, links and resources.

Teachers TV

www.teachers.tv

Teachers TV offers video materials on a whole range of teaching-related subjects. Whatever issue or interest you have, you should be able to find something relevant here.

The Times Educational Supplement (TES)

www.tes.co.uk

The TES website has developed over the years into a very useful source of support and ideas. The forums section offers a busy place to chat to other teachers and the resources section gives you access to loads of free downloads and resources.

Woodlands Junior School

www.woodlands-junior.kent.sch.uk

Although essentially a school website, the Woodlands Junior School site is widely recognised in the educational community as a great source of ideas and materials. The site contains useful seasonal ideas and lots of information about British cultures and customs.

Index

• **S** •

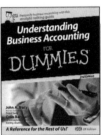

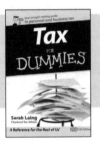

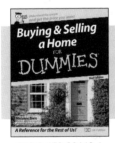
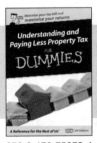

FOR DUMMIES®

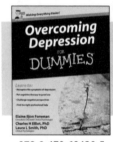

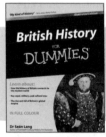
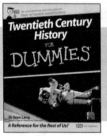
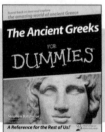

FOR DUMMIES®

The easy way to get more done and have more fun

LANGUAGES

978-0-7645-5194-9

978-0-7645-5193-2

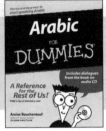

978-0-471-77270-5

MUSIC

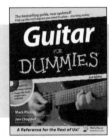

978-0-7645-9904-0

978-0-470-03275-6
UK Edition

978-0-7645-5105-5

SCIENCE & MATHS

978-0-7645-5326-4

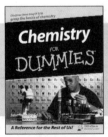

978-0-7645-5430-8

978-0-7645-5325-7

Art For Dummies
978-0-7645-5104-8

Baby & Toddler Sleep Solutions For Dummies
978-0-470-11794-1

Bass Guitar For Dummies
978-0-7645-2487-5

Brain Games For Dummies
978-0-470-37378-1

Christianity For Dummies
978-0-7645-4482-8

Filmmaking For Dummies, 2nd Edition
978-0-470-38694-1

Forensics For Dummies
978-0-7645-5580-0

German For Dummies
978-0-7645-5195-6

Hobby Farming For Dummies
978-0-470-28172-7

Jewelry Making & Beading For Dummies
978-0-7645-2571-1

Knitting for Dummies, 2nd Edition
978-0-470-28747-7

Music Composition For Dummies
978-0-470-22421-2

Physics For Dummies
978-0-7645-5433-9

Sex For Dummies, 3rd Edition
978-0-470-04523-7

Solar Power Your Home For Dummies
978-0-470-17569-9

Tennis For Dummies
978-0-7645-5087-4

The Koran For Dummies
978-0-7645-5581-7

U.S. History For Dummies
978-0-7645-5249-6

Wine For Dummies, 4th Edition
978-0-470-04579-4

Available wherever books are sold. For more information or to order direct go to www.wiley.com or call +44 (0) 1243 843291

13902_p3

FOR

DUMMIES®

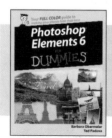